Letter from the Publisher

**Publisher and
Creative Director:**
B. Martin Pedersen

Chief Visionary Officer:
Patti Judd

Design Director:
Hee Ra Kim

Designers:
B. Martin Pedersen
Hee Ra Kim
Hiewon Sohn

Associate Editor:
Colleen Boyd

Design Interns:
Charlotte Benes
Sophia Di Iorio
Lela Johnson
Hana Williams

Editorial Interns:
Kathryn Bailey
Paige Cook
Brooke McCormick

Writer:
Claire Lui

Japanese Advisors:
USA: Toshiaki & Kumiko Ide
Japan: Taku Satoh
Sakura Nomiyama

Chief Executive Officer:
B. Martin Pedersen

Cover Image:
"LASCALA FACE"
By Eduardo del Fraile Studio

Published by:
Graphis Inc.
389 5th Ave., Suite 1105
New York, NY 10016
Phone: 212-532-9387
www.graphis.com
help@graphis.com

Distributed by:
National Book Networks, Inc.
15200 NBN Way
Blue Ridge Summit, PA 17214
Phone: 800-462-6420
customercare@nbnbooks.com

ISBN 13: 978-1-931241-98-4

In this issue, we feature, as always, a broad spectrum of highly accomplished talents in the creative arts, all of whom share one defining trait in common: passion. They are driven by their passions to create innovative work that is original and groundbreaking.

We've long recognized their skills and mastery, since many are past winners of multiple Graphis Platinum and Gold awards.

In addition to exploring their work in this journal, we invite you to visit our website, graphis.com, for the most up-to-date information about how to submit entries, read our blog, get inspired with our store of design books and magazines, and explore the Master Portfolios. We are presently in the process of updating the site to be more responsive, and we hope you are enjoying the updated mobile experience.

Design: Eduardo del Fraile (Spain), Graphis Master, is the founder and creative director of Eduardo del Fraile Studio. He served as the president of the D&AD packaging design jury in 2018 and has won multiple awards from the One Show, Laus Barcelona, and Pentawards.

Hajime Tsushima (Japan) founded his own design firm, Tsushima Design, in 1995. He has served on the jury for the China International Poster Biennale and the Poster Stellars Intercontinental Poster Competition. He is an associate professor at Osaka University of Arts.

Advertising: The Gate (USA) is an international full-service advertising agency with offices in New York, San Francisco, London, Edinburgh, and Shanghai.

Photography: Peter Whyte (Tasmania) is a commercial and fine art photographer whose work has won awards from Graphis and PX3 Prix de la Photographie Paris. He also has had solo exhibitions in Sydney, Melbourne, and Hobart.

Michael Schoenfeld (USA), Graphis Master, has worked with international clients including Intel, Moran Eye Global Outreach, and YESCO.

Art/Illustration: Michael Doret (USA), Graphis Master, grew up near Coney Island in Brooklyn. His book, *Growing Up in Alphabet City*, will be published in 2022 by Letterform Archive.

Education: Dong-Joo Park and Seung-Min Han (South Korea), both Graphis Masters, are professors at Hansung University's Design & Arts Institute. They have taught many prize-winning students featured in past Graphis New Talent Annuals.

Products: The ICON A5 (USA) is an amphibious light-sport aircraft. **Phoenix i Wheelchair** by Phoenix Instinct (UK) is the first lightweight wheelchair with smart technology, while **Revolve Air** by Andrea Mocellin (Italy) is a collapsible wheelchair.

Architecture: The Voyager Station by the Orbital Assembly Corporation (USA) hopes to be the first space hotel. **Gaia** by Pin-Up Houses (Czech Republic) is a tiny house built out of a shipping container.

Advisory Board: Quinnton Harris (USA) is Retrospect's co-founder and CEO. Harris also recently led the #hellajuneteenth movement, getting more than 600 companies committed to observing Juneteenth as a paid holiday.

B. Martin Pedersen
Publisher & Creative Director

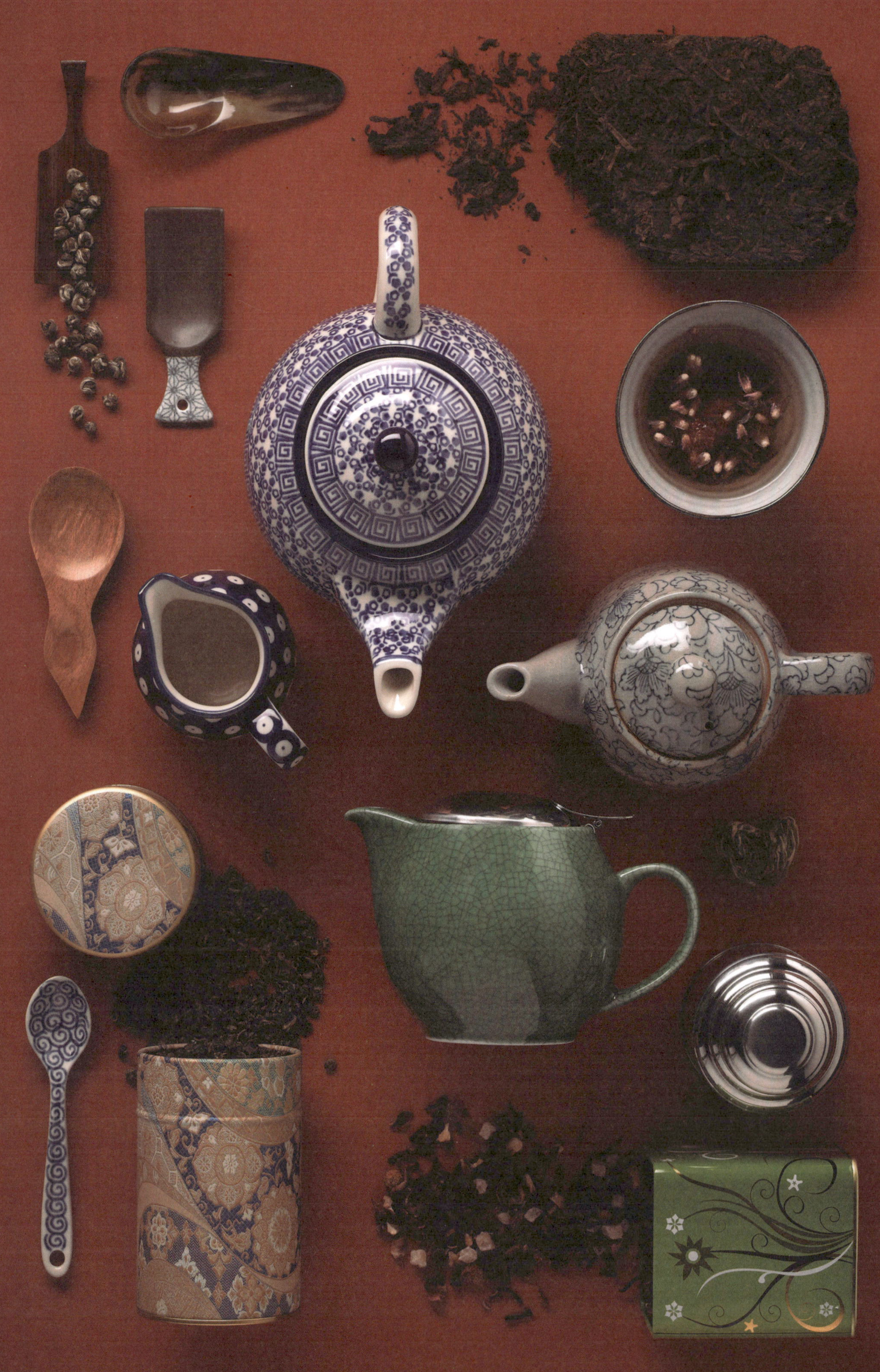

Contents

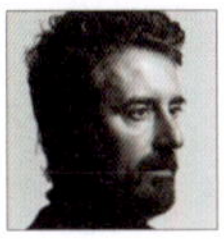

(Opposite page) Title: The Art of Tea 002; Year: 2012; Client: Norman & Dann; Photographer: Peter Whyte

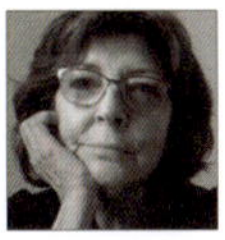

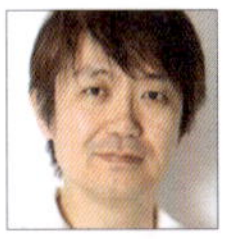

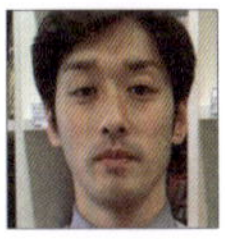

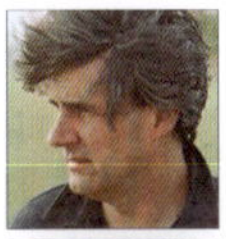

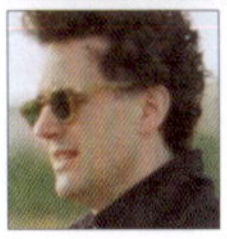

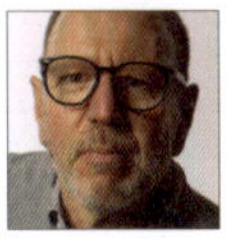

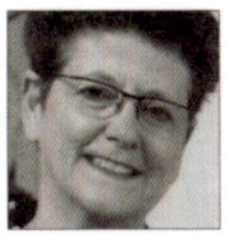

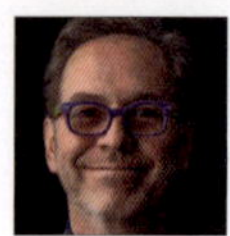

68 **Michael Schoenfeld (Graphis Master) / USA**

Michael Schoenfeld has been lucky. Very lucky. To be alive at such a pivotal time in history; to have been allowed to earn a living doing such a wonderful thing as taking pictures. To have, through no effort of his own, won such an unwarranted place in the ovarian lottery. Make no mistake, hard work has always played a pivotal role. But once he discovered that the greatest passion he had was using photography to allow him to meet and photograph interesting people, Michael essentially felt as if the gods had bestowed some gift upon him. Thank you for that.

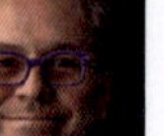

Introduction by Ron Crump

For more than twenty-five years, Ronald Crump has worked in marketing and creative communications. He brings a proven history of developing marketing and communication strategies that have successfully boosted sales, built brand awareness, and increased market share in diverse industries including technology, finance, OEM manufacturing, retail, B2B, and B2C. Ronald is known as a task-focused, creative, interactive team player with meticulous attention to detail. Some of the brands he has worked with include Intel, T-Mobile, and HP Inc.

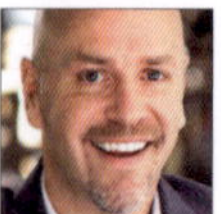

ART/ILLUSTRATION:

84 **Michael Doret (Graphis Master) / USA**

Michael grew up in Brooklyn near what are now the remains of the collection of amusement parks known as Coney Island. At the time, his father worked for MGM in Manhattan's Times Square. Consequently, the inspiration for his work came from his early years growing up near the lights, signage, and brilliant colors found near his Brooklyn neighborhood, and which also surrounded his father's office. Later in life he found similar inspiration in such diverse sources as matchbook covers, enamel signs, packaging, and numerous and varied artifacts of the mid-century America he grew up in. Over the years, his work has earned dozens of awards, and Michael has taught workshops and lectured at many institutions. His book, *Growing Up in Alphabet City*, will be published in 2022 by Letterform Archive.

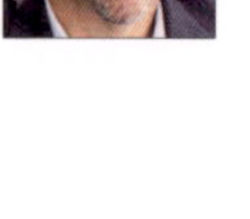

Introduction by John Sabel

John Sabel is the former executive vice president of creative print marketing at the Walt Disney Studios. His concepts and creative direction branded all theatrically released live-action and animated films for Disney Studios, DisneyToons, Disney-Pixar, Marvel, Dreamworks, and Lucasfilms. Some of the more memorable film campaigns he's worked on are *Iron Man, Guardians of the Galaxy, The Avengers, The Rock, Armageddon, The Royal Tenenbaums, Pirates of the Caribbean, Pearl Harbor, Maleficent, Cinderella, Alice in Wonderland, Wreck-It Ralph, Tangled, Lincoln, Toy Story 3, Monsters University, Up, Inside Out*, and *Star Wars: The Force Awakens*.

PRODUCT:

100 **Icon A5 by ICON / USA** *by Claire Lui*

ICON Aircraft's mission is to accelerate the democratization of personal flight. The company's goal is to create a consumer-friendly, safe, technologically advanced aircraft that makes the adventure of flying more accessible to mainstream consumers. ICON's first aircraft is the A5, an amphibious sport plane that fuses aeronautical engineering with world-class product design and unprecedented safety features. The A5 has won some of the world's most prestigious design awards and has inspired a global following. ICON Aircraft's manufacturing headquarters is located in Vacaville, California.

102 **Phoenix i Wheelchair / UK** *by Colleen Boyd*

Phoenix Instinct was founded by award-winning designer Andrew Slorance, a wheelchair user for thirty-five years following SCI. Prior to starting Phoenix Instinct, Andrew had a long career in TV production before he designed the Carbon Black wheelchair. Phoenix Instinct is dedicated to creating innovative, life-enhancing independence equipment. The first product Andrew designed for Phoenix Instinct was wheelchair luggage. Now the winner of the Toyota Mobility Unlimited Challenge, the company is developing the world's first ultra-light intelligent wheelchair. Andrew's mission is to create products that advance independence through great design.

103 **Revolve Air by Andrea Mocellin / Italy** *by Colleen Boyd*

Andrea Mocellin gained a bachelor's with honors at the IED in Turin. He later attended the Royal College of Art in London, graduating with a master's degree in vehicle design. His experiences have included working as chief designer at Granstudio, as senior designer at Lilium, NIO, and Alfa Romeo/Maserati, as creative designer for Pininfarina, Audi AG, GM Forum, and Cleto Munari, and as an interior designer in London. Various projects he has worked on have been exhibited during the Beijing and Geneve Motor Show, Ever in Monaco, MART in Rovereto, and the London Transport Museum.

ARCHITECTURE:

106 **Voyager Station by Orbital Assembly Corporation / USA** *by Claire Lui*

The Orbital Assembly Corporation is headquartered in Fontana, California. Orbital Assembly is working on creating semi-autonomous, robotic machines capable of building and assembling large structures in space quickly and efficiently. The company is developing the technologies and structures to be the world's first large-scale space construction company, enabling humanity to work, play, and thrive in the space ecosystem. Orbital Assembly plans on launching the first space hotel that will produce its own simulated gravity. The hotel is designed to welcome national space agencies conducting low-gravity research, as well as space tourists.

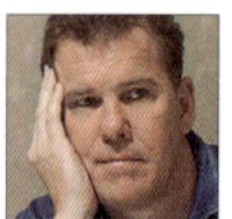

(Opposite page) HONEY SWEET HONEY, 2021; Design by Eduardo del Fraile Studio

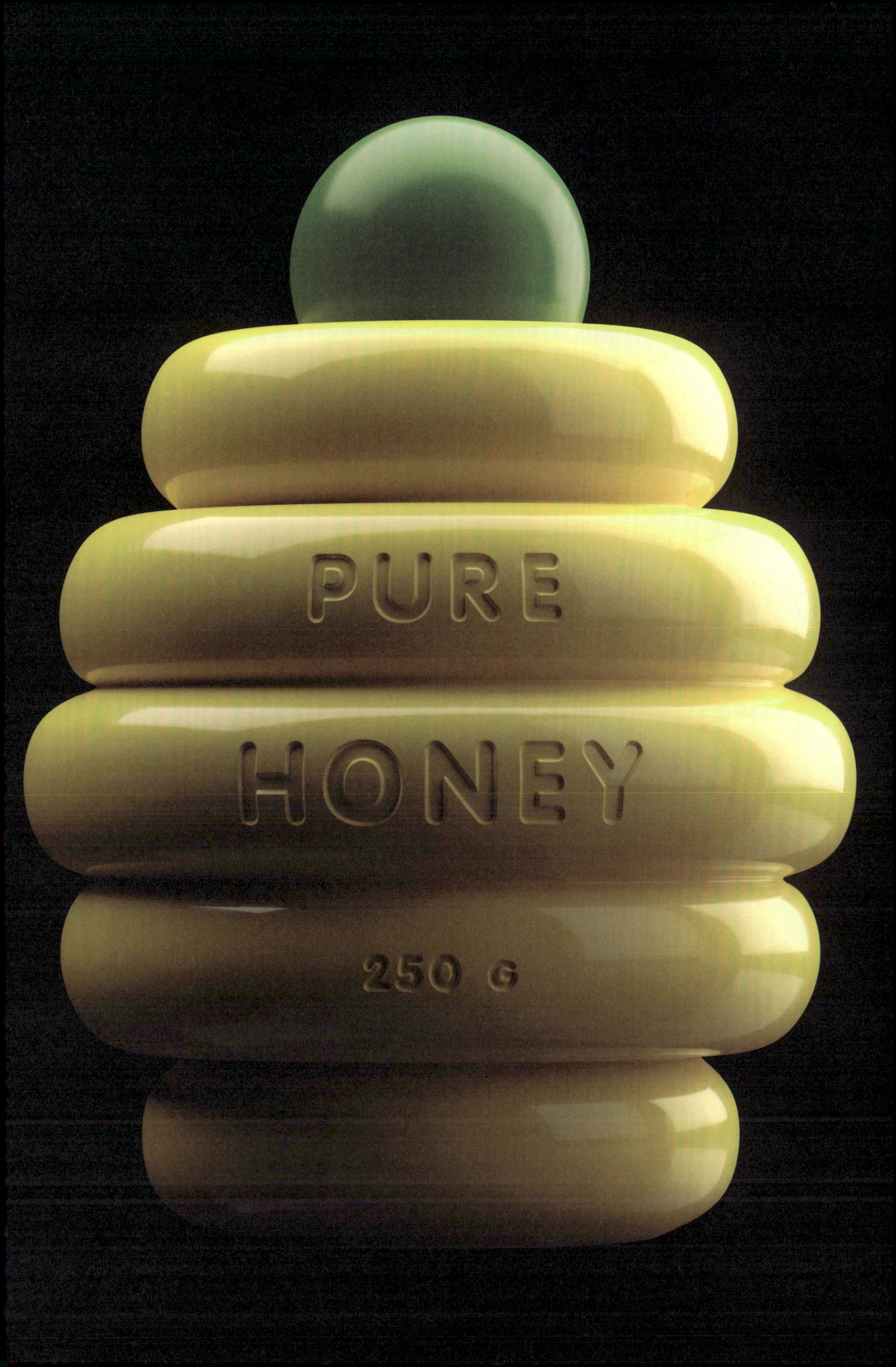

PURE
HONEY
250 G

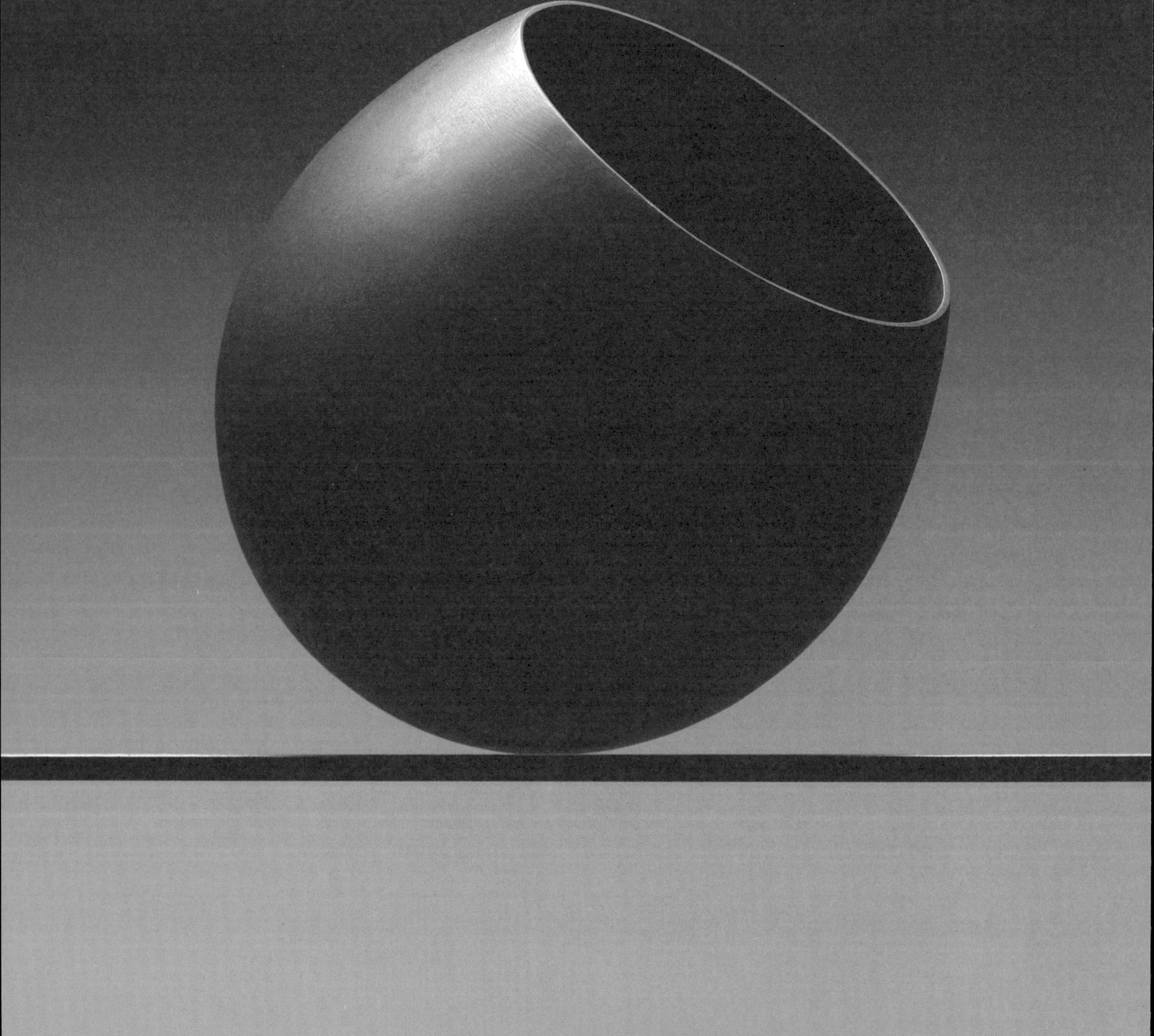

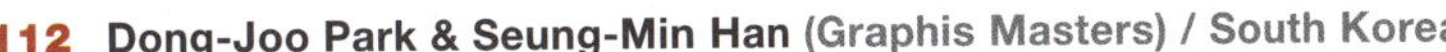

108 Gaia by Pin-Up Houses / Czech Republic *by Claire Lui*

Pin-Up Houses is an architecture studio based in Prague, working both within and outside the traditional boundaries of architecture. Pin-Up Houses mainly focuses on small, DIY wooden house designs that have an emphasis on affordable living. The studio's plans are designed to translate the firm's experience as professional tiny house architects and constructors for the abilities and budgets of amateur builders. Joshua Woodsman, founder and primary architect of Pin-Up Houses, is the author of *How to Build a Tiny House*, which is a compilation of the firm's practical tiny-house knowledge.

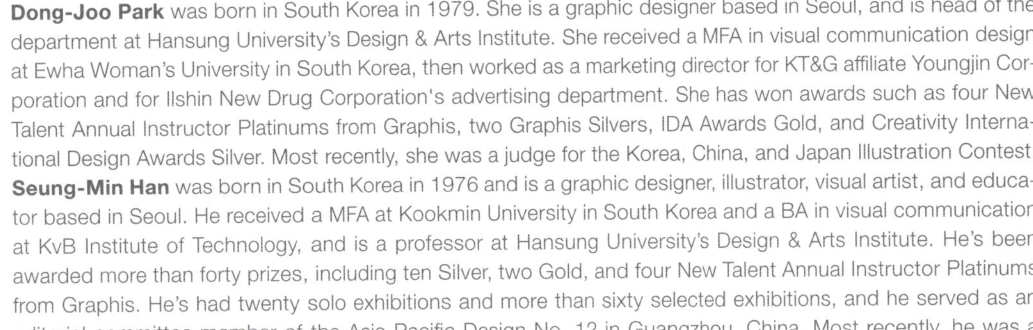

EDUCATION:

112 Dong-Joo Park & Seung-Min Han (Graphis Masters) / South Korea

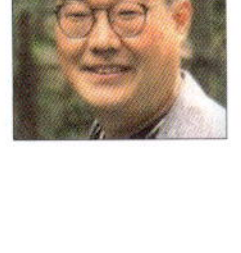

Dong-Joo Park was born in South Korea in 1979. She is a graphic designer based in Seoul, and is head of the department at Hansung University's Design & Arts Institute. She received a MFA in visual communication design at Ewha Woman's University in South Korea, then worked as a marketing director for KT&G affiliate Youngjin Corporation and for Ilshin New Drug Corporation's advertising department. She has won awards such as four New Talent Annual Instructor Platinums from Graphis, two Graphis Silvers, IDA Awards Gold, and Creativity International Design Awards Silver. Most recently, she was a judge for the Korea, China, and Japan Illustration Contest.

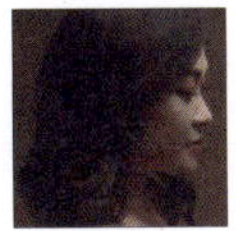

Seung-Min Han was born in South Korea in 1976 and is a graphic designer, illustrator, visual artist, and educator based in Seoul. He received a MFA at Kookmin University in South Korea and a BA in visual communication at KvB Institute of Technology, and is a professor at Hansung University's Design & Arts Institute. He's been awarded more than forty prizes, including ten Silver, two Gold, and four New Talent Annual Instructor Platinums from Graphis. He's had twenty solo exhibitions and more than sixty selected exhibitions, and he served as an editorial committee member of the Asia-Pacific Design No. 12 in Guangzhou, China. Most recently, he was a judge for the Korea, China, and Japan Illustration Contest.

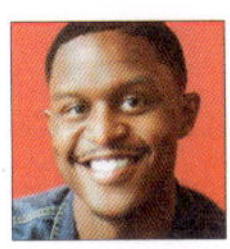

Introduction by Yumi Jung

Yumi Jung earned her bachelor's degree in industrial design and completed her master's degree in interior and spatial design at the University of the Arts in London. Currently, she is a brand consultant in the design marketing center at Daehong Communications in South Korea, mainly in charge of designing corporate identities and managing brand development. Based on her professional career and academic knowledge, she also gives lectures about personal branding at different universities and graduate schools.

128 From Graphis Books: Recent and Forthcoming Titles

ADVISORY BOARD:

136 Quinnton Harris / USA

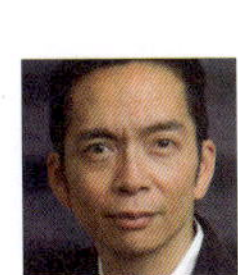

Retrospect co-founder and chief executive officer, Quinnton J. Harris is a creative leader and entrepreneur living in Brooklyn, New York. His new venture focuses on building products and digital experiences that are radical, culturally nuanced, and more accessible for untapped or overlooked market opportunities. Previously, he served as Publicis Sapient Group creative director within experience design as well as co-leader of global computational design, which focused on evolving the organization's design systems practice. He played a critical role in accelerating CXO John Maeda's vision for fostering a more inclusive, multidimensional, and cohesive experience design capability. He also served as head of Experience for San Francisco. In early 2020, he completed a short tenure as John Maeda's chief of staff, finding much success in pushing critical CXO initiatives, implementing systems for global collaboration, and enhancing internal communication strategies. Quinnton recently led the #hellajuneteenth movement and got over 600 companies committed to observing Juneteenth as a paid holiday for its employees. Prior to joining Publicis Sapient, he served as inaugural creative director at Blavity, Inc., and before that led design at Walker & Company Brands, a start-up consumer products and tech company notably acquired by Procter & Gamble. He is an MIT alum, graduating with a SB in mechanical engineering and dual minors in architecture and visual arts.

Introduction by John Maeda

John Maeda is an American technologist and product experience leader bridging business, engineering, and design via working inclusively. He's the SVP chief customer experience officer at Everbridge, working on the future of critical event management technologies for saving lives and keeping businesses and society running. John is an MIT-trained computer scientist, both risk manager (MBA effect) and risk taker (learner effect), and a seasoned for-profit/nonprofit growth executive. He's the author of five books, including the new *How To Speak Machine* and the bestselling *Laws of Simplicity*. He also recently was the EVP/CXO of IT consultancy Publicis Sapient, serving digital transformation needs globally and across industries, plus FED/SLED with the LEAD (Light, Ethical, Accessible, Dataful) system. John is also on the board of directors at Sonos and the Smithsonian Design Museum, was the former president/CEO of the Rhode Island School of Design, and was a partner at Kleiner Perkins Venture Capital in Silicon Valley. During his early career, Dr. Maeda was an MIT research professor in computational design, is represented in the permanent collection of the Museum of Modern Art, and is a recipient of the White House's National Design Award. He has appeared as a speaker all over the world, from Davos to Beijing to Sao Paulo to New York, and his TED talks have received millions of views.

144 Graphis Advisory Board Member Biographies

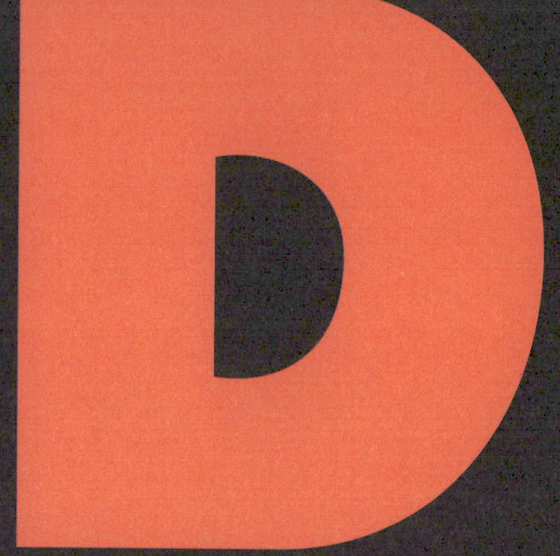

DESIGN

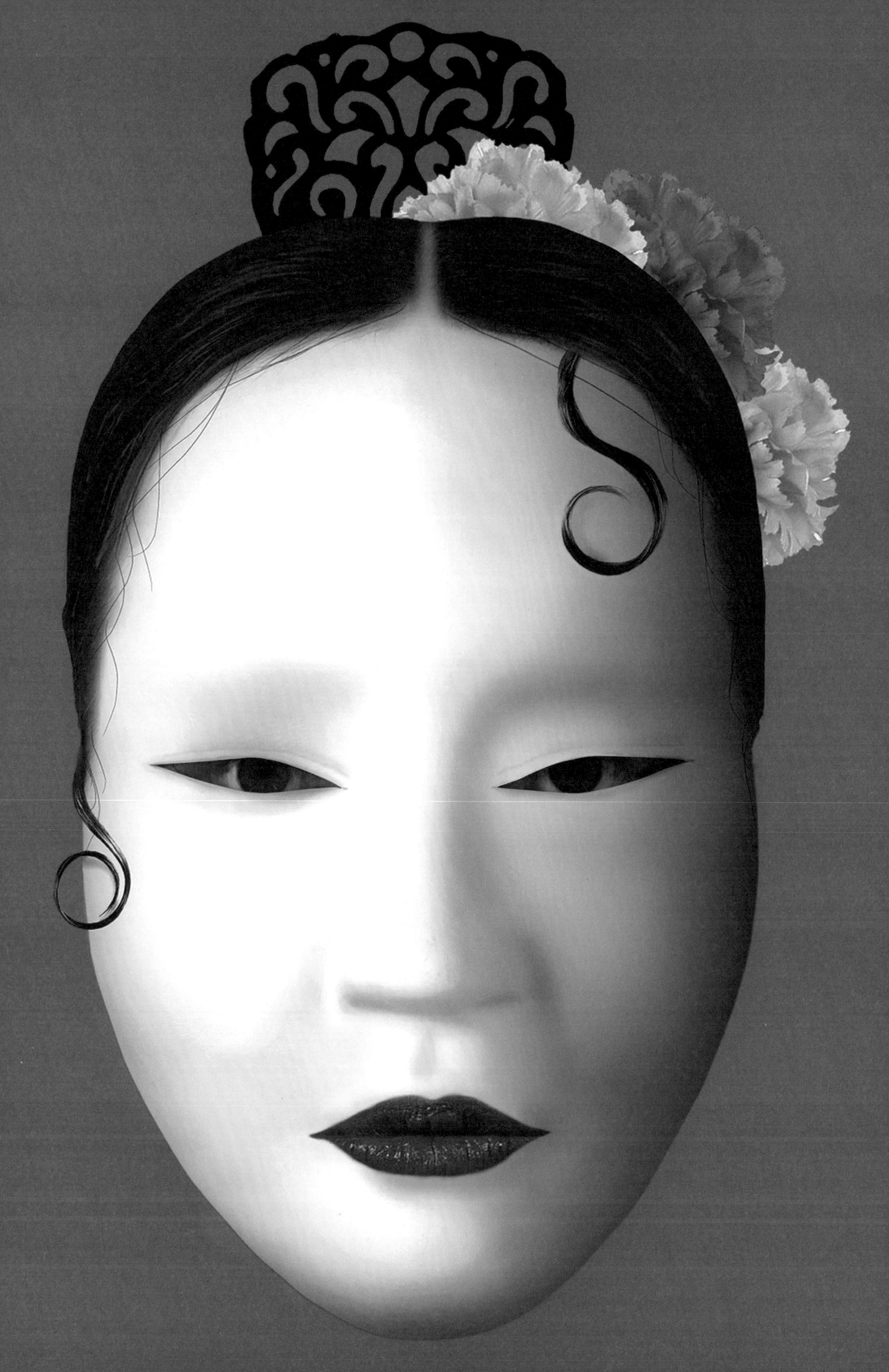

WORKING ON KONG WITH EDUARDO WAS GREAT. A WELL EXECUTED IDEA WAS PRESENT, AND WE'VE SEEN HOW THIS PROJECT HAS KNOCKED DOWN WALLS WITH A BEAUTIFUL STORY. WE'RE VERY PROUD AND HAPPY TO HAVE TAKEN PART IN THIS.

Carlos Sacristan, *Director, Kong Spirit*

BY OBSERVING HIS WORK, YOU REALIZE HE INHABITS TIME, KEEPING THE ESSENCE OF CHILDHOOD INTACT AND CREATING UNDER THE ILLUSION OF THAT ESSENCE, THROUGH WHICH HE IS ABLE TO ACHIEVE AN ASTOUNDING SIMPLICITY.

Ana Gea, *Co-founder of Gràffica Magazine*

EDUARDO'S WORK AND CREATIVITY ALLOWED US TO GIVE OUR COMPLEX ITS OWN PERSONALITY, IDENTITY, AND HISTORY. THROUGH HIS TALENT, AND TECHNIQUE, HE TRANSFORMED OUR PROJECT AND HELPED US ACHIEVE OUR GOALS.

David Conesa, *Head of Communication at Grupo Orenes*

HE IS THE KING MIDAS OF DESIGN: EVERYTHING HE TOUCHES TURNS INTO GOLD. HIS WORKS ARE A PERFECT MARRIAGE OF INTELLIGENCE, CREATIVITY, STRATEGY, AND HEART.

Maria Pradera, *Creative Director, Yinsen Studio*

HE GETS UNDER THE SKIN OF PRODUCTS AND WEARS THEM AS A FASHION DESIGNER DOES WITH MODELS. HE IS TREMENDOUSLY CREATIVE, AND HIS CREATIONS ALWAYS HAVE A DISTINCTIVE AND PERSONAL IMPRINT.

Lorenzo Abellán, *Director, Carchelo Wines*

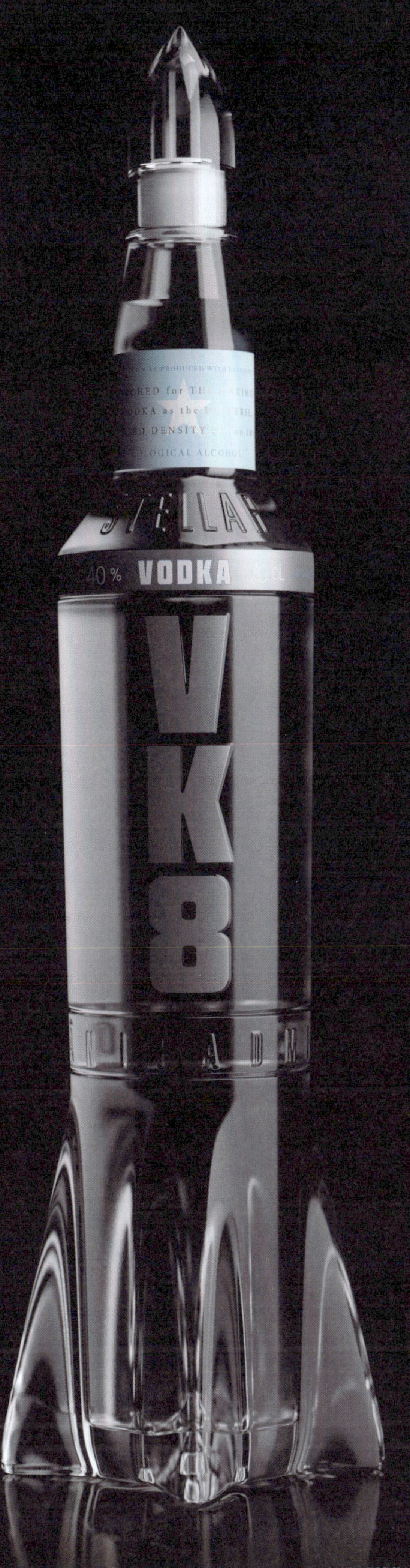

(Page 9) LASCALA SPANISH WINE IN CHINA, 2013 / (Above) Rocket Bottle VK8 VODKA 2019/2020

In his beautiful studio on the coast of Alicante, Eduardo del Fraile keeps cooking up great designs that will later travel across the world on labels, brands, books, or even objects. De Fraile's successful style is characterized by a symbolic morphing of concepts, words, and shapes, which efficiently and elegantly embody and help convey the valued propositions of his clients. He listens and observes, considers each and every case carefully with his small team of close collaborators, and then confidently leads the way towards a version of the brand that no one suspected was there: playing with conflicting and decontextualized elements and sprinkling them with a zest of witty irony, Del Fraile brings surprise and emotion to everyday products. With the same poise and conviction he uses for his clients, Eduardo has recently undertaken a few projects in order to push the boundaries of his design skills and test the waters of entrepreneurship. Based on his previous trajectory, he will undoubtedly succeed in this as well, so it's worth keeping an eye on!

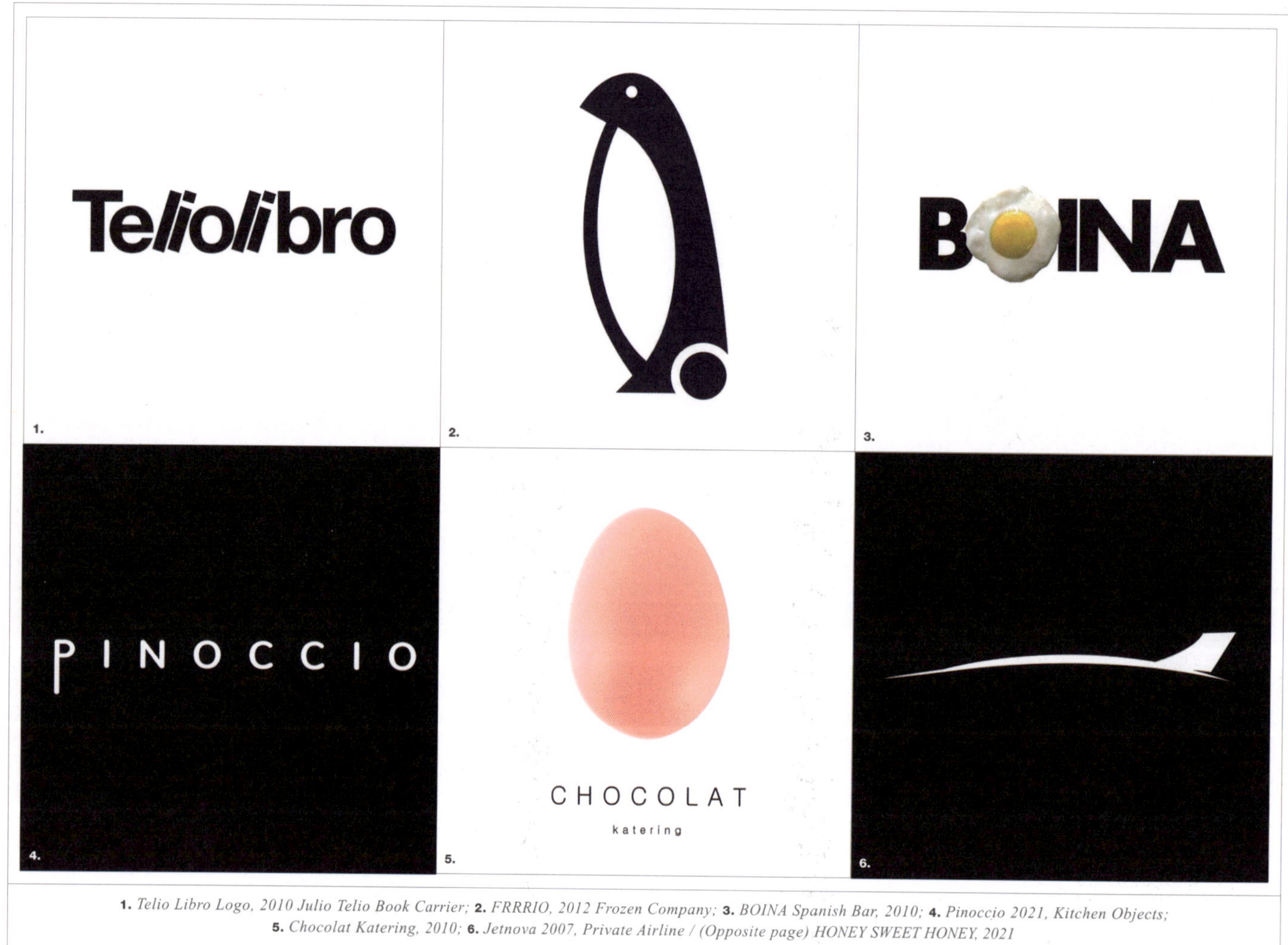

1. *Telio Libro Logo, 2010 Julio Telio Book Carrier;* **2.** *FRRRIO, 2012 Frozen Company;* **3.** *BOINA Spanish Bar, 2010;* **4.** *Pinoccio 2021, Kitchen Objects;* **5.** *Chocolat Katering, 2010;* **6.** *Jetnova 2007, Private Airline / (Opposite page) HONEY SWEET HONEY, 2021*

I TRY TO BE A PART OF ALL THE STAGES OF PRODUCTION, AND THANKS TO THIS I AM CONSTANTLY LEARNING. **Eduardo del Fraile,** *Founder & Creative Director, Eduardo del Fraile Studio*

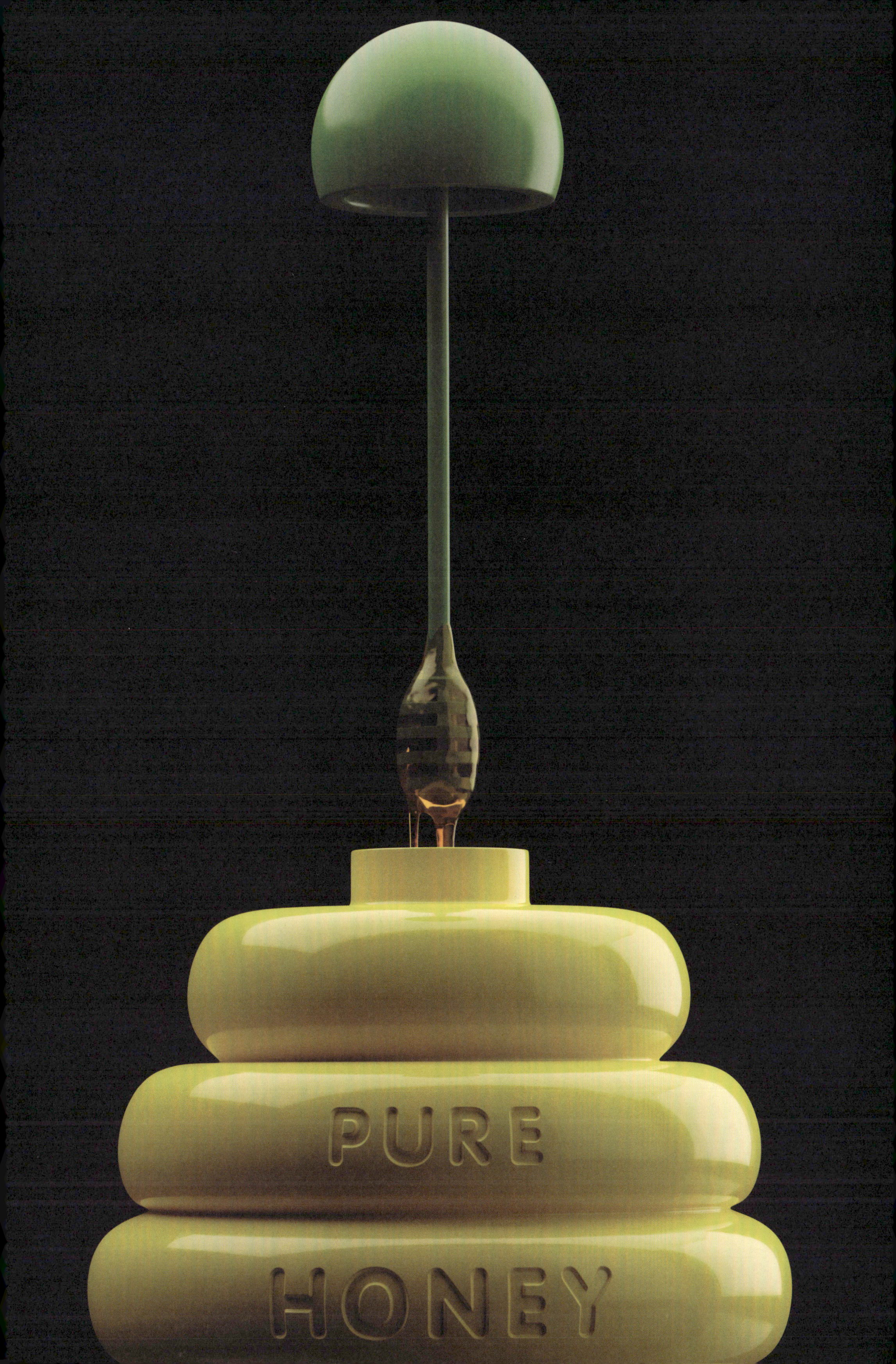

PURE
HONEY

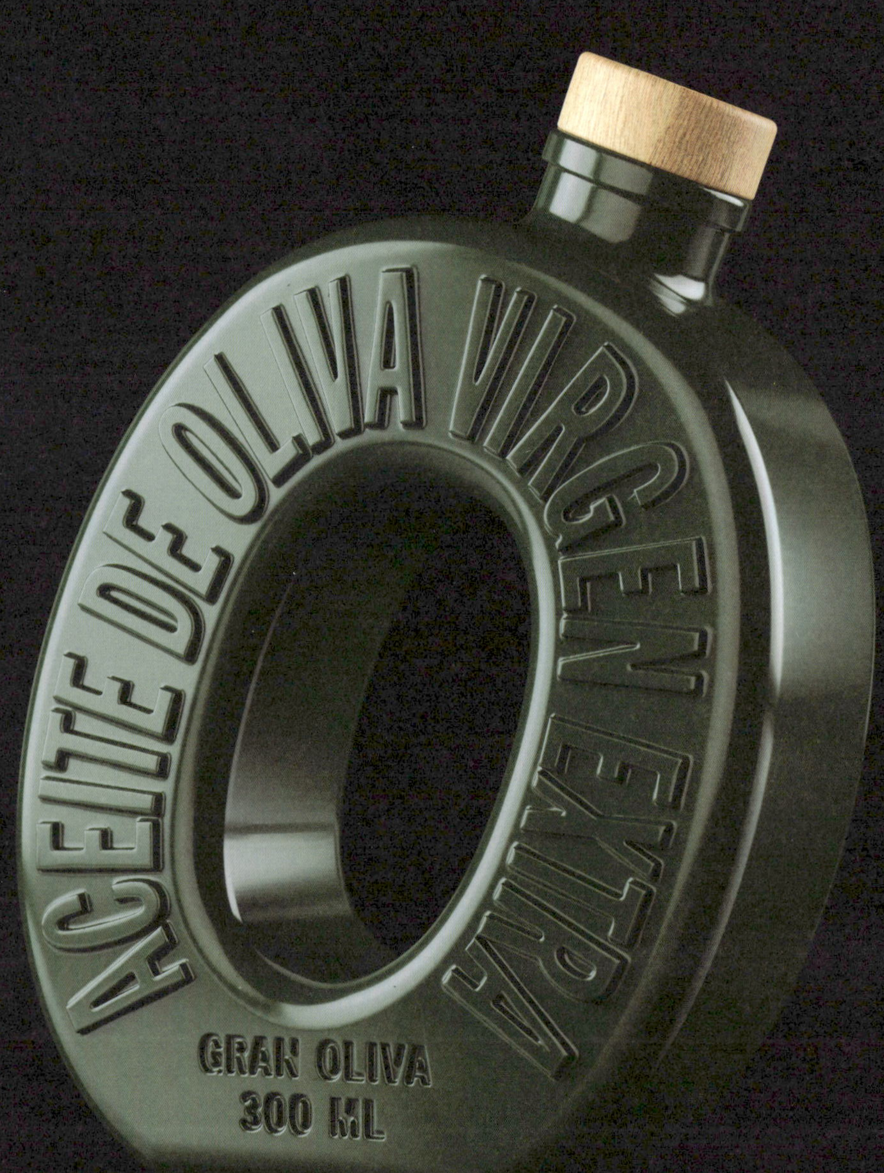

(Above) GRAN OLIVA, 2021/2022 BIOFRUITS / (Opposite page) LASCALA SPANISH WINE IN CHINA, 2013

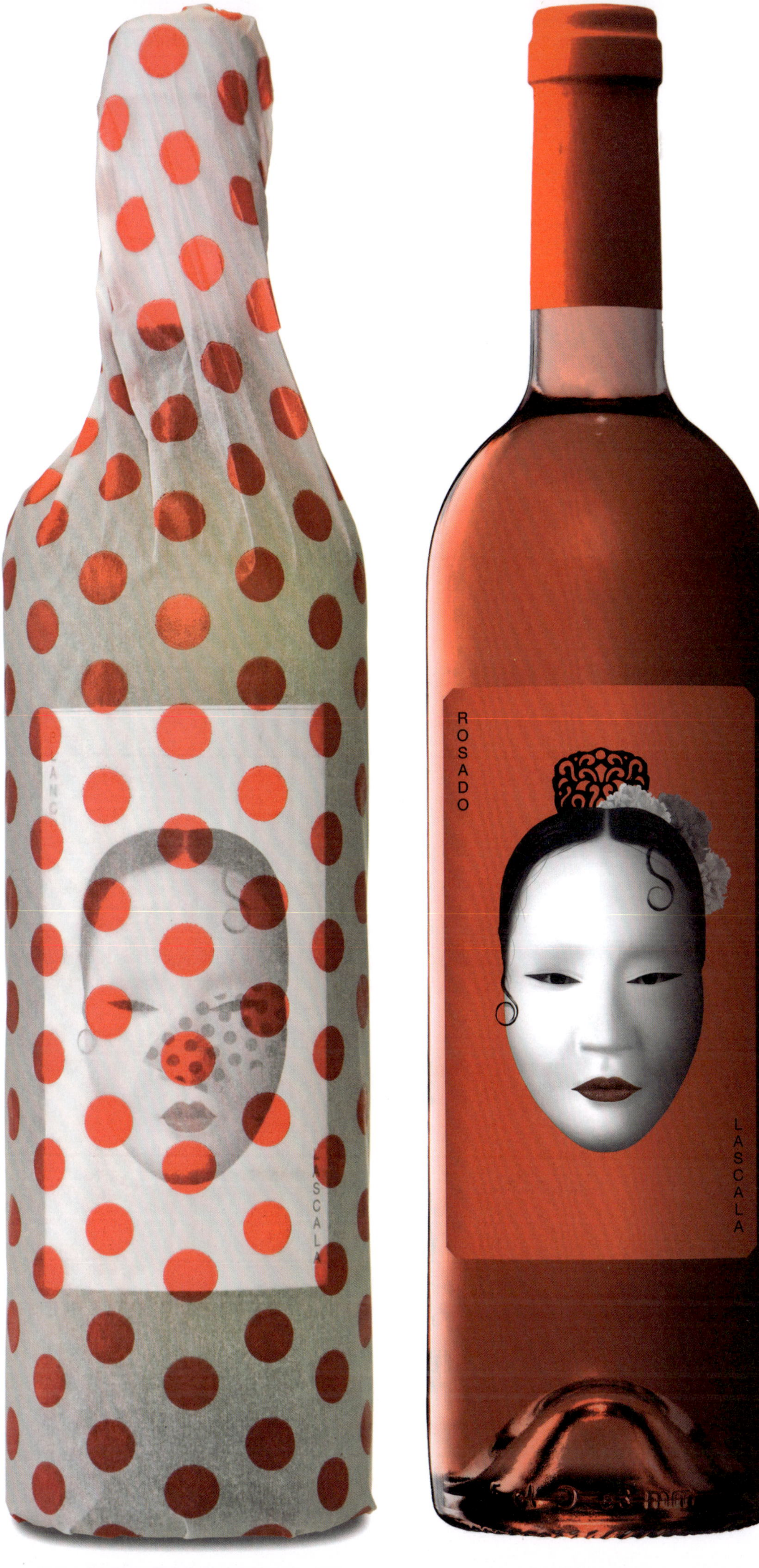

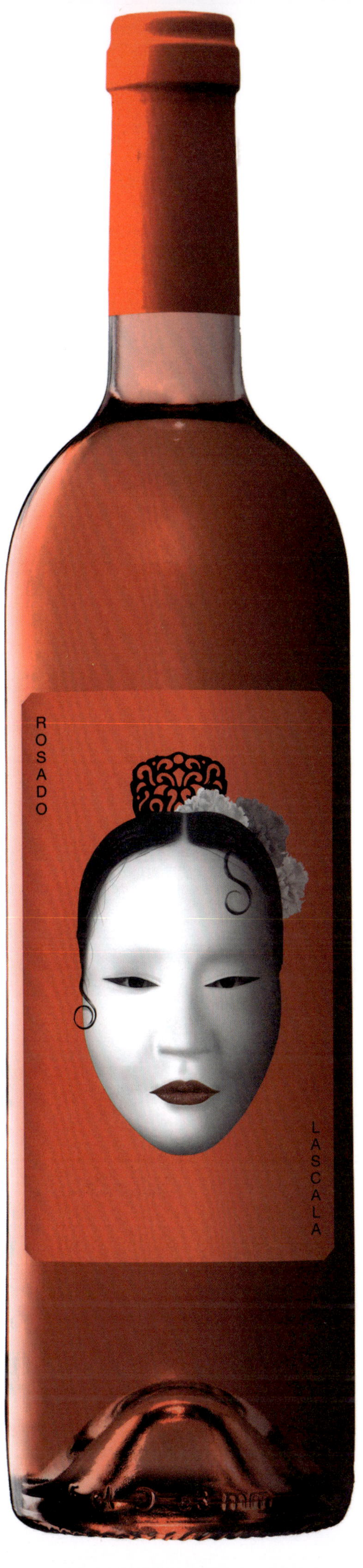
ROSADO
LASCALA

Who is or was your best mentor?
During my studies in Barcelona at Escola Elisava, I had two professors who knew how to develop talent: Enric Jardi and Jordi Almuni. It was during the 1992 Olympics in Barcelona and, at that time in Spain, Mariscal was responsible for bringing design to the general population. His illustrations and his way of communicating them transmitted happiness. However, the coolest thing in those days was to have magazines like *Raygun* or Emigre's typographic work. Personally, I was drawn more towards Scandinavian design since it organized my mind.

At HDK Goteborg, the deceased HC Erikson made you understand the magnitude of the design profession. Both schools reflect two key positions. Escola Elisava is more oriented to the tradition of Catalan design and is represented by the researching spirit of Enric Bricall, one of the key figures in the design scene. He's credited with putting the design teaching system on the map. HDK Goteborg is more rational, with a very specific design tradition such as the Swedish school, where I felt respect towards the materials, nature, and design's important role in society.

With these two approaches, I was able to understand how the various branches of design can coexist in the same building. This has also broadened my expectations by better understanding its various disciplines.

What career achievement are you most proud of?
I was very honored to be part of the packaging jury at the D&AD, and years later (2018) I was called again to be president of the same packaging jury.

I followed their annual publication every year when I was a student. I believe the work of this type of organization gives a solid base to the profession. I grew up with those yearbooks and with the ones from Graphis; both were a part of the studios where I worked and later on in mine.

What is your work philosophy?
This is a studio represented by the name of a designer. I've always liked old Chinese movies in which the karate school respected its founder's philosophy. I've been practicing yoga for many years, and I try to combine this discipline with my work. The studio functions like a restaurant, with delicate cuisine and just the right amount of customers.

I work with two design assistants on a regular basis and have been doing this for twenty years. I try to be a part of all the stages of production, and thanks to this I'm constantly learning.

I design by linking clear concepts with very formal synthetic systems and a marked art direction. The studio's evolution and my own interest give more and more direction to product design. It's as if the designs are growing and becoming more physical; it's more fun and interesting. Now the whole studio has more volume. I call it a symbolic product.

What is the most difficult challenge you've had to overcome?
I think, without a doubt, the development of KONG SPIRIT, a project that supports the Eastern gorilla and is based on the original adventure of Dian Fossey. The spirit drink is inspired by the gorilla's habitat. The amount of bottles produced in each batch corresponds with the official number of surviving gorillas. The company proposes a spirit drink from the standpoint of the soul of the animal. It was founded by my studio. The Dian Fossey Gorilla Fund and GRACE Gorillas supported us in the project, and we rely on their certificates, as well as other information, to obtain the official number of gorillas to produce each batch. Their support has been a great part of the project.

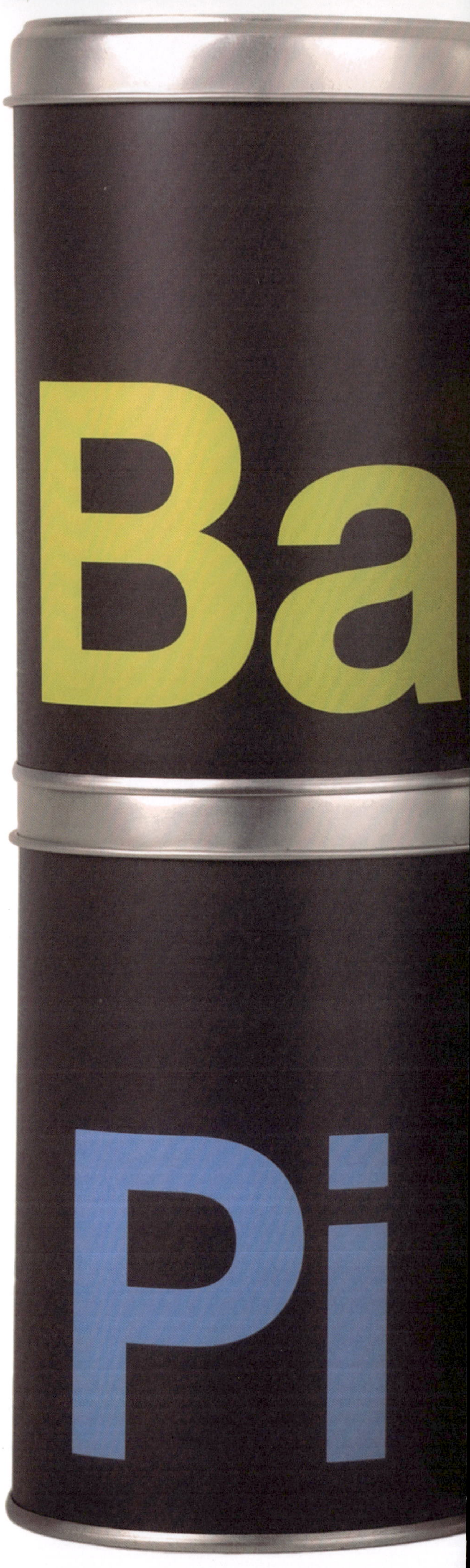

SALT for Jose Ros Soso Factory, 2010

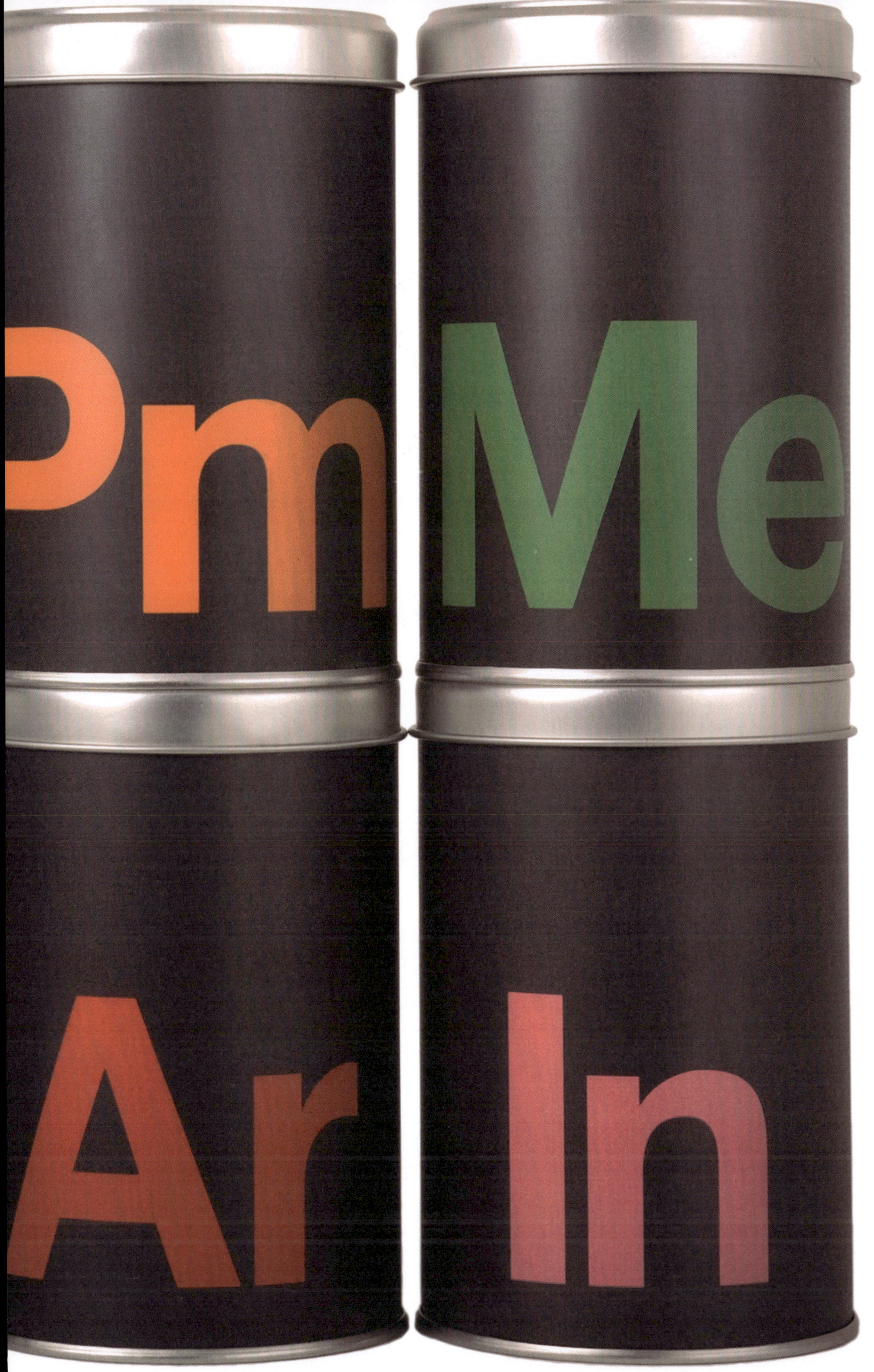

It was a complete development concept elaboration. I invested a large part of the studio's savings. It was a leap of faith where we had to take into account many factors, and we achieved great things. A few partners came to be a part of the project during its development, such as the beloved Ricardo de Santiago from Txoco S.L., and Almudena, who later became my wife and who was my emotional support while making something so beautiful come to life.

After four years of struggle that entailed the creation of a bottle in the shape of a twelve-year-old mountain gorilla carved in clay, the communication of a global concept around the gorilla, the creation of a spirit drink that was inspired by the 146 types of herbs, fruits, and trees that make up the gorilla's diet and that won several awards at beverage festivals for its quality and differentiation, and building the structural axis of the global company, we decided that we should do this with a stronger and more consolidated group. We built a great, unique, and special ship and partnered with a business group to help us navigate the seas. In other words, it was at this point in time when KONG took on a life of its own.

*What interests do you have outside of
your job?*
Yoga, cinema, and above all learning from nature. I'm very interested in Chinese medicine because it doesn't approach the problem from a single standpoint; it expands and looks at it as a whole. The solution comes through knowledge and intuition.

*Why are you so interested in working on the
shape or volume of a design?*
I think that the work is more complete. There are more elements at stake. You need more technical knowledge. Working on the volume poses many questions, and the graph takes on another dimension. It isn't the same when you have a customer pointing to a bottle and saying, "I want to try the Rocket Vodka."

The simplest answer is usually the most obvious one, and I think that bringing graphic design closer to the industrial sometimes generates more powerful answers.

*What is the story behind the creation of
Eduardo del Fraile Studio?*
It was a leap into the void in every way. Twenty years ago, I decided to go my own way after working at two design agencies. The first one was in Barcelona and was more focused on great

teamwork. The second one was with Jose Maria Nuño de la Rosa, a signature studio located in Murcia in southern Spain where I learned that a small structure can generate great work dynamics.

My first office was the very room where I slept in my parents' house. I began to land big clients, and I was still finishing the office for the studio. So, my mother Pilar (who was an artist in her time) served as the receptionist. Those were very fun and intense days. Everything came into place with a very nice loft. First, my sister Ana helped in administration, and currently my wife Almudena does many tasks around the studio.

It's the result of many years of intense work. One of the most beautiful surprises was when clients from other cities in Spain and from other countries such as Japan, South Korea, and Italy began to knock on my door.

*What would you like to change about
design today?*
When we become more professional, we tend to limit disciplines. On the other hand, when you investigate something new, the opposite happens.

When we did the pasta work, there were colleagues who didn't understand the purpose of doing it. It wasn't a brand, a label, or a poster. It was simply going to the base of the product itself and changing it symbolically. It's interesting that there are jobs that open other roads for a profession.

In which area would you like to do more research?
Definitely in the process and behavior of the materials.

Waiting for the craftsman who's been working with you to produce a piece is very exhilarating. In recent years, there has been great development in the research of production volume and its materials.

We've worked for environmental agencies in many projects, and they've trained us to become acquainted with the world of recycling in all its stages.

We've also worked with biodegradable polymers or making packages from the peels of oranges, polymers that pose as an option to the PET, or with thermoformed organic materials such as rice paste, clay, and porcelain. All these are technical solutions that are involved in the design process. I find them all very interesting and have had the opportunity to solve some assignments or studio projects with them.

Eduardo del Fraile Studio www.eduardodelfraile.com
See their Graphis Master Portfolio on graphis.com.

WHEN WE BECOME MORE PROFESSIONAL, WE TEND TO LIMIT DISCIPLINES. ON THE OTHER HAND, WHEN YOU INVESTIGATE SOMETHING NEW, THE OPPOSITE HAPPENS. **Eduardo del Fraile,** *Founder & Creative Director, Eduardo del Fraile Studio*

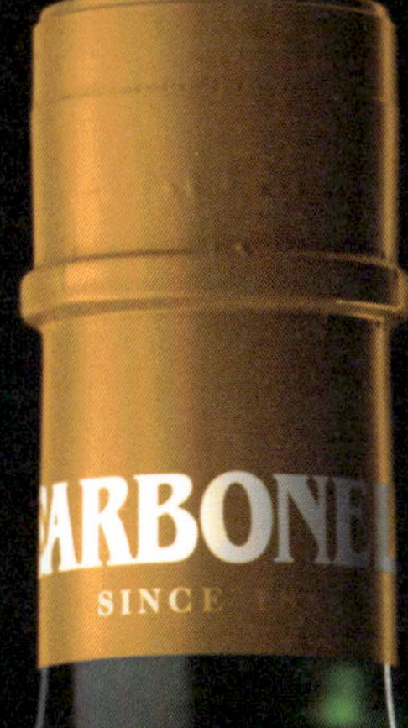
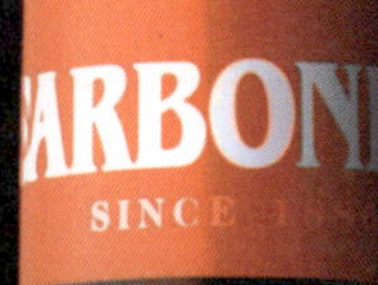
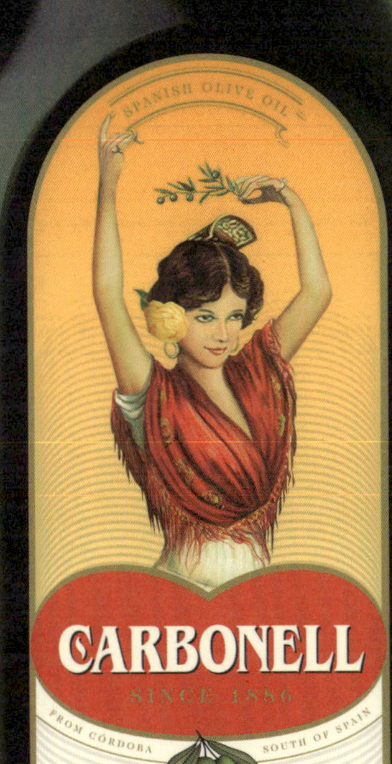

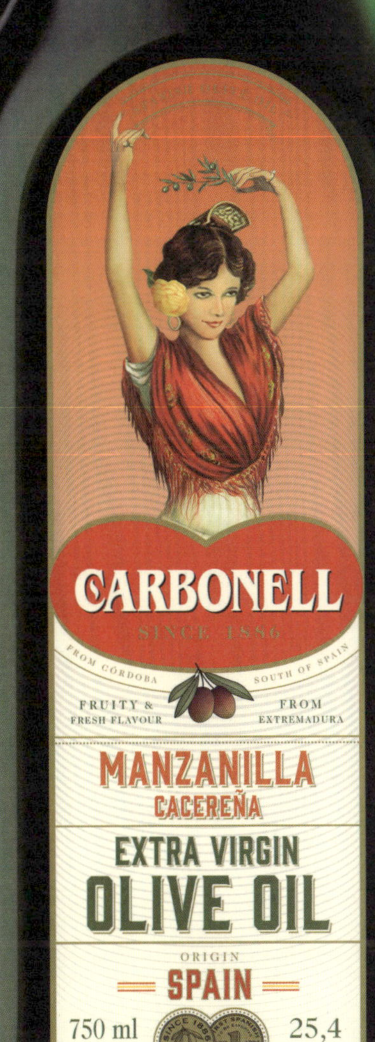

(Opposite page, above) Redesign for Carbonell USA Range, 2020/2021

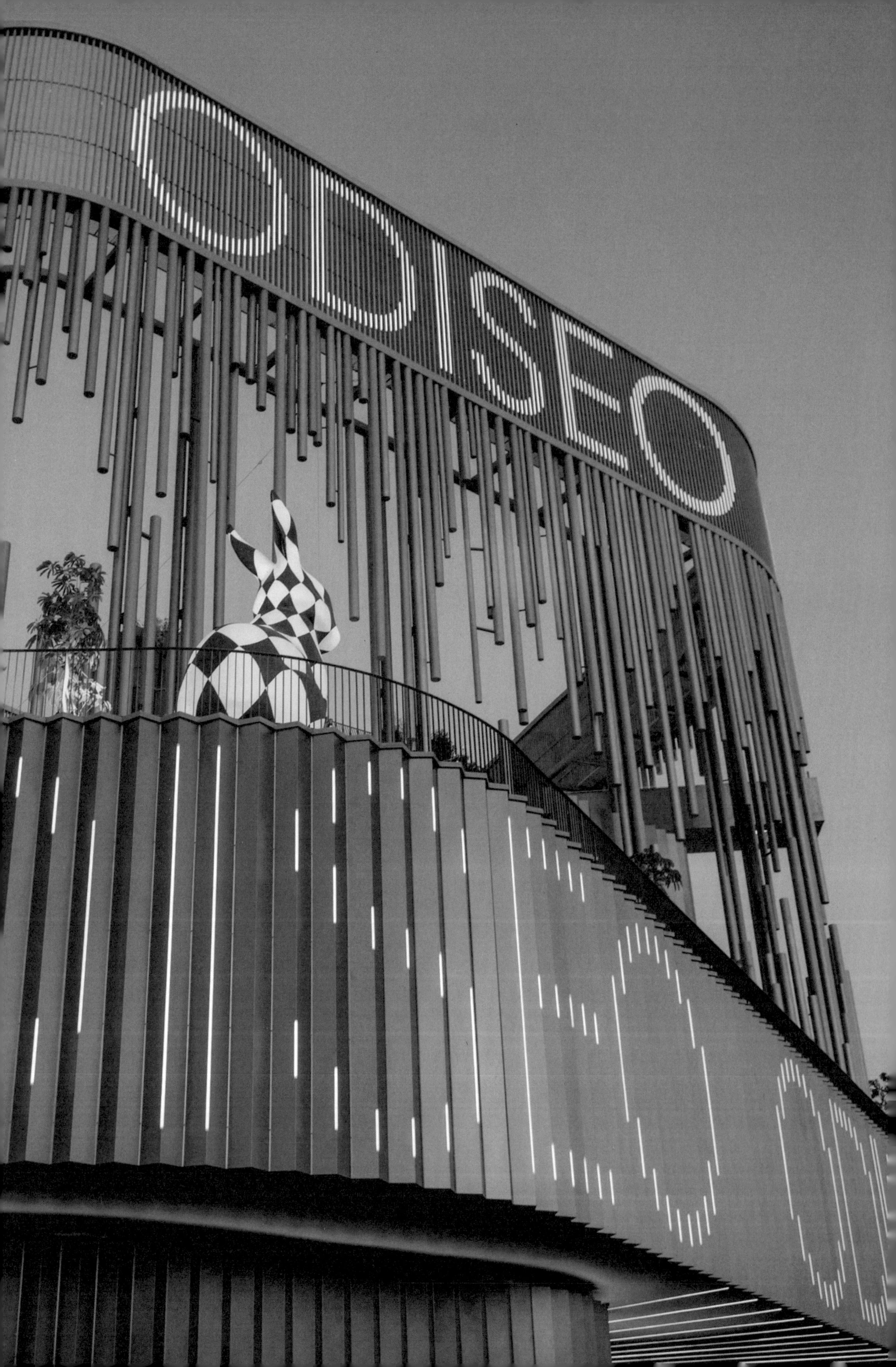
ODISEO

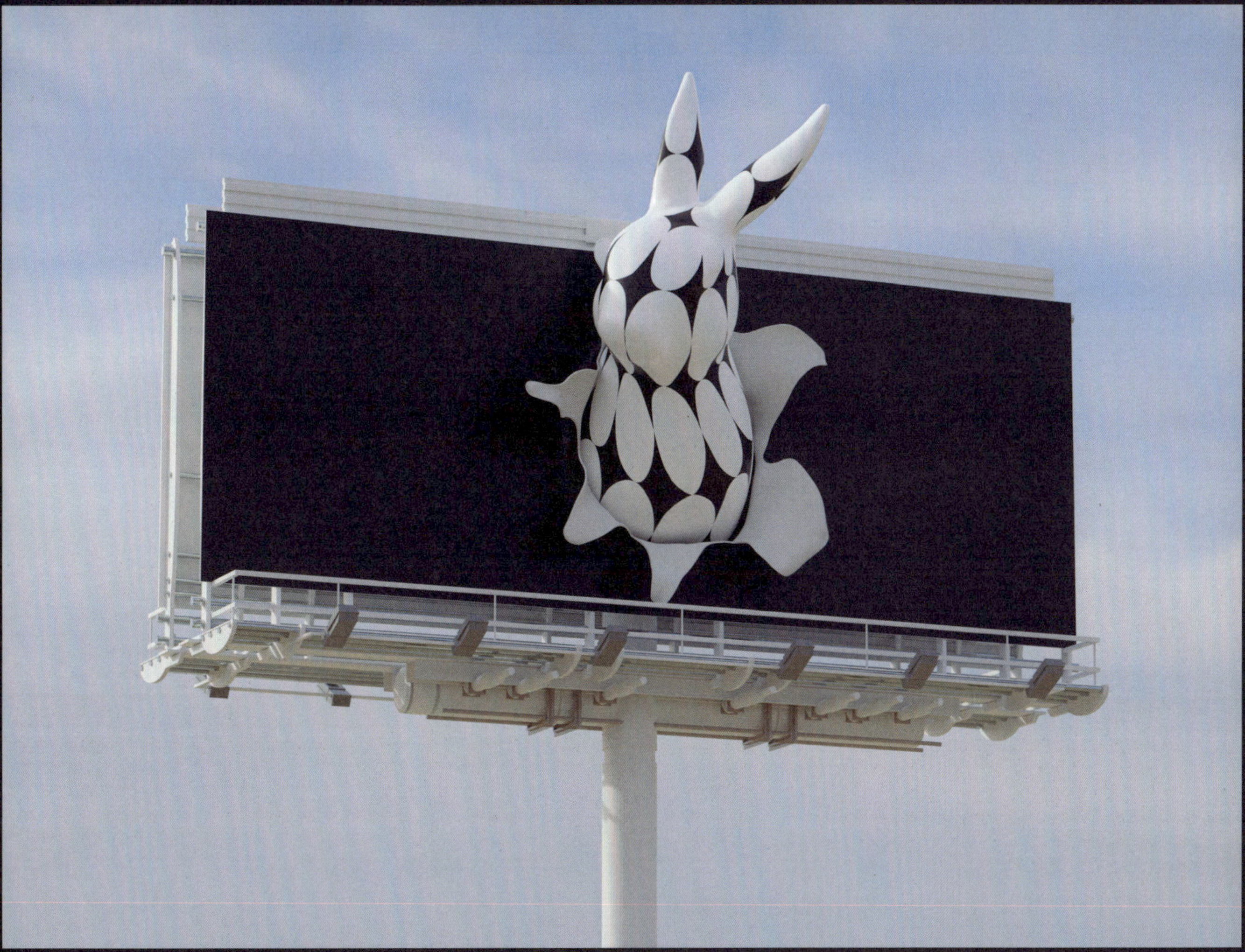

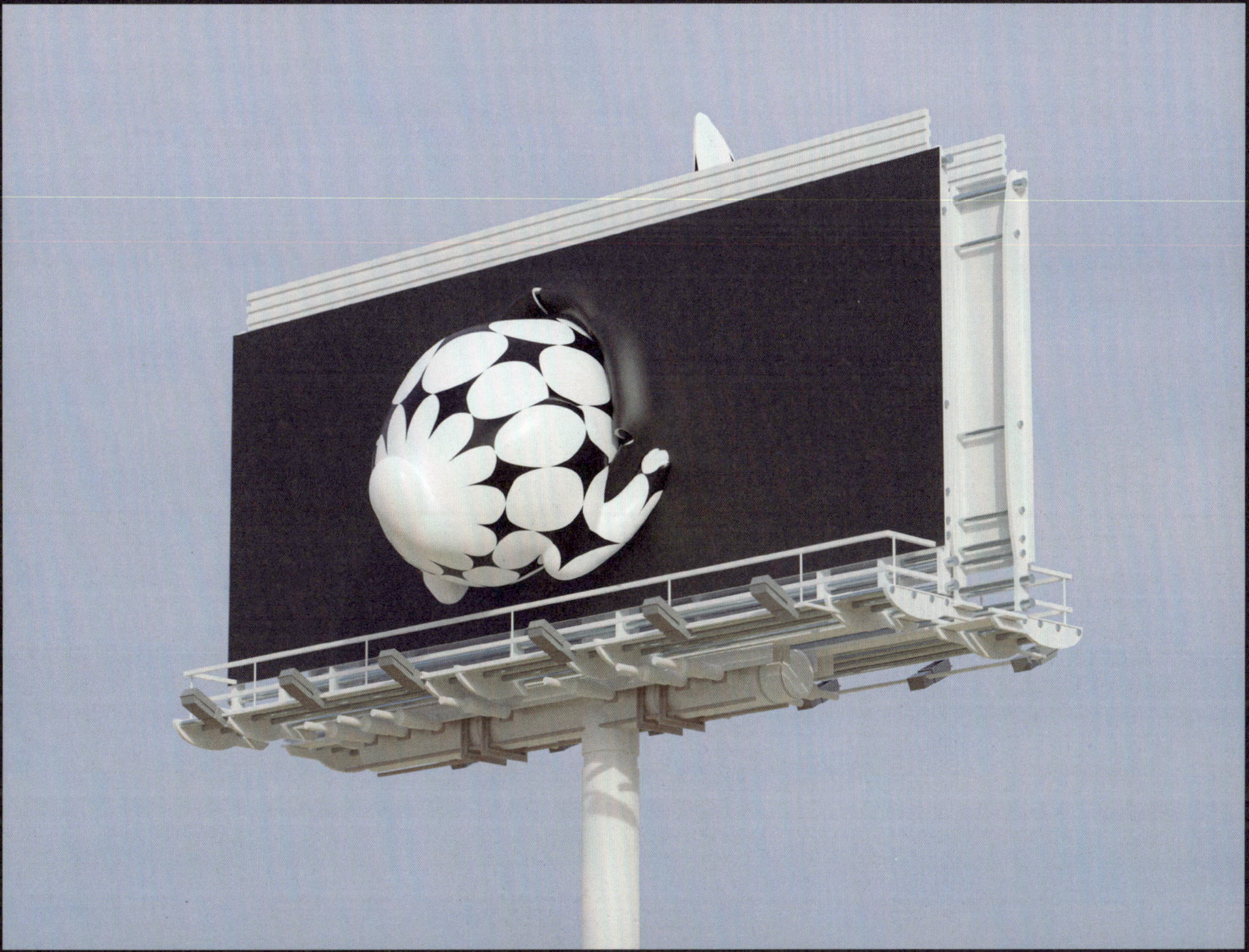

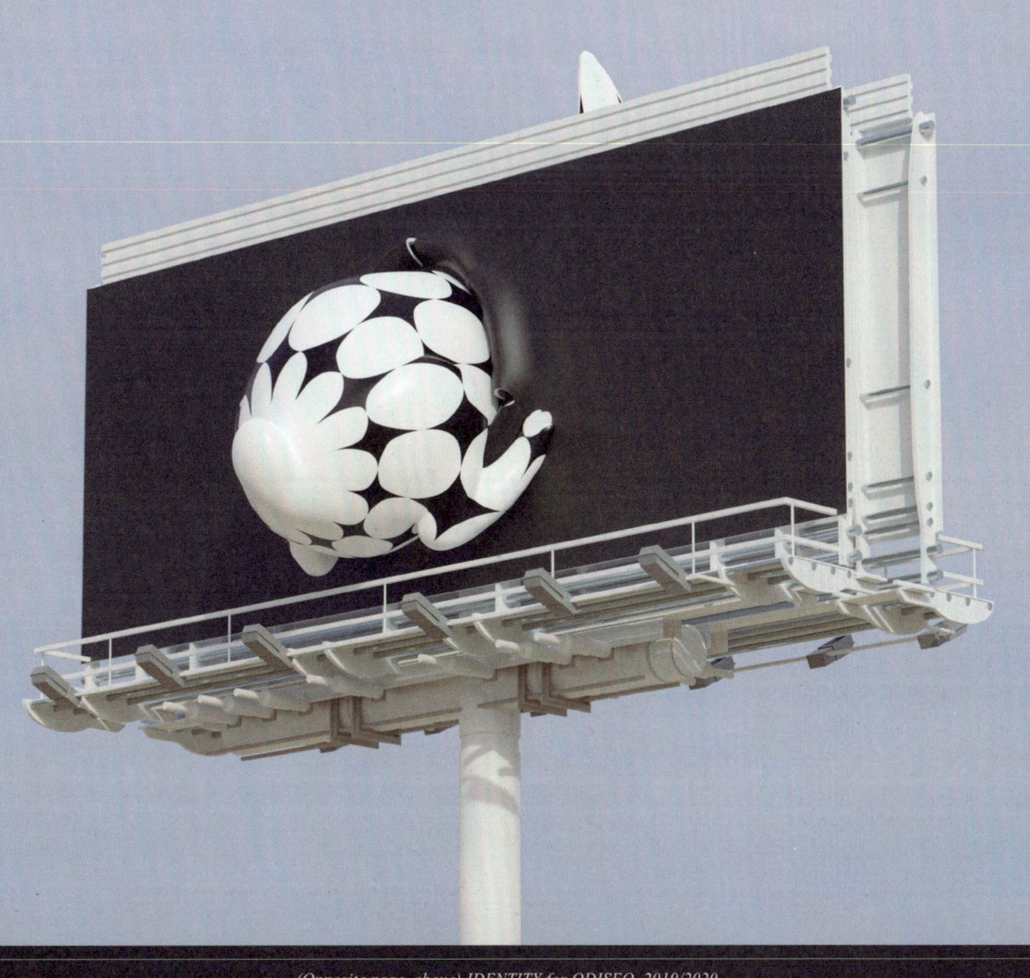

(Opposite page, above) IDENTITY for ODISEO, 2019/2020

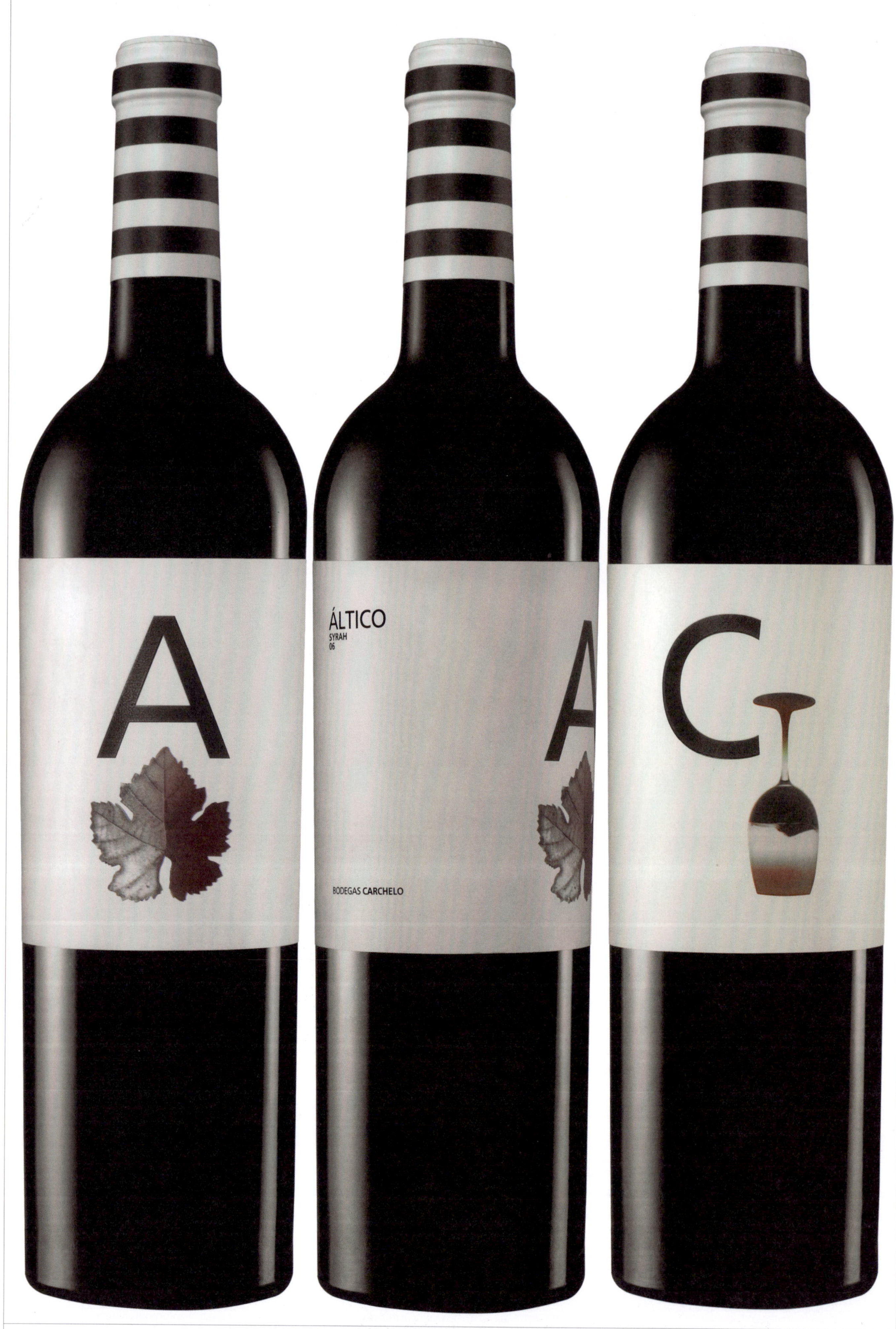

Bodegas Carchelo Design Range Wines, 2009/2012

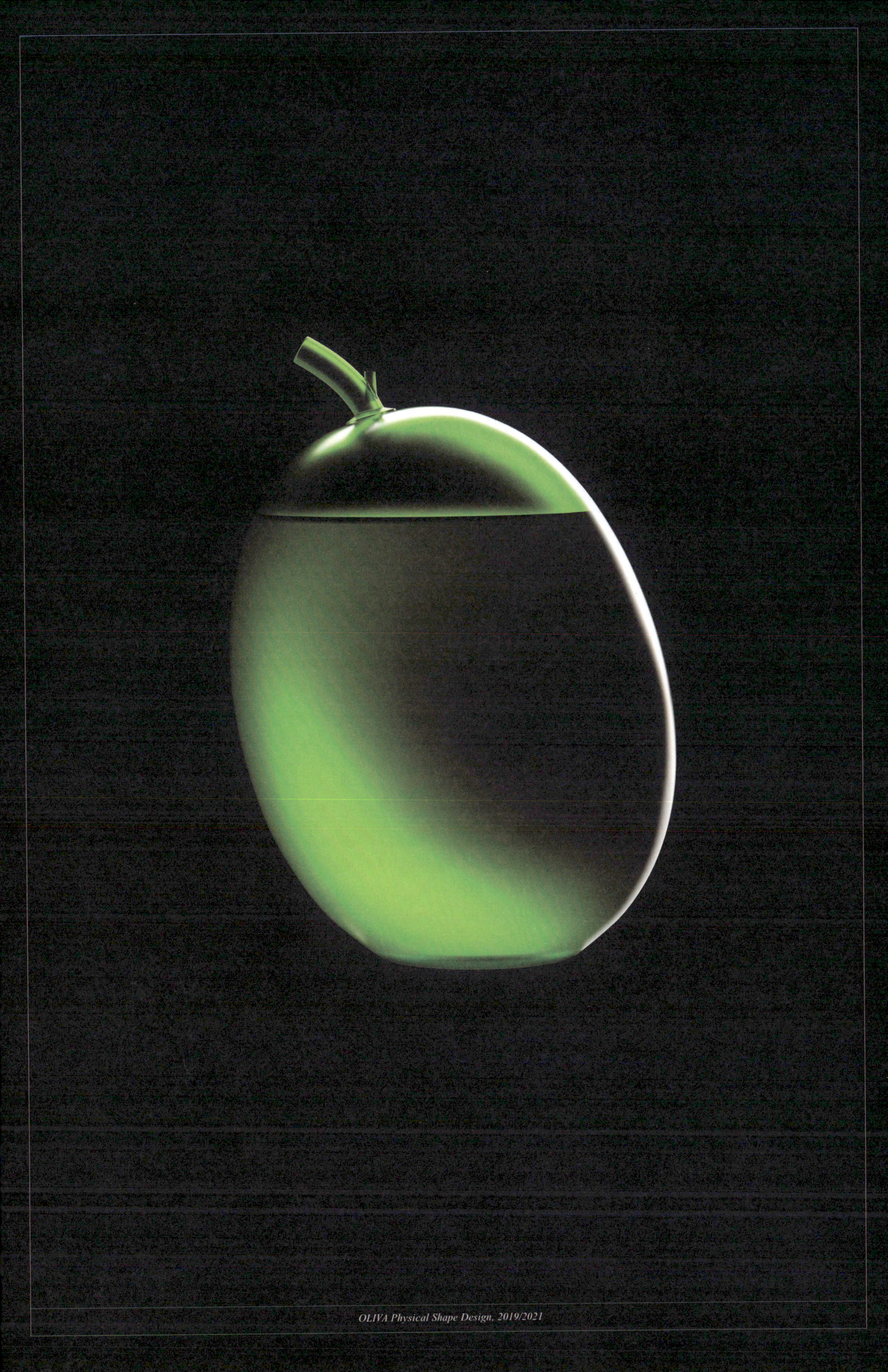

OLIVA Physical Shape Design, 2019/2021

HAJIME IS A GOOD GRAPHIC DESIGNER AND IS
IN PERFECT HARMONY WITH JAPANESE TRADITIONS,
SHAPES, AND NEW EXPRESSIONS. HIS DESIGN
PERFECTLY EMBODIES OUR SIXTY YEAR TRADITION,
HISTORY, TECHNOLOGY, AND INNOVATION.
Hidetoshi Maehama, *Chairman, Maehama Kogyo Co., Ltd.*

HE'S A TALENTED DESIGNER WHO HELPED US
CREATE OUR COMPANY LOGO, PRODUCT BINDER,
AND BROCHURE. WE'VE SINCE THEN RECEIVED
DESIGN AWARDS THANKS TO HIM. WE HOPE HE'LL
CONTINUE TO SUCCEED IN THE FUTURE.
Toshiaki Hirai, *Account Executive, Studio Zen Wallcoverings*

HIS IMAGINATION GOES FAR BEYOND EXPECTATIONS.
HIS DESIGNS HAVE THE POWER TO DRAW THE
VIEWER INTO THEIR DEPTHS; THE MORE YOU LOOK,
THE MORE YOU LOVE THEM. THE DESIGN FOR OUR
IROHERB PROJECT WILL LAST FOR MANY YEARS.
Takahiro Ishikawa, *President, Nest House*

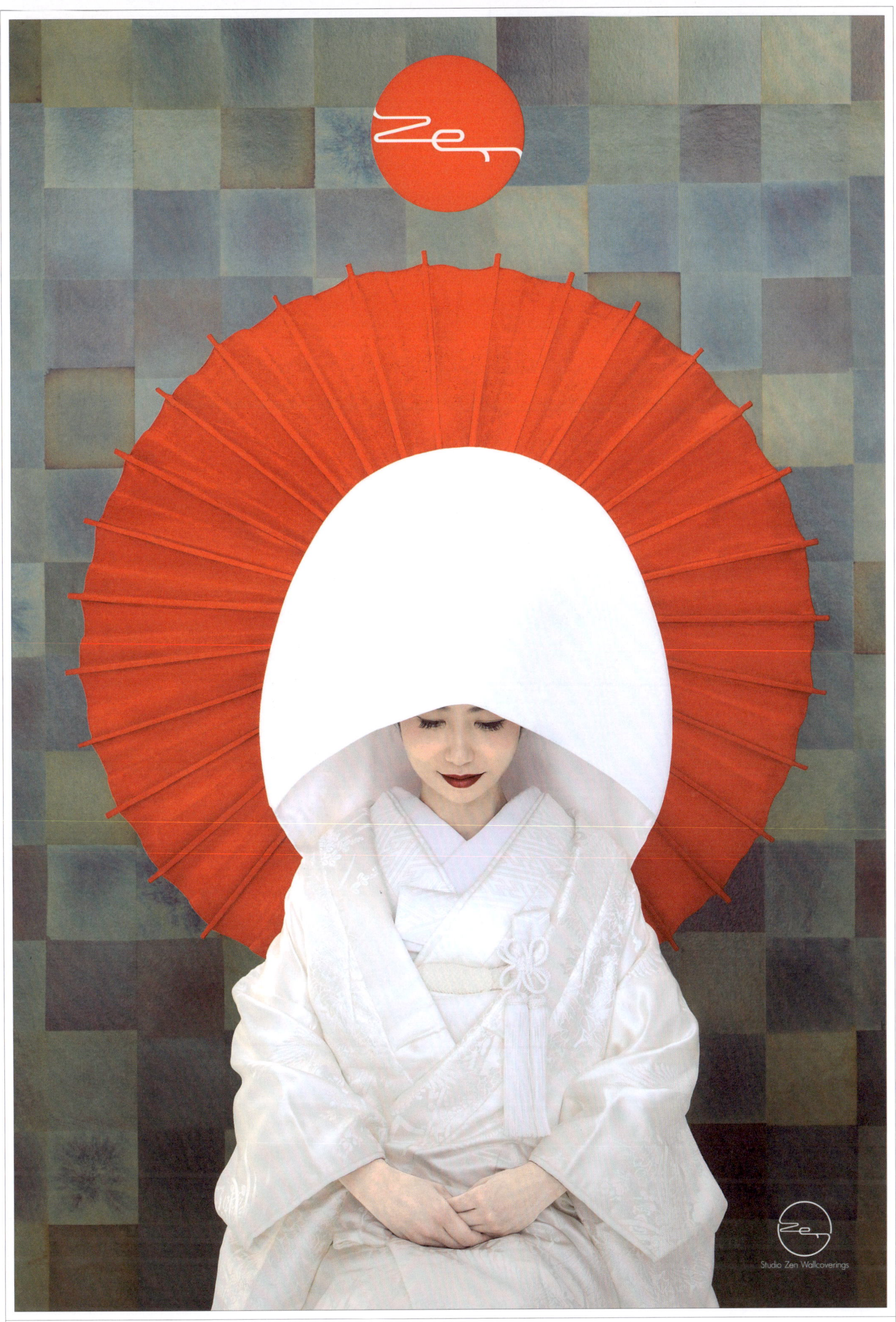

Title: Studio Zen Wallcoverings; Client: Studio Zen Wallcoverings; Art Director: Hajime Tsushima; Creative Director: Yukiko Tsushima; Designer: Hajime Tsushima; Photographer: Takeshi Shimizu; Model: Eimy; Design Firm: Tsushima Design

We met Mr. Tsushima for the first time when we asked him to design a label for sake wines, one of Japan's traditional drinks. Since then, we have been working together for five years on web design, package designs, and so forth. He is a designer with high technical skills, and at the same time a special person to us because he embodies clients' thoughts and wishes while at times inspiring many ideas and surprises.

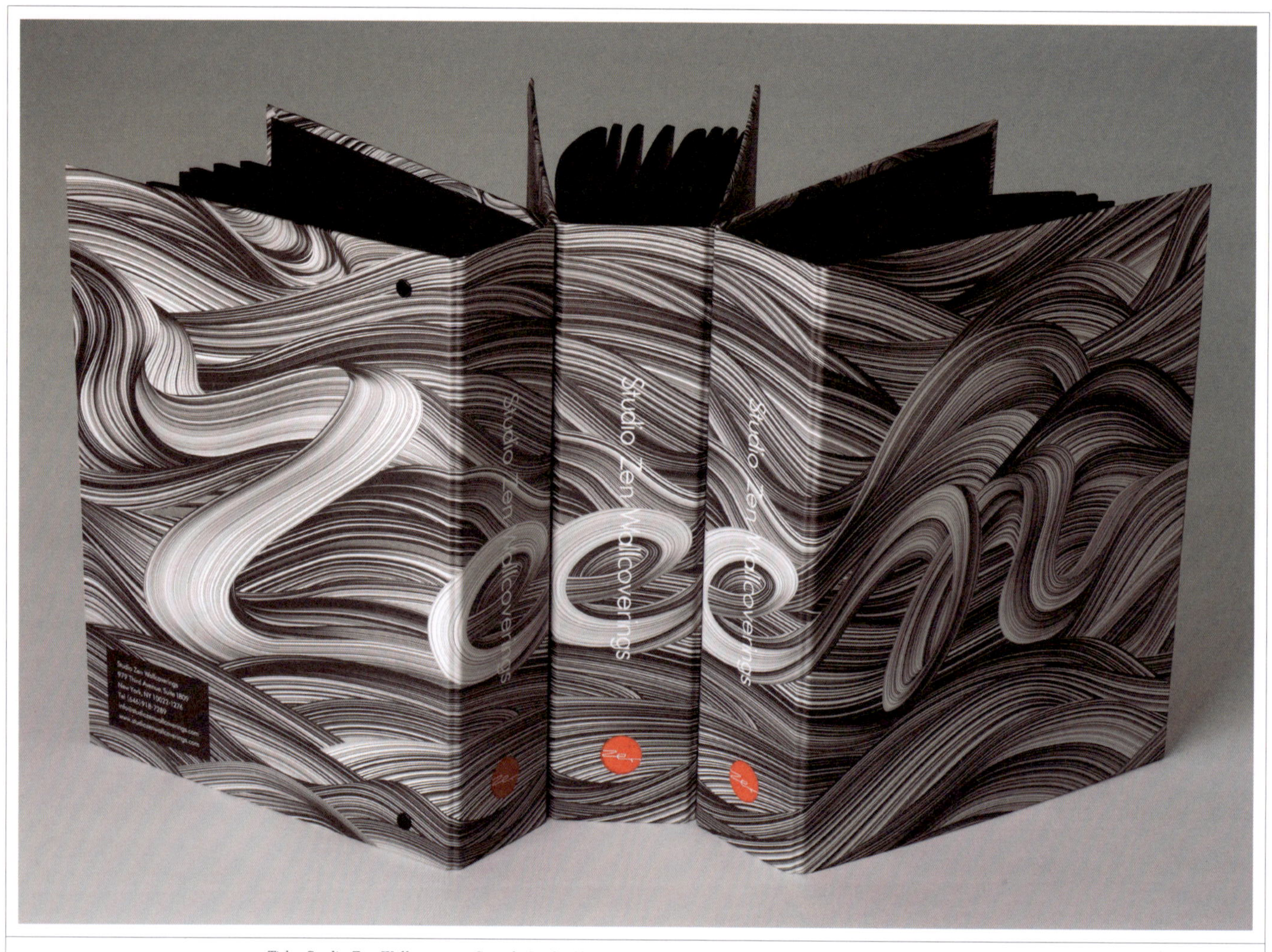

Title: Studio Zen Wallcoverings Sample Book; Client: Studio Zen Wallcoverings; Art Director: Hajime Tsushima;
Creative Director: Yukiko Tsushima; Designers: Hajime Tsushima, Yukiko Tsushima; Design Firm: Tsushima Design

I BELIEVE THAT THE POWER OF MY DESIGN IS
THE MOST IMPORTANT THING TO MAKE
CUSTOMERS AND VARIOUS PEOPLE HAPPY.

Hajime Tsushima, *Founder & Art Director, Tsushima Design*

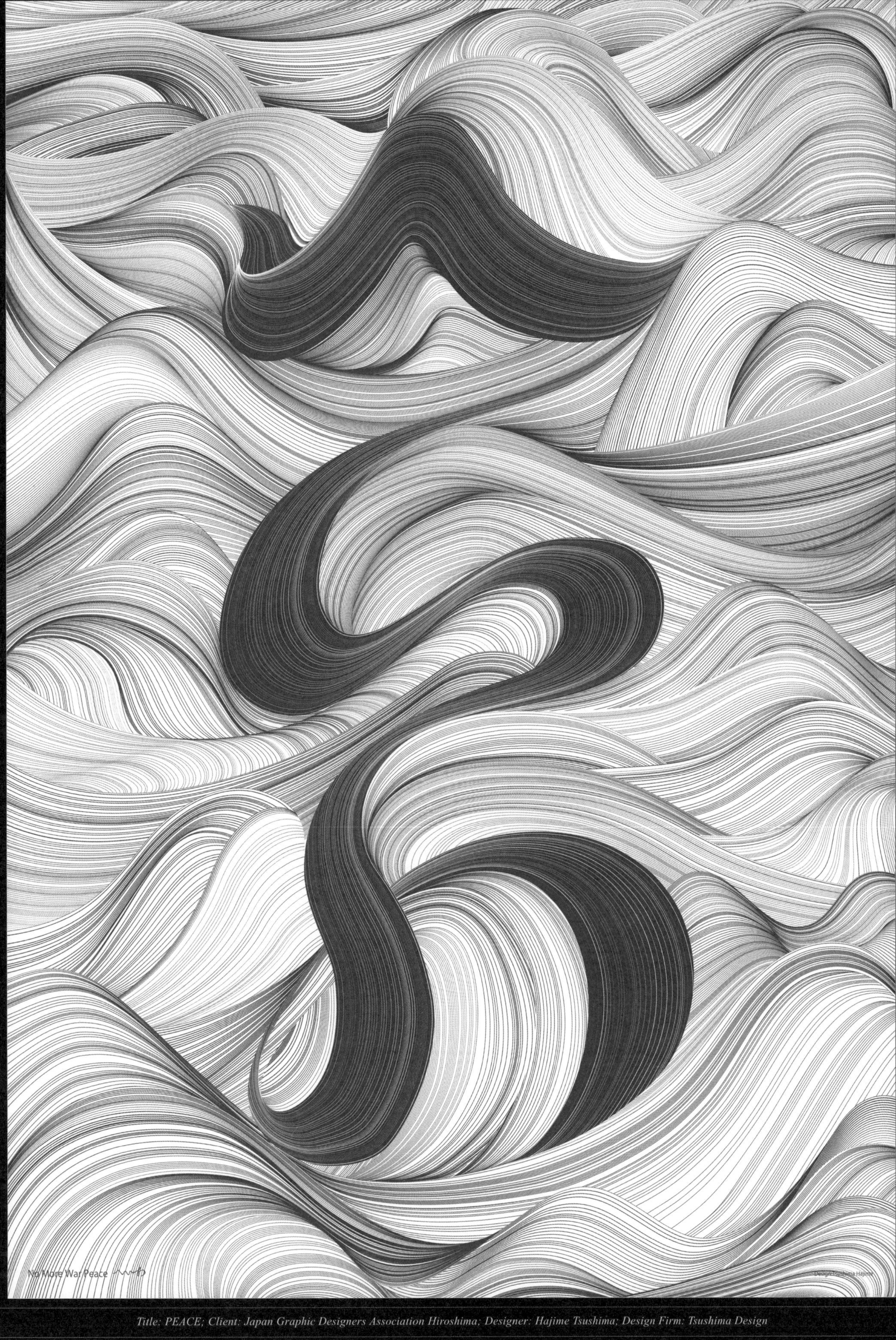

Title: PEACE; Client: Japan Graphic Designers Association Hiroshima; Designer: Hajime Tsushima; Design Firm: Tsushima Design

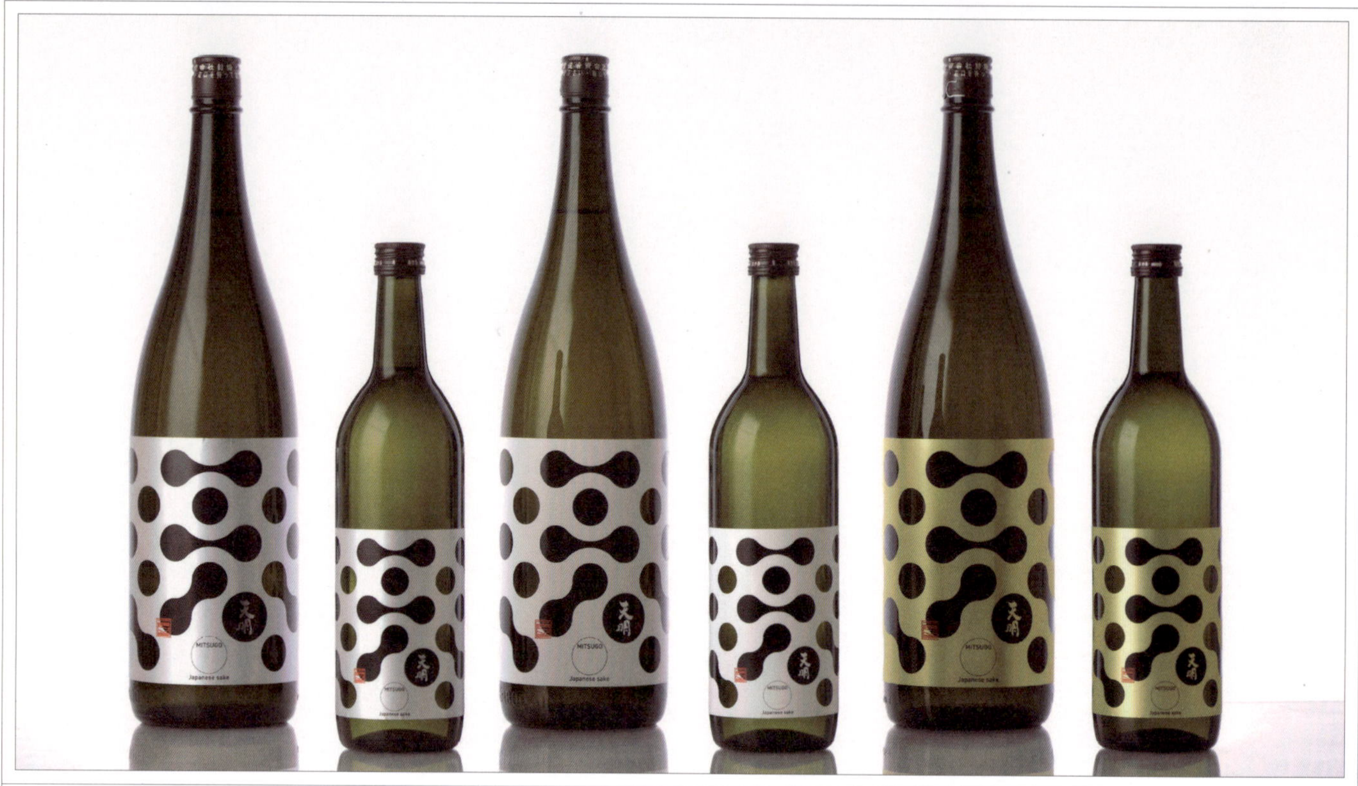

Title: TENMEI; Client: SAKE-SHOW YAMADA; Art Director: Hajime Tsushima; Creative Director: Yukiko Tsushima; Designers: Hajime Tsushima, Yukiko Tsushima; Producer: Tomohisa Hirata; Design Firm: Tsushima Design

What inspired or motivated you into your career?
I was influenced by the painters Maruyama Oukyo and Ito Jakuchu from the Edo period in Japan.

What is the story behind the creation of Tsushima Design?
I stopped working as a product designer at an environmental facility playground equipment manufacturer. I started a company because I wanted to create a graphic design company myself.

What is your work philosophy?
I believe that the power of my design is the most important thing to make customers and various people happy.

Who is or was your greatest mentor?
I have no specific mentor.

What is it about design that you are most passionate about?
My belief is the power of my graphic design makes people happy.

What has been your most memorable project?
It's my New York wallpaper showroom branding.

What is the most difficult challenge you've had to overcome?
My challenge is expressing my personality as a creator and my passion for creation. The other is the importance of always creating new things.

Who among your contemporaries today do you most admire?
I respect all designers in the world.

*Who have been some of your favorite people
or clients you have worked with?*
Studio Zen Wallcoverings and SAKE-SHOE YAMADA.

What is your proudest professional achievement?
I do my best work in every piece of work from time to time. I am proud of all my work, not just the most proud.

What would be your dream assignment?
It would be to influence or impress people beyond the limits of ethnicity, history, country, etc. with the posters I made. I hope we can communicate.

What is the greatest satisfaction you get from your work?
I think it's best to please my clients and the people in the market.

What part of your work do you find most demanding?
I often create works that are both delicate and intricate, so I can't overlook the details.

What professional goals do you still have for yourself?
I want to keep sending various messages through graphic design.

What advice would you have for students starting out today?
I always want to tell them to never give up.

What interests do you have outside of your work?
My hobby is road biking.

What would you change if you had to do it all over again?
I've never thought about starting over again. We are always heading toward the future.

Where do you seek inspiration?
I think inspiration is very important. I always have a notebook because I can be inspired at unexpected moments.

How do you define success?
I think it's very important to keep winning prizes. It's also important to send a message.

Where do you see yourself in the future?
I want to go all over the world.

Tsushima Design www.tsushima-design.com

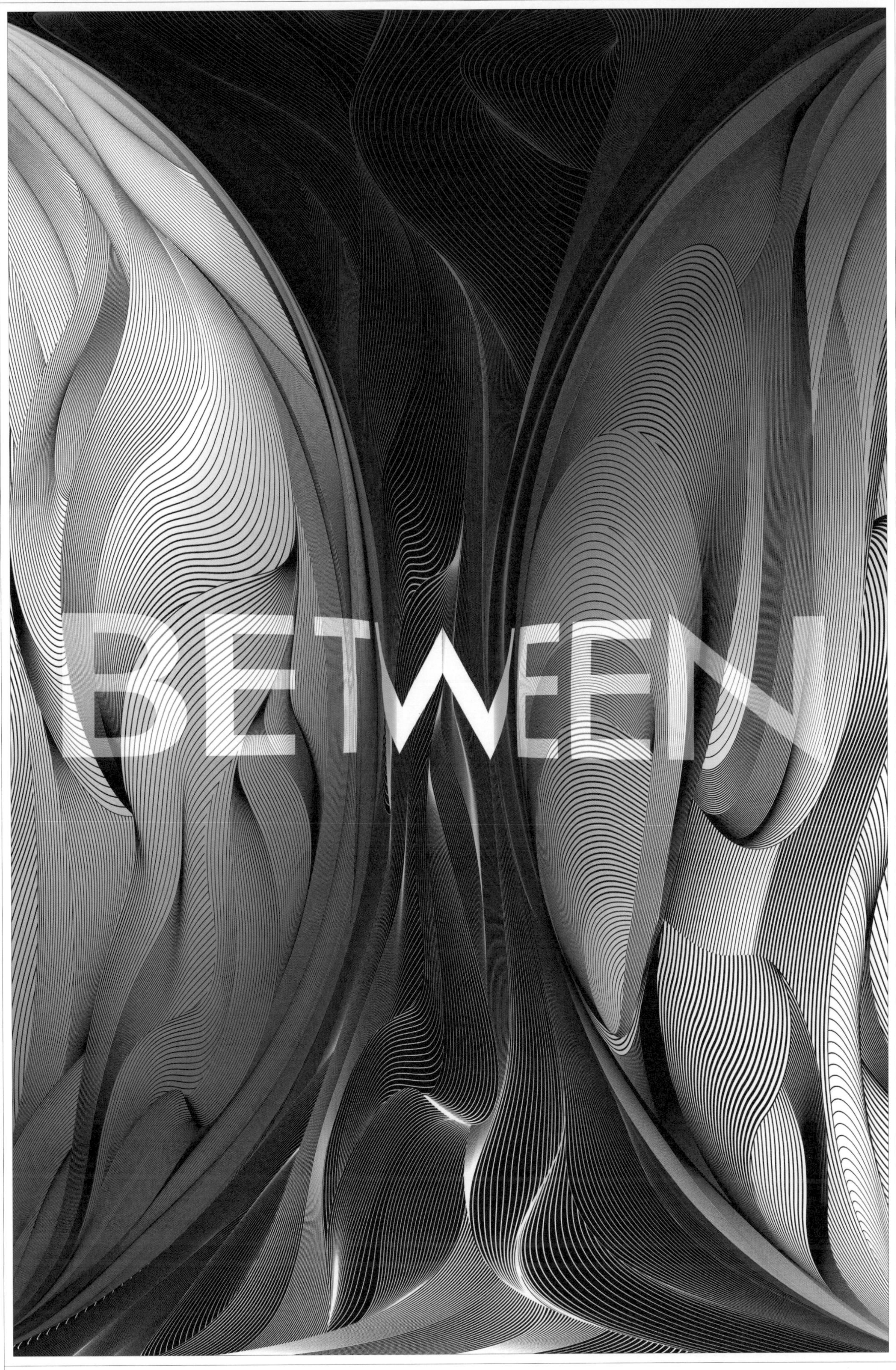

Title: *BETWEEN; Client: Shenzhen International Poster Festival Organizing Committee; Designer: Hajime Tsushima; Design Firm: Tsushima Design*

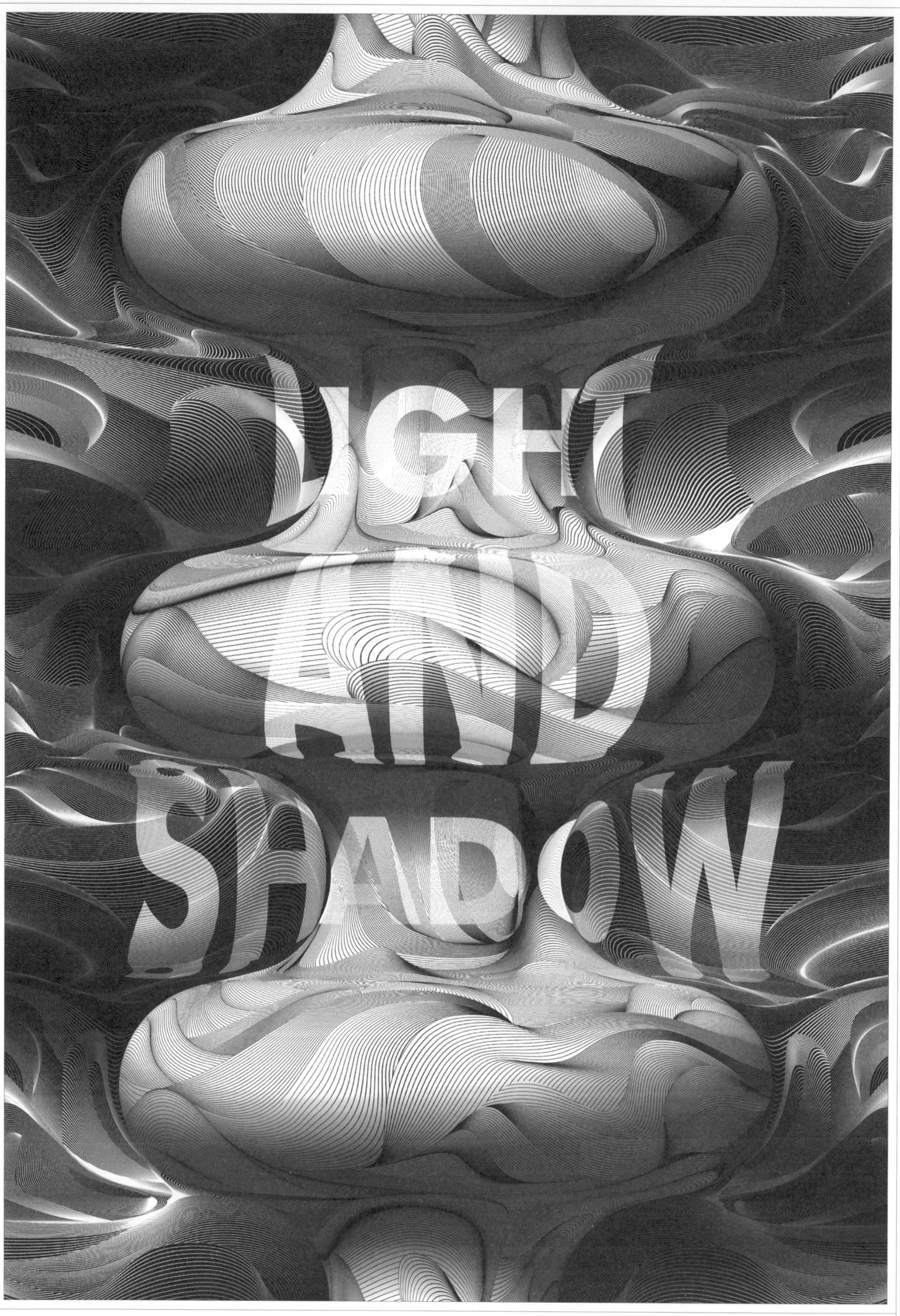

Title: *LIGHT & SHADOW*; Client: *Japan Graphic Designers Association Hiroshima*; Designer: *Hajime Tsushima*; Design Firm: *Tsushima Design*

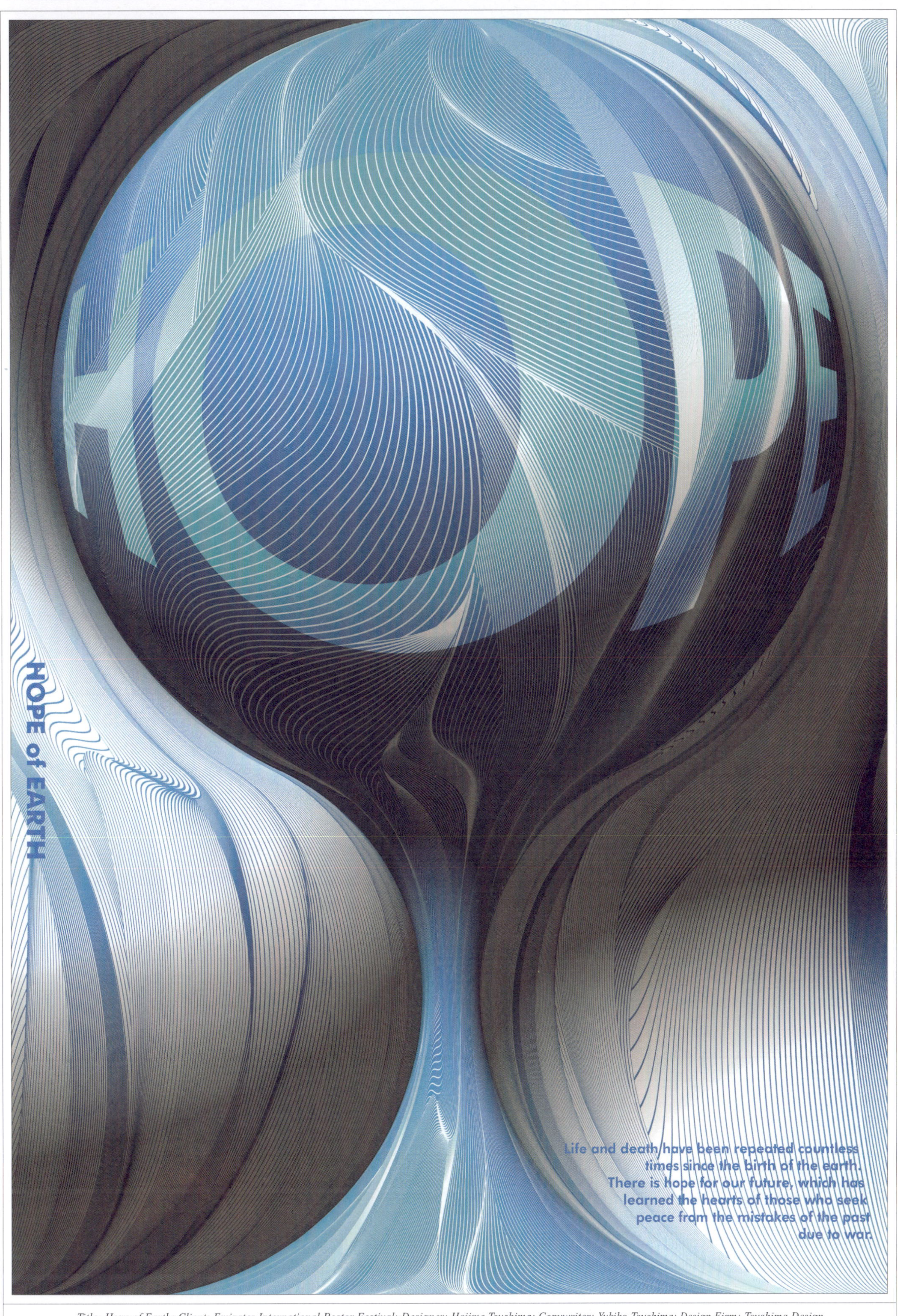

Title: Hope of Earth; Client: Emirates International Poster Festival; Designer: Hajime Tsushima; Copywriter: Yukiko Tsushima; Design Firm: Tsushima Design

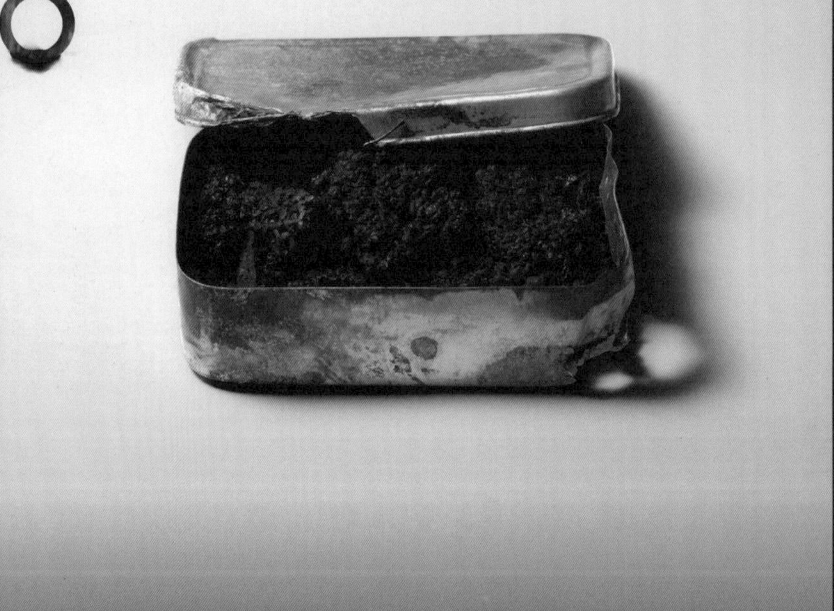

HIROSHIMA APPEALS POSTERS BOOK 1983-2017
BLACK BENTO
くろい
おべんとう
1945年8月6日8時15分、広島。
HIROSHIMA at 8:15 a.m. in August 6 1945
Giver   Shigeko Orimen
Holder Shigeru Orimen

At Hiroshima Peace Memorial Museum, there are the remains of a lunch box that was exposed to the atomic bomb. The owner of the lunch box was Shigeru, a first year junior high school student. On the morning of August 6, he left home early in the morning to work in removing buildings. The dishes in the lunch box had been made by his mother using the first harvest from their garden on land which Shigeru had reclaimed. He was delighted by the lunch box which his mother had made with love for him.*
The lunch box is also a symbol of love and peace. We were unable to take my eyes off of its pitiful, damaged form. The theme of love is all the more important at the site of an atomic bombing. How is it possible to express this? While pondering this question, I sought guidance from the lunch box, filled as it was with selfless love, as I produced the Hiroshima Appeals Posters 1983-2017. It is my hope that the Hiroshima Appeals project can move as many people as possible with what is not forgotten, what continues to be told, and what can be achieved.

*From Database of Hiroshima Peace Memorial Museum

BLACK BENTO

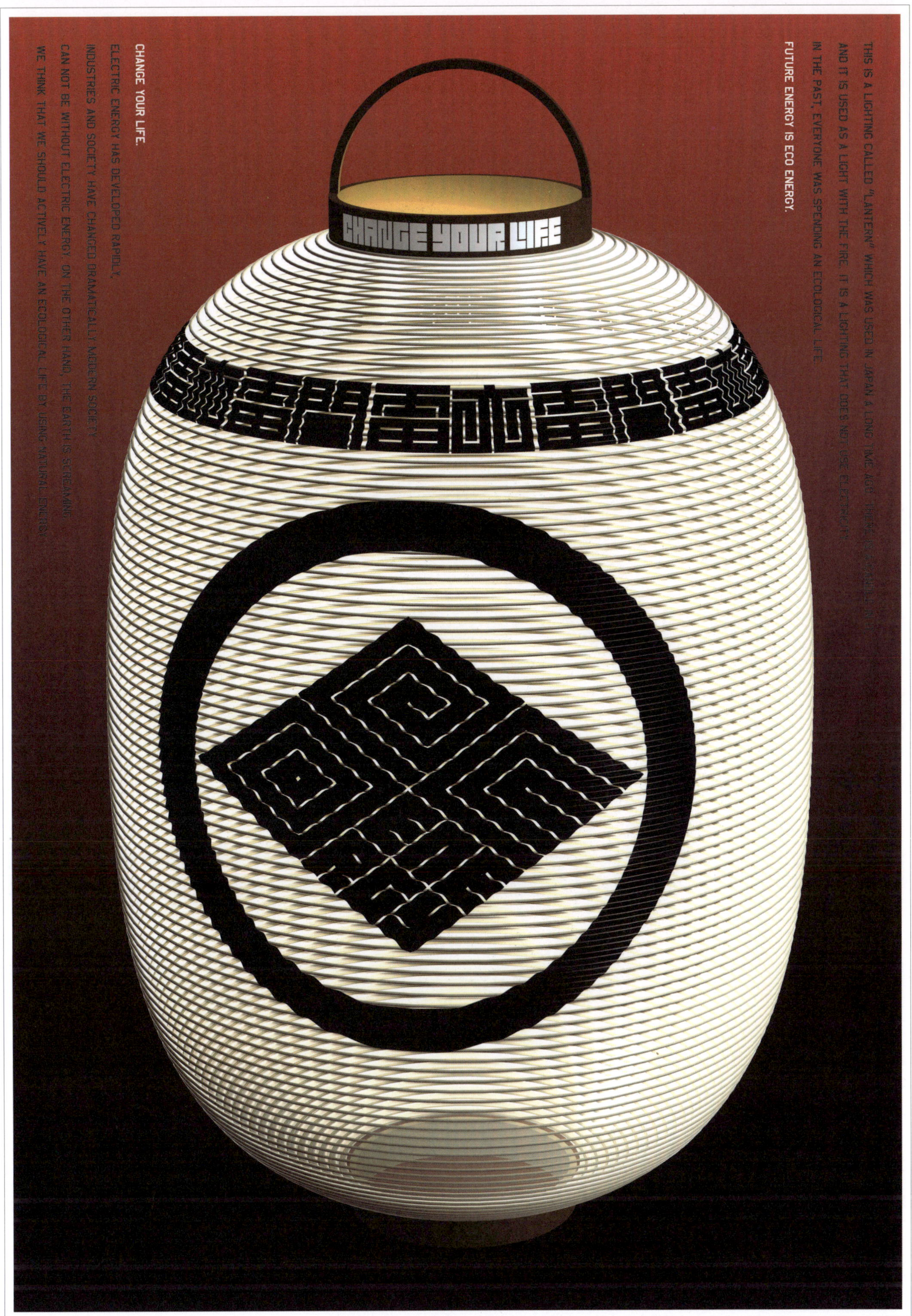

Title: Future Energy; Client: World Expo Museum;
Designer: Hajime Tsushima; Design Firm: Tsushima Design

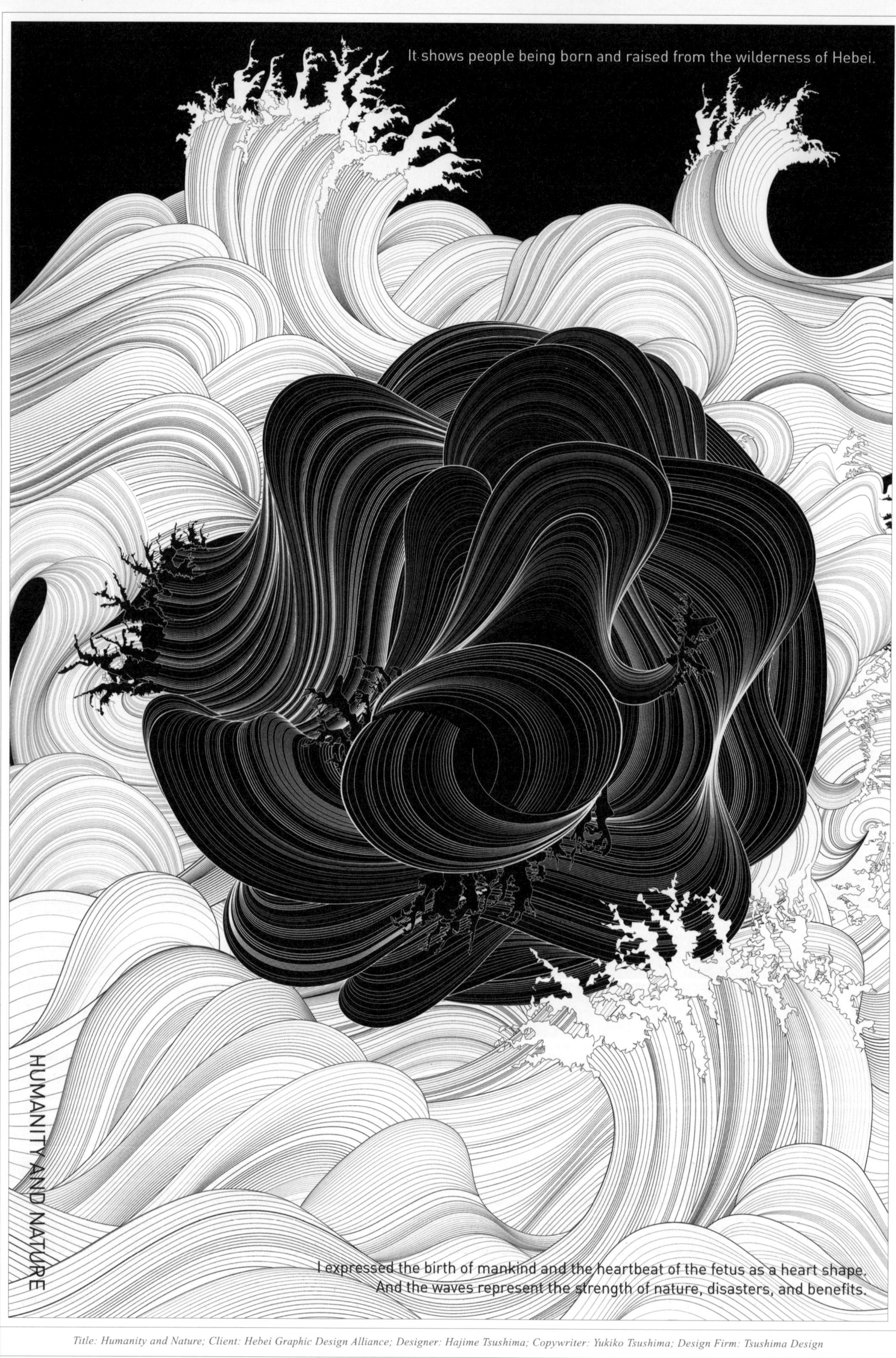

Title: Humanity and Nature; Client: Hebei Graphic Design Alliance; Designer: Hajime Tsushima; Copywriter: Yukiko Tsushima; Design Firm: Tsushima Design

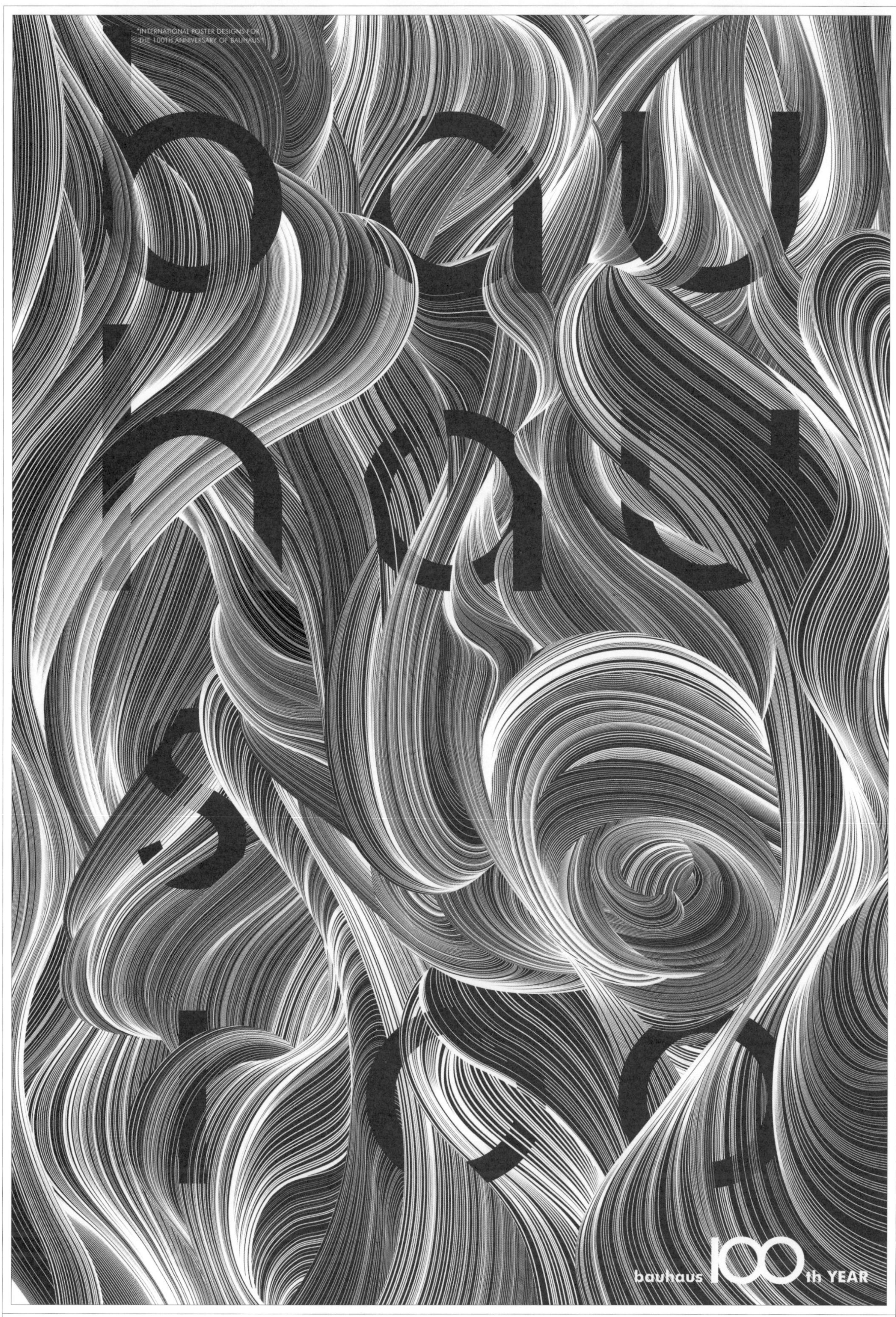

Title: THE 100TH ANNIVERSARY OF BAUHAUS; Client: Giresun University; Designer: Hajime Tsushima; Design Firm: Tsushima Design

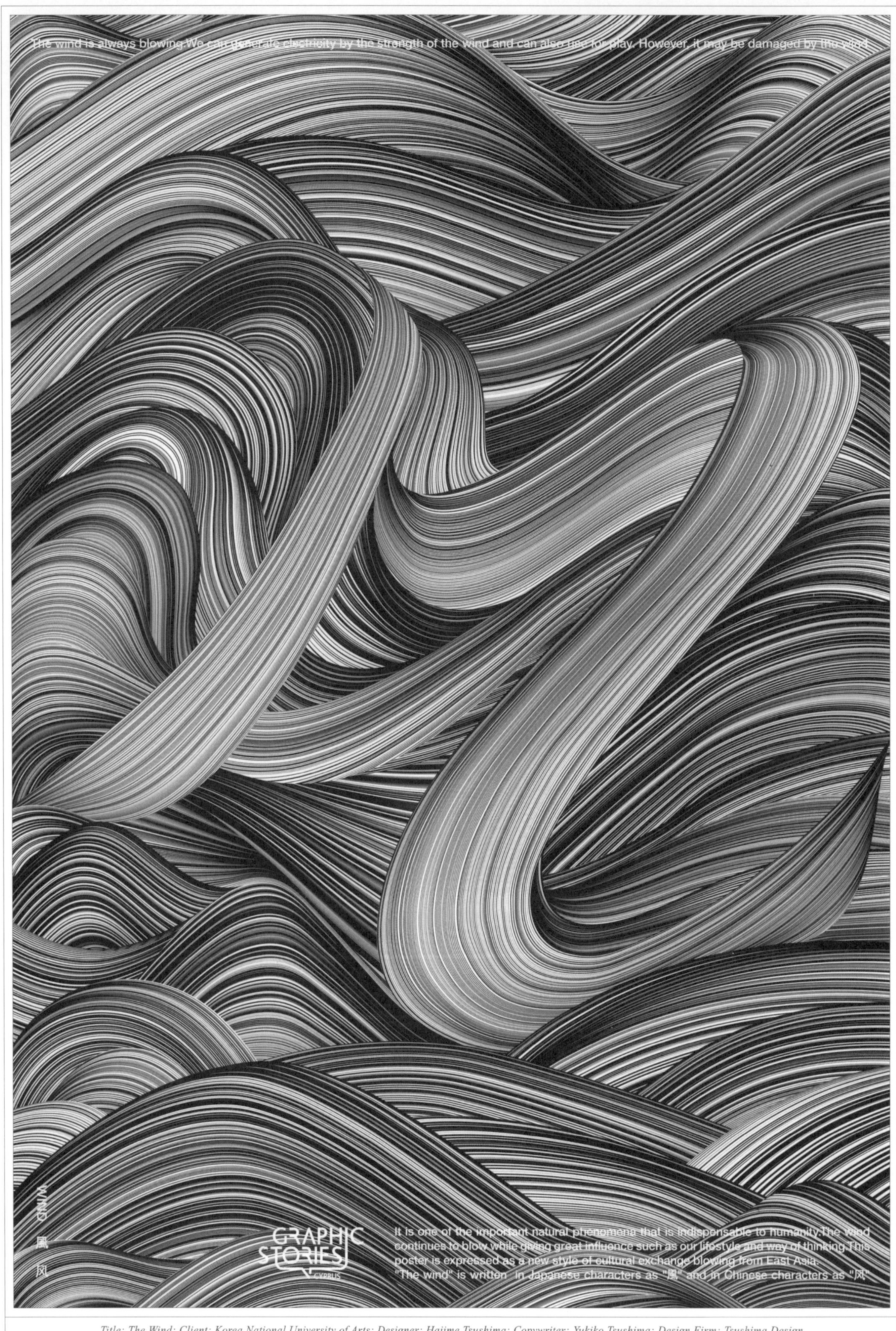

Title: The Wind; Client: Korea National University of Arts; Designer: Hajime Tsushima; Copywriter: Yukiko Tsushima; Design Firm: Tsushima Design

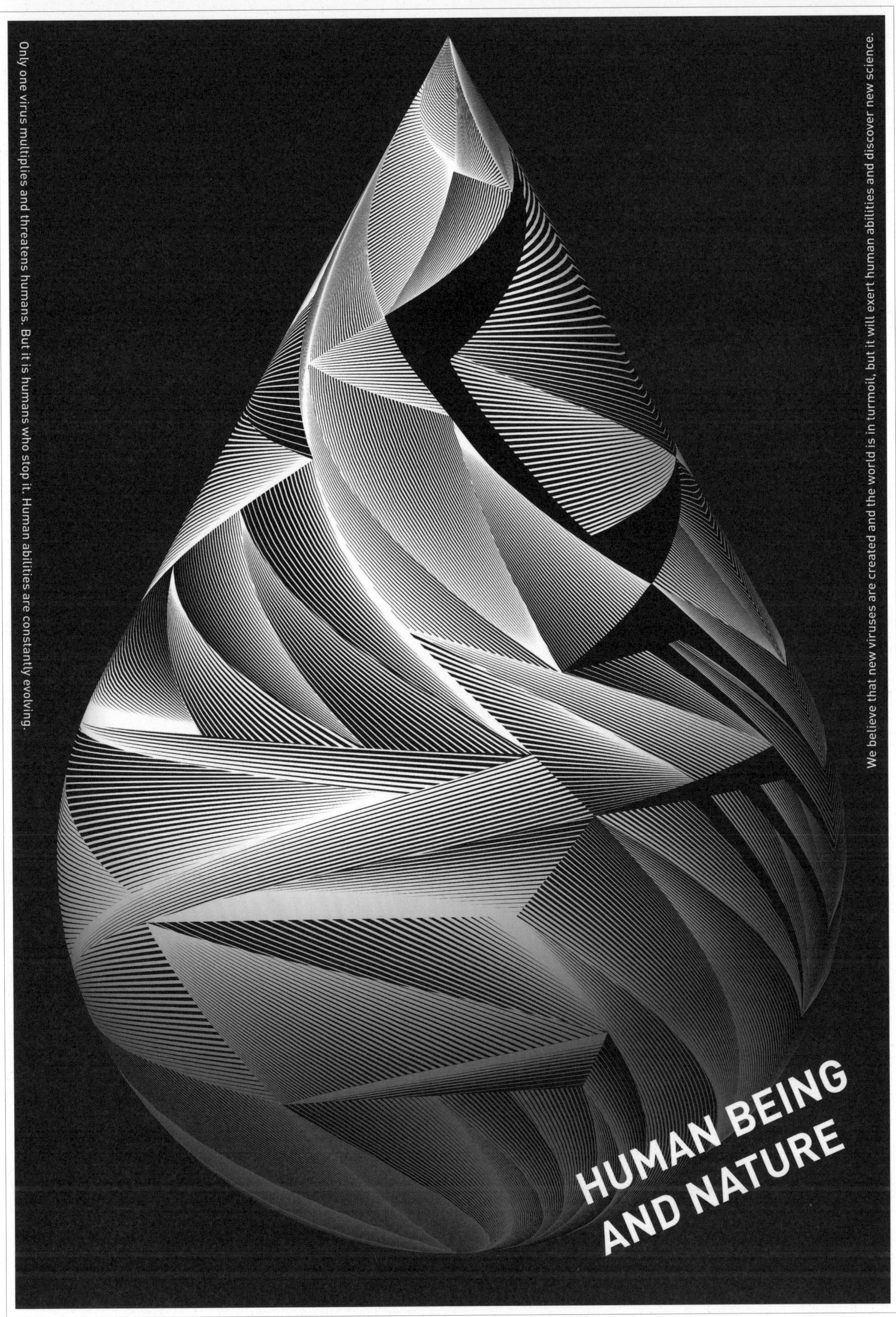

Title: Human Being and Nature; Client: China Advertising Association; Designer: Hajime Tsushima; Design Firm: Tsushima Design

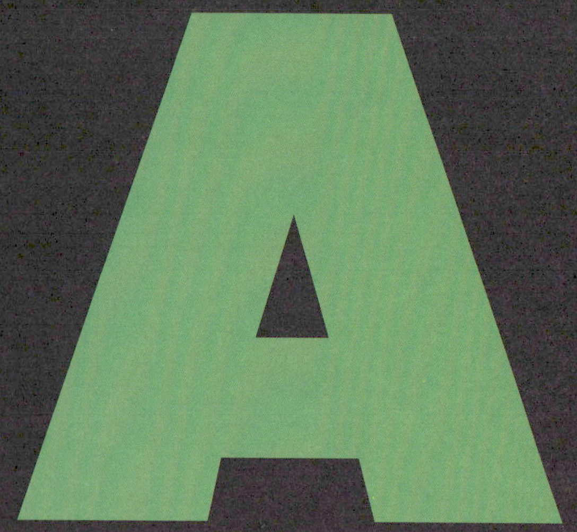

A

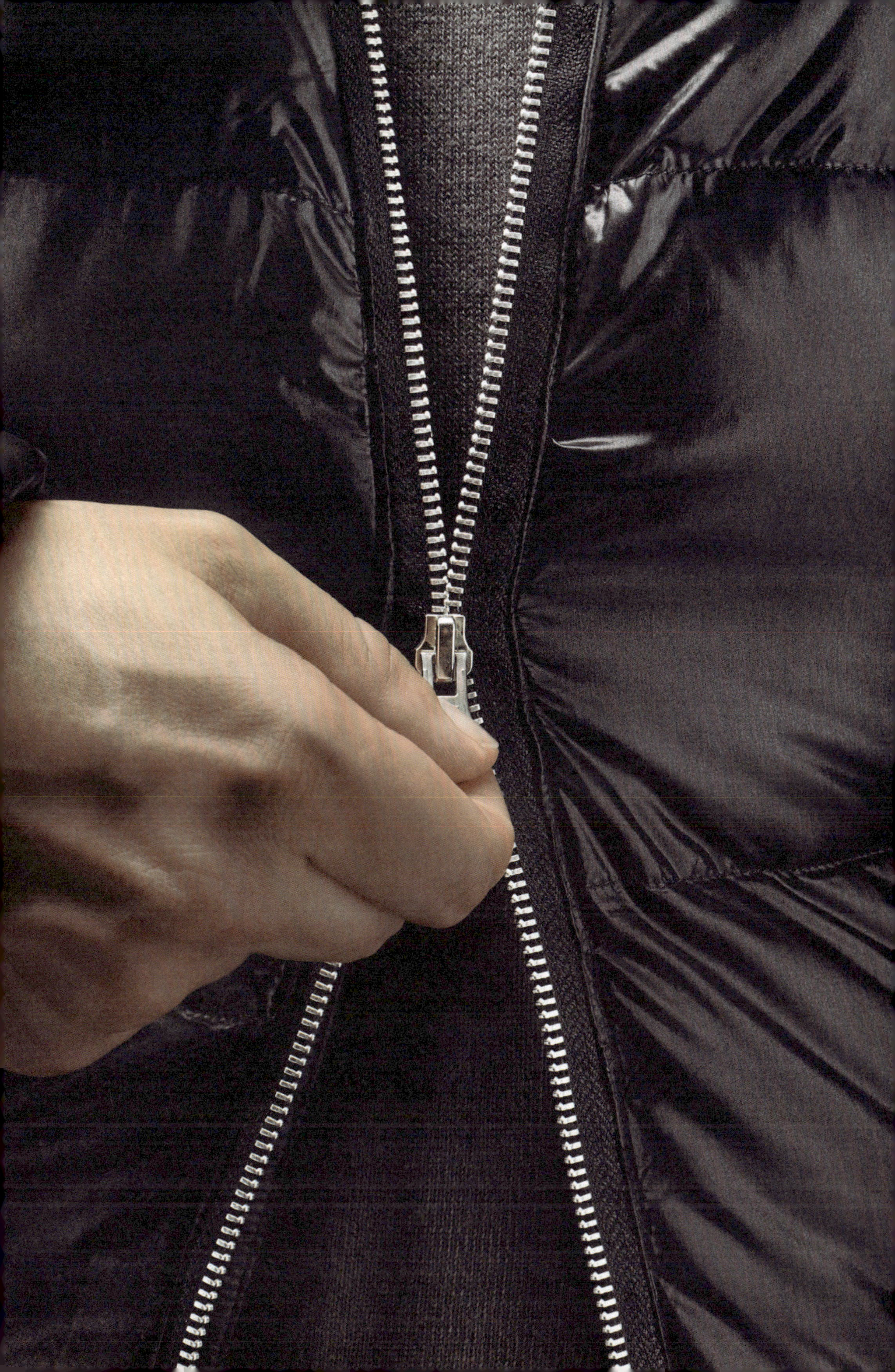

DAVID'S A TRUE LEADER; HE VALUES INPUT, HE TRUSTS YOU, AND HE LETS YOU EXPLORE CREATIVE CHOICES. HIS TASTE IS IMPECCABLE, AND HE'S NOT AFRAID TO CHALLENGE YOU, MAKING THE END RESULT FAR BETTER THAN ANTICIPATED.

Peter Holcomb, *Founder & Creative Partner, Sound Lounge*

THE GATE IS ONE OF THOSE AGENCIES THAT'S A BIT HARD TO PIN DOWN. THEY'RE KNOWN FOR BEING A FANTASTIC B2B AGENCY WITH A COMMITMENT TO CREATIVITY, WHICH IS A RARE THING.

BUT THEN YOU LOOK AT THEIR CLIENTS, AND THEY DO ALL SORTS OF CONSUMER WORK. YOU JUST DON'T OFTEN SEE THIS KIND OF CROSSOVER WITH SUCH A GREAT CREATIVE TRACK RECORD.

David Baldwin, *Lead Guitar, Baldwin&*

YOU WORK WITH ALL SORTS OF PEOPLE IN YOUR LIFE. SOME YOU LOVE AS PEOPLE. SOME YOU LOVE FOR THEIR WORK. BUT WITH VERY FEW DO YOU ACTUALLY LOVE BOTH. FOR ME, ELINOR IS AMONG THOSE EXCEPTIONAL FEW.

Ari Halper, *Founder of Sauce Idea Lab*

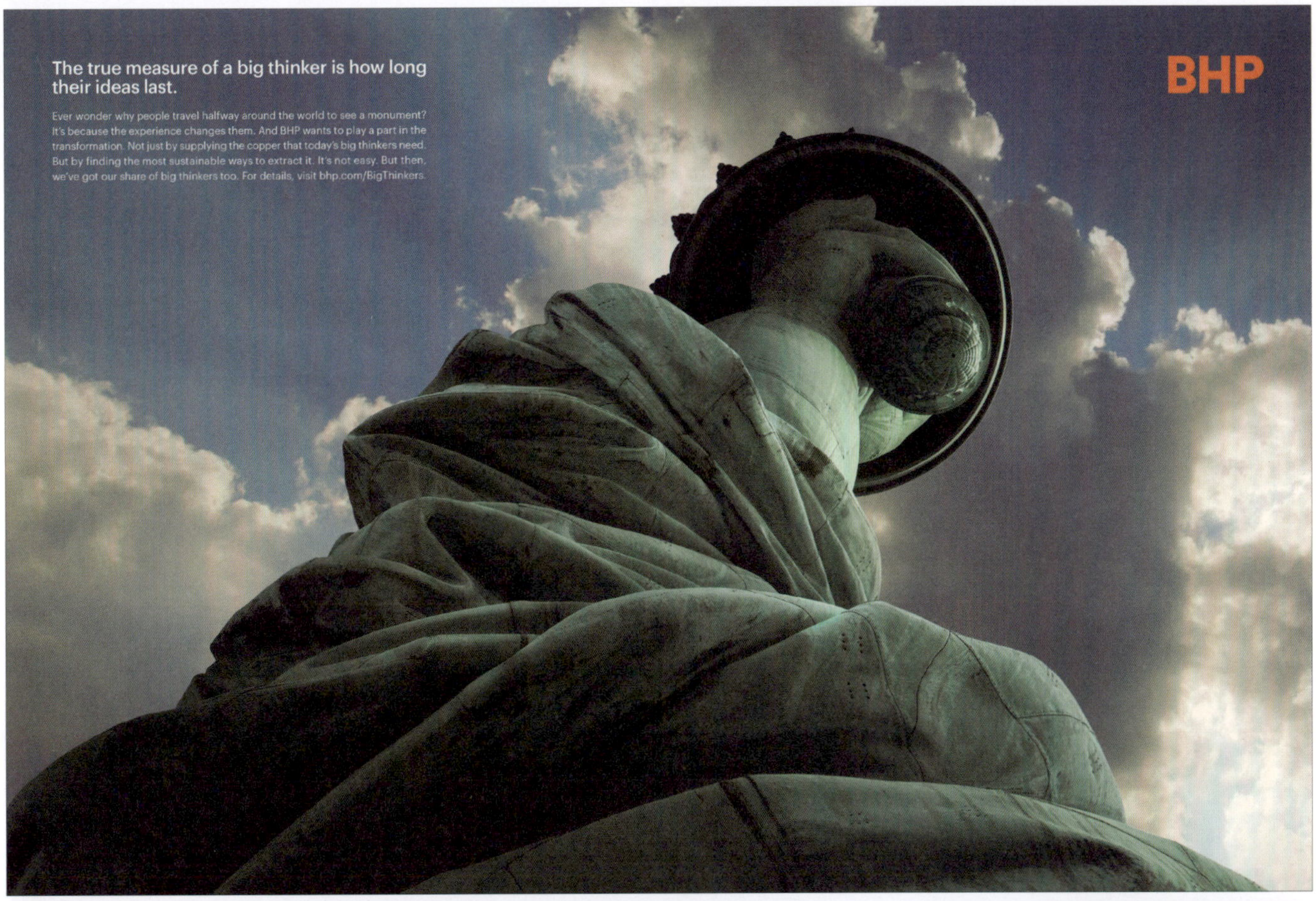

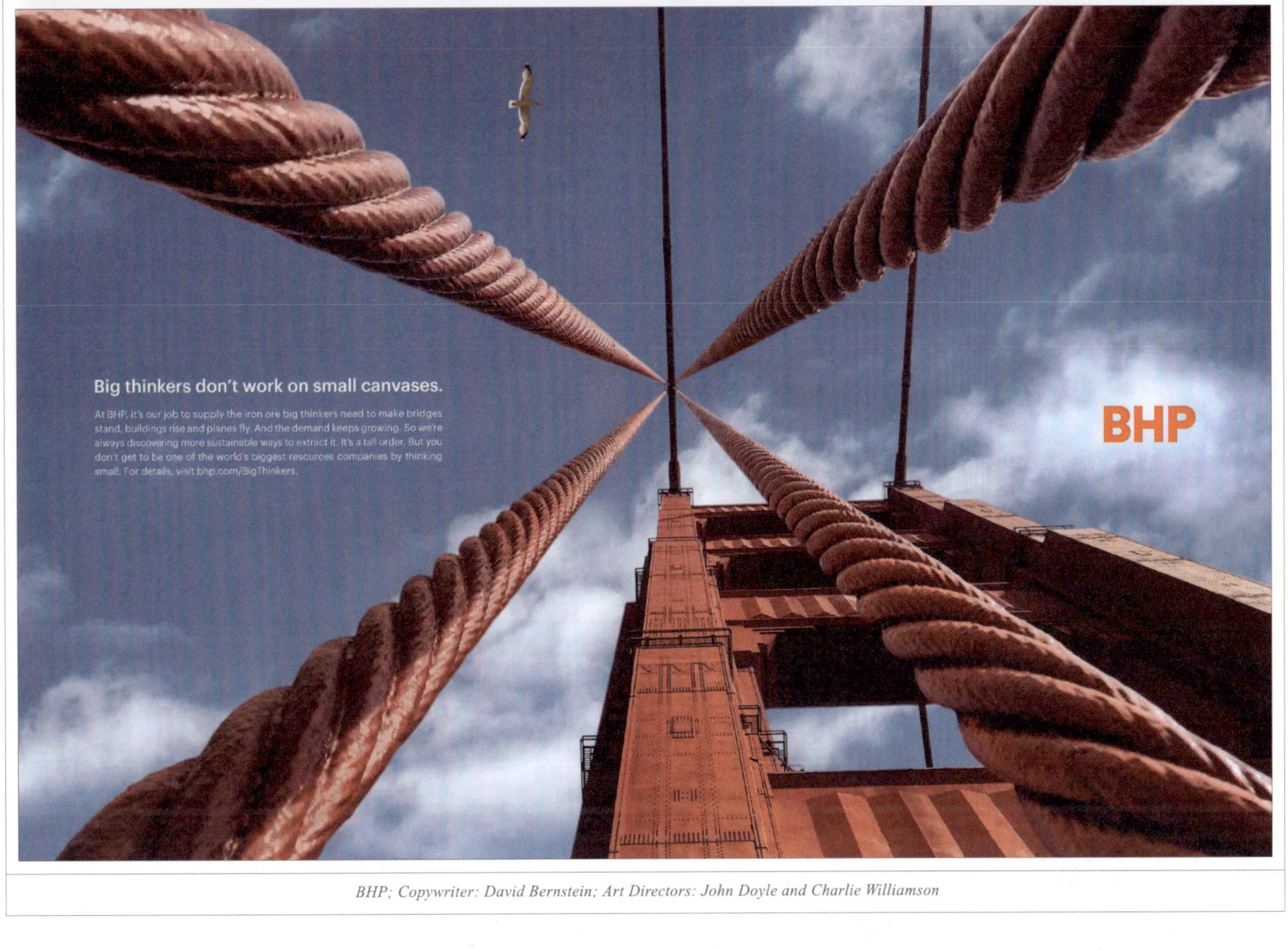

BHP; Copywriter: David Bernstein; Art Directors: John Doyle and Charlie Williamson

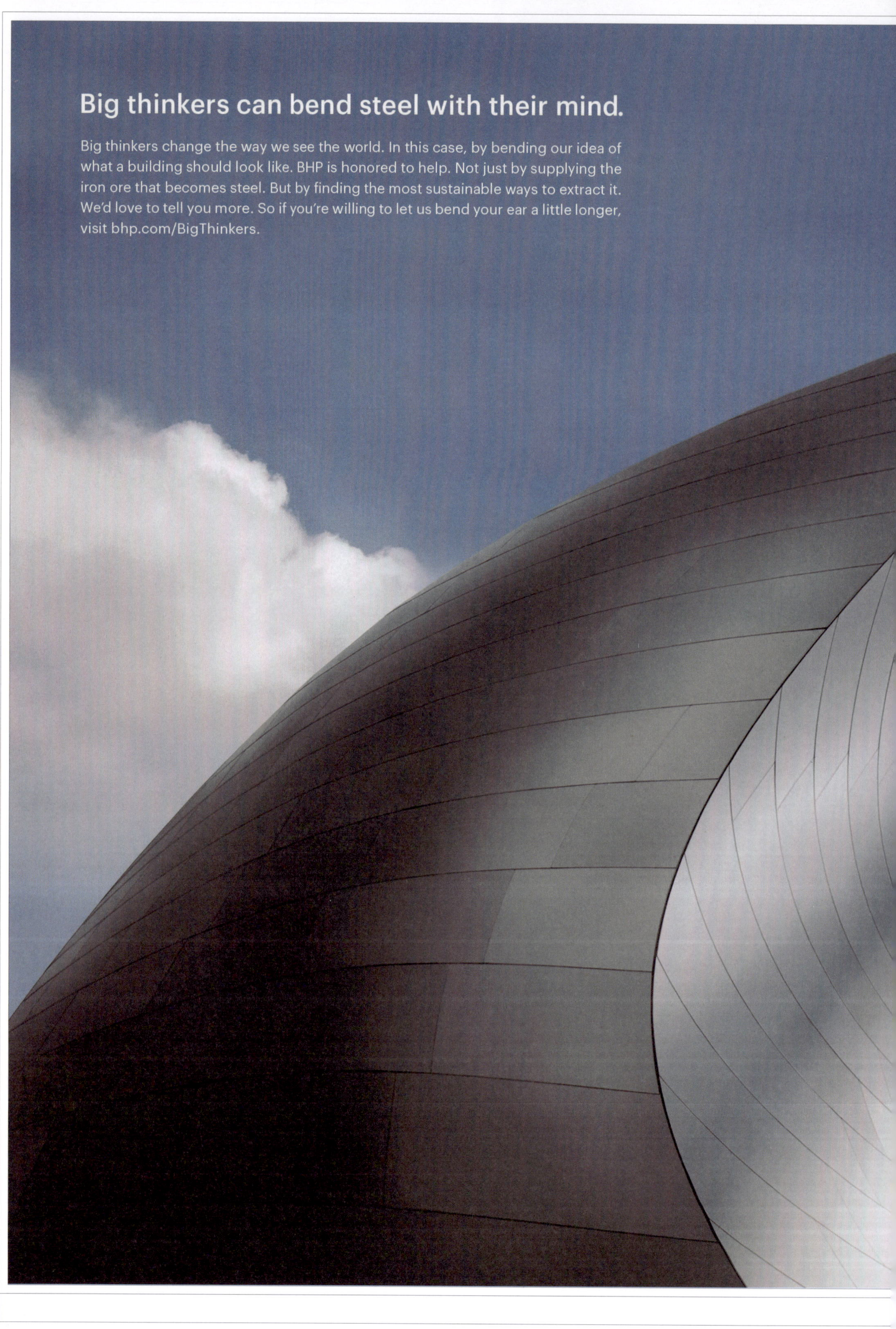

Big thinkers can bend steel with their mind.

Big thinkers change the way we see the world. In this case, by bending our idea of what a building should look like. BHP is honored to help. Not just by supplying the iron ore that becomes steel. But by finding the most sustainable ways to extract it. We'd love to tell you more. So if you're willing to let us bend your ear a little longer, visit bhp.com/BigThinkers.

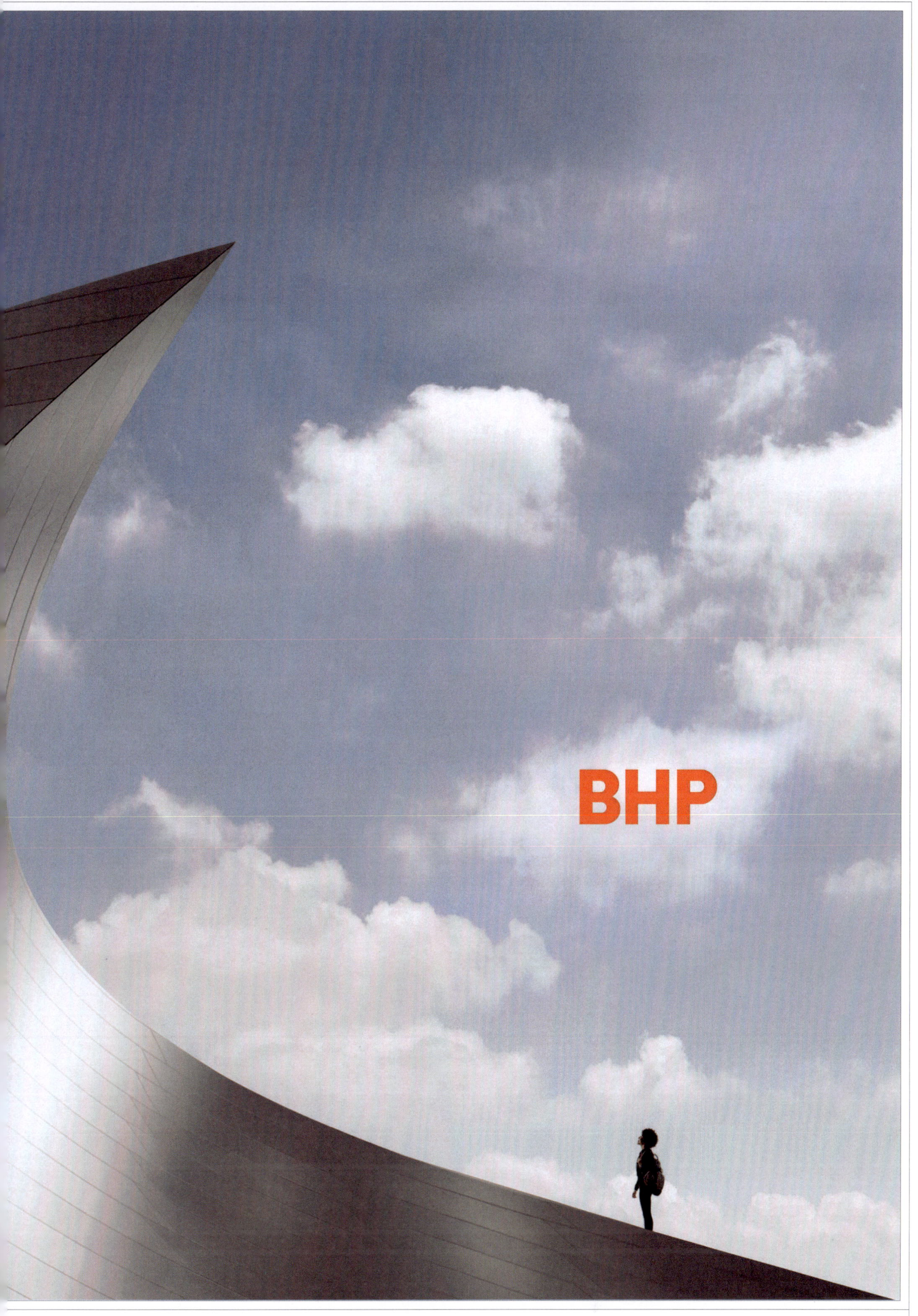

BHP; Copywriter: David Bernstein; Art Directors: John Doyle and Charlie Williamson

Introduction by Tom and Charles Guard *Film/Commercial Directors*

Every script that comes out of The Gate shines with something special: wit, ambition, and a unique emotional magic. David Bernstein and his team consistently write beautifully human ideas that are a joy to realize. But what really sets the agency apart is their process. In today's risk averse culture where scripts are seemingly signed off years in advance, David is always open to taking stories further and always hungry to hear the idea he hadn't thought of, which not only makes him the rarest and most generous of creatives, but an absolute pleasure to work for. He brings out the very best in everyone around him.

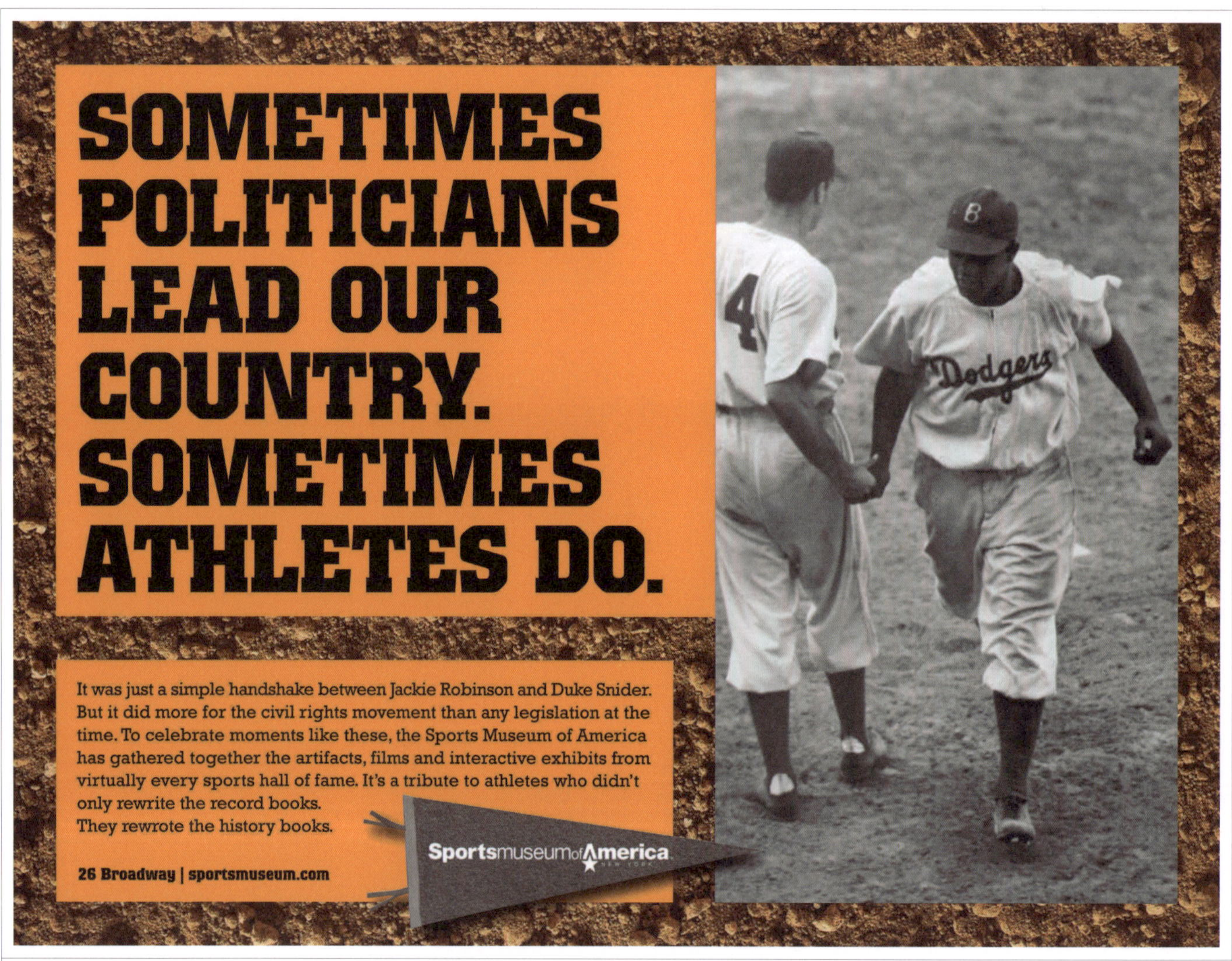

Sports Museum of America; Copywriter: David Bernstein; Art Director: Graham Clifford

DON'T BE PRECIOUS WITH YOUR IDEAS. WRITE AS MANY AS YOU CAN. EVENTUALLY YOU'LL COME UP WITH A FEW KEEPERS.

David Bernstein, *Chief Creative Officer, The Gate*

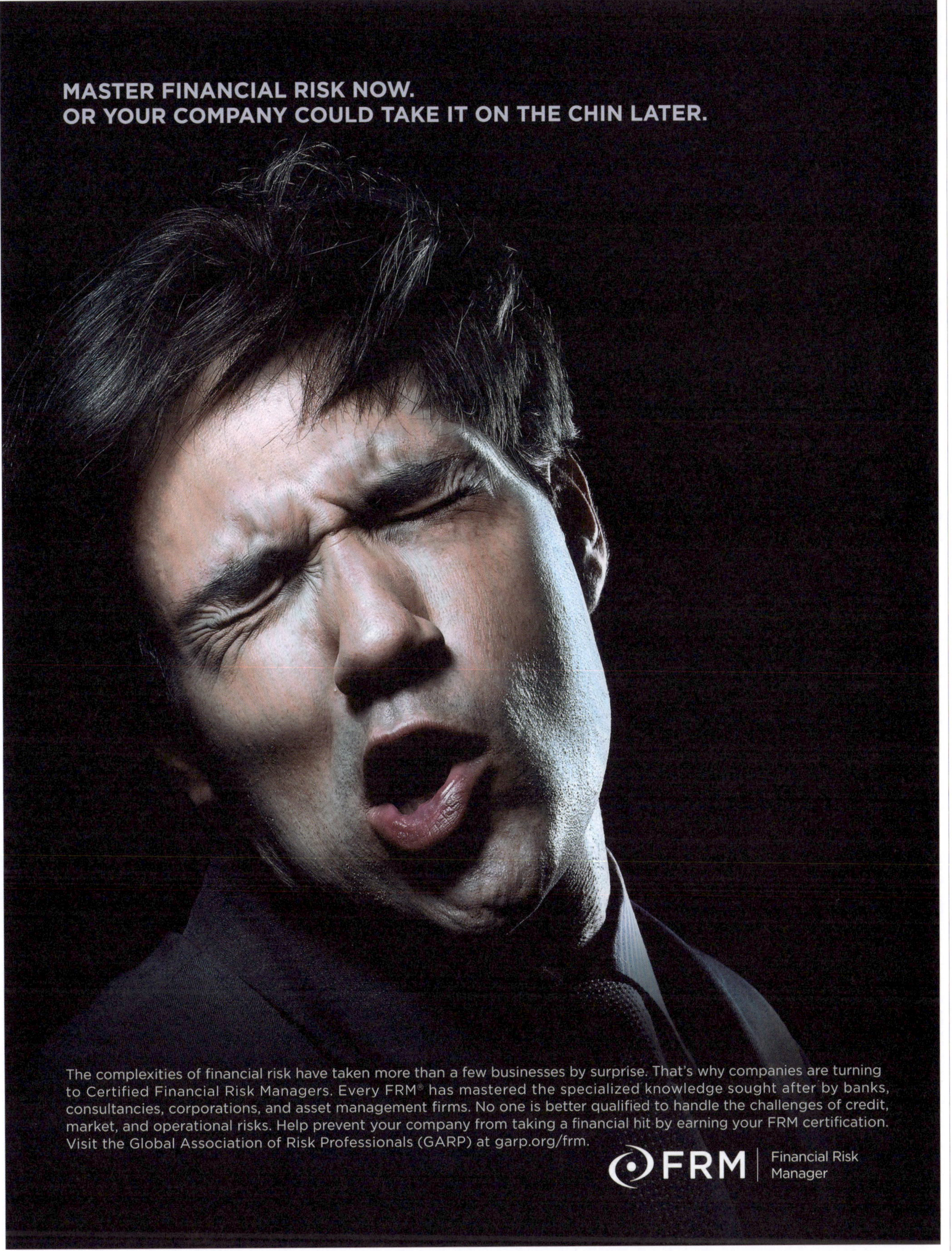

GARP; Copywriter: Mike Abadi; Art Director: Tim Ryan

What inspired or motivated you into your career?
David Bernstein (D.B.), Chief Creative Officer: When I was nineteen, I got a summer internship in the creative department at TBWA, working for the guys who created the Absolut Vodka campaign. They taught me how to write ads and drink Guinness. They were smart, witty, and always seemed to be having fun. After that summer, I was hooked on advertising.
Charlie Williamson (C.W.), Associate Creative Director: I always knew I wanted to make things. It just took me a while to figure out what those things were. I started out creating computer programs in high school and college, then explored architecture. Eventually, I realized all the designing I was doing for fun could actually be a career.
Elinor Beltrone (E.B.), Creative Director: My parents. I grew up in a pretty artsy family. I was born in Paris, in the heart of Montmartre. My father was a fashion photographer, and my mother was a fashion stylist and fine arts painter. Most of my school vacation was spent traveling to the U.S. and being on photo shoots. Often, when I was doing my homework at the kitchen table, my dad was next to me looking at composites and casting models. From a very young age, I knew I wanted to have a creative profession. And for a very long time, I thought I would become a photographer. But then, I went to the School of Visual Arts and took an introduction to advertising class and knew that was what I wanted to do.
Mike Abadi (M.A.), Associate Creative Director: Bad advertising. The more I saw, the more it bothered me that people were actually paid for their lack of imagination. Then I found a book about DDB's classic Volkswagen ads and realized you could get paid for doing good stuff, too.

What is your work philosophy?
D.B.: Don't be precious with your ideas. Write as many as you can. Eventually, you'll come up with a few keepers.
Scott Singow (S.S.), Associate Creative Director: This is, after all, a business. I put my head down and tackle the task at hand. I'm focused and not thinking about anything else. I generally work best in two hour bursts. I take a fifteen minute break, and then it's back to work. In the business, I'm what's known as a "grinder." Grind away enough, and eventually you'll come up with a solution.

Who is or was your greatest mentor?
D.B.: A writer and creative director named Joe O'Neill. He ran the great San Francisco agency Hal Riney for many years. Prior to that, he produced some famous work for BMW, Club Med, and Irish Tourism. The thing about Joe was that he didn't have one style. He had a dozen of them. When I started working for him, I could only write in snarky headlines and TV scripts. I was only coloring with one crayon. By the time I moved on, he'd taught me how to use the whole box.
E.B.: I don't have one great mentor. But I do have several big influences; people who touched my career, one way or another, and changed it for the better. I'll start with Sal DeVito, who was my first boss. He led the most competitive agency I ever worked at, which was where I also met my future husband. Ari Halper and Steve Krauss, who I owe the many opportunities to work on award-winning clients and projects. Finally, my current CCO, David Bernstein, who has always trusted me to lead and let me grow into who I am today.
S.S.: My greatest mentors were the Communication Arts Advertising Annual and the One Show Annual. I studied those books religiously. I learned why those ads were in there. I learned who was doing the best work, both people and agencies. And even though I've been doing this for a while, I still look forward to (and get excited by) seeing great work.

Who were some of your greatest past influences?
D.B.: Besides the previously mentioned Joe O'Neill, I always wanted to write TV spots like Hal Riney and print ads like Tom McElligott and Tim Delaney.
S.S.: First, there was the great Volkswagen work from DDB, with the thinking behind them and the simplicity of how they were executed. They still inspire me. Nike, of course. Got Milk? The list goes on.
M.A.: I'm influenced as much by someone's inner fortitude as by their outsized talent. So while I've been guided by the creative vision of advertising icons like Bill Bernbach and Tom McElligott, I'm also driven by their ability to fight for their ideas whatever the obstacles.

Who among your contemporaries today do you most admire?
D.B.: David Droga, Gerry Graf, David Baldwin, Jeff Goodby, and Dan Wieden.

What would be your dream assignment?
D.B.: I was lucky enough to work on BMW years ago. I'd love to work on a luxury car again.

What is it about the advertising industry that excites you most?
C.W.: What I've always loved about advertising is the continued learning. To work on a client, you need to really study it and know their business inside out. I've learned all sorts of things over the years that I never would've otherwise, like what it takes to become a certified management accountant.

Who has been some of your favorite people or clients you have worked with?
D.B.: Chuck Willis, the editor, Peter Holcomb, the mixer, Lex Rudge, the colorist, and Bob Shriber, the producer. There are too many directors to list, so I'll just mention one (which is really two): the Guard brothers. I've shot with them in London, Los Angeles, Milan, and Warsaw. And every single time, they've delivered something far better than the raw storyboard I gave them. Their storytelling never hits a false note. Their film is lush. And their personalities make the whole experience a pleasure.

The Gate has five different offices in three different countries. What makes each office unique?
D.B.: While there are differences based on culture, I think what's more important are the similarities. We have the same work ethic (everyone sweeps the floors), the same standard, and the same desire for long-lasting client relationships.

What is your greatest professional achievement?
D.B.: Years ago, I did a poster campaign for the New York Mets that ran in the subway stations. It was so popular, people kept stealing them off the walls. Eventually, the client had to do a second run at the printers to replace them. Winning awards is nice, but watching someone risk jail time to have your ad hanging in their bedroom is better.

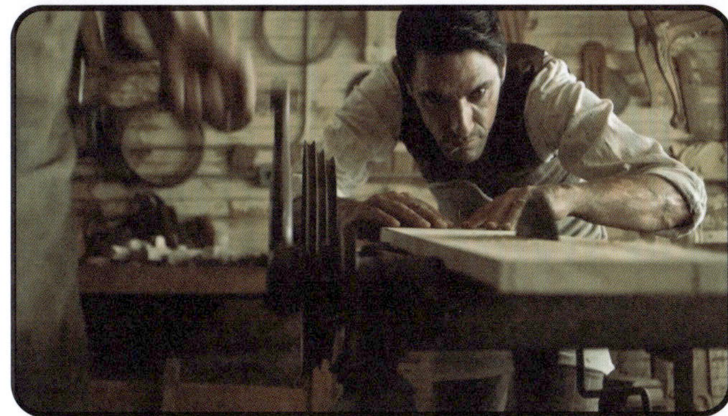

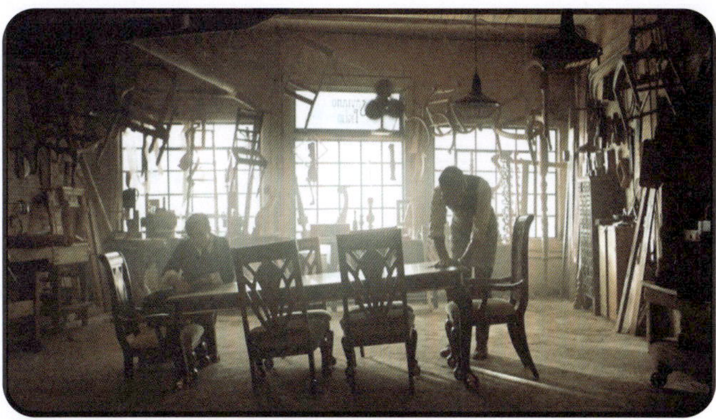

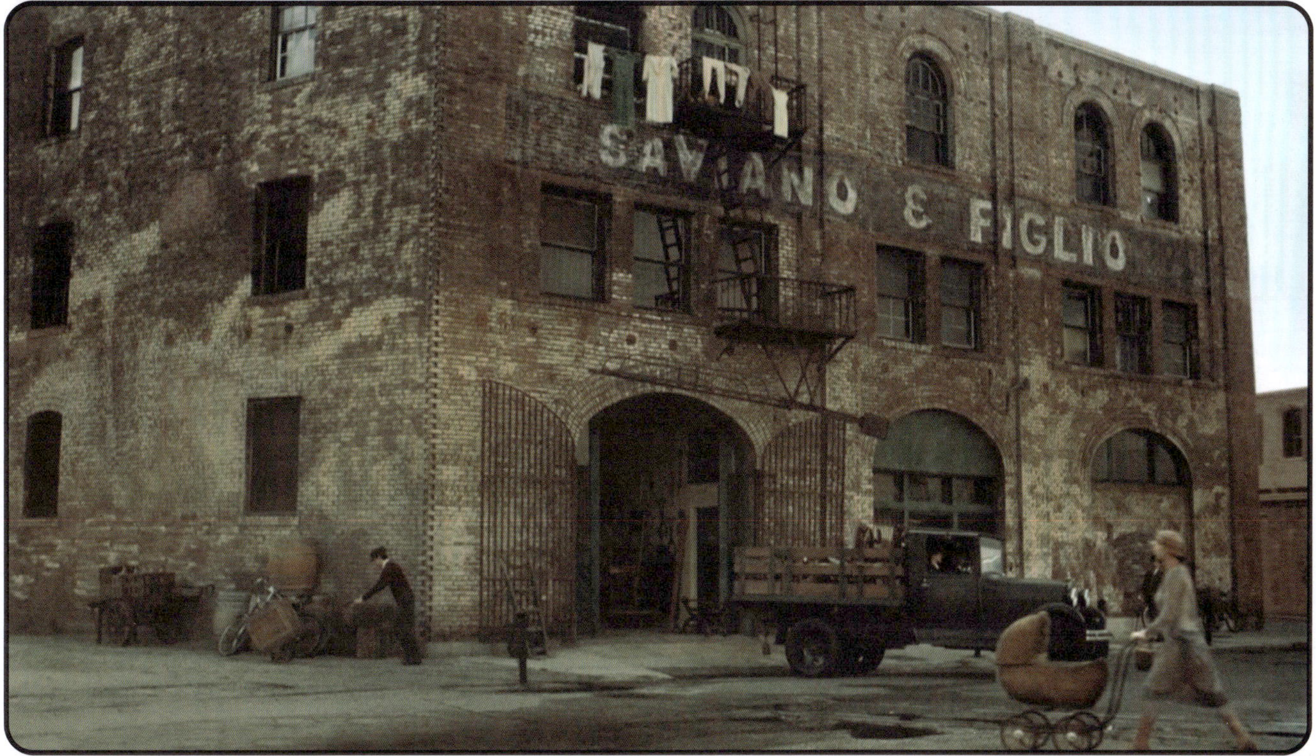

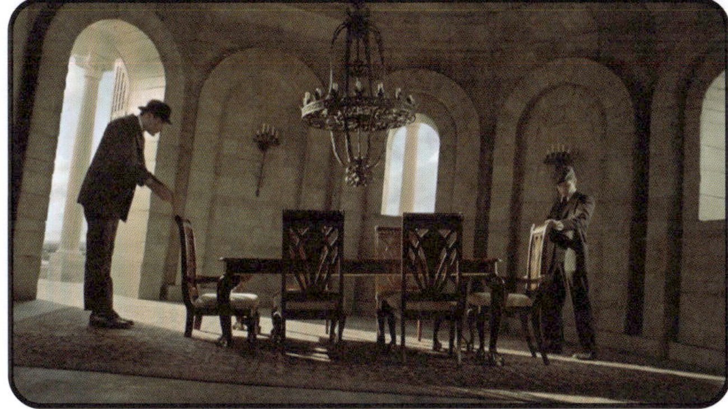

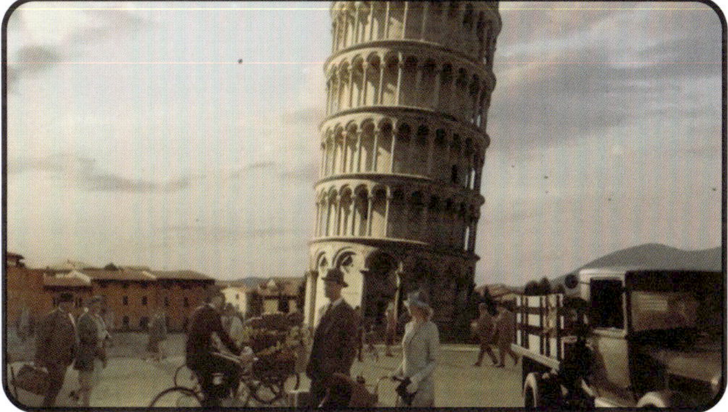

Copywriter: David Bernstein | **Art Director:** Michael English | **Client:** State Street Global Advisors

Description: Investors like SPDR exchange trade funds because they're more precise than mutual funds. So, our commercials always showed how hard it was to be precise. In this case, it was by making a precisely unlevel table appear level when it reached its home inside the Leaning Tower of Pisa.

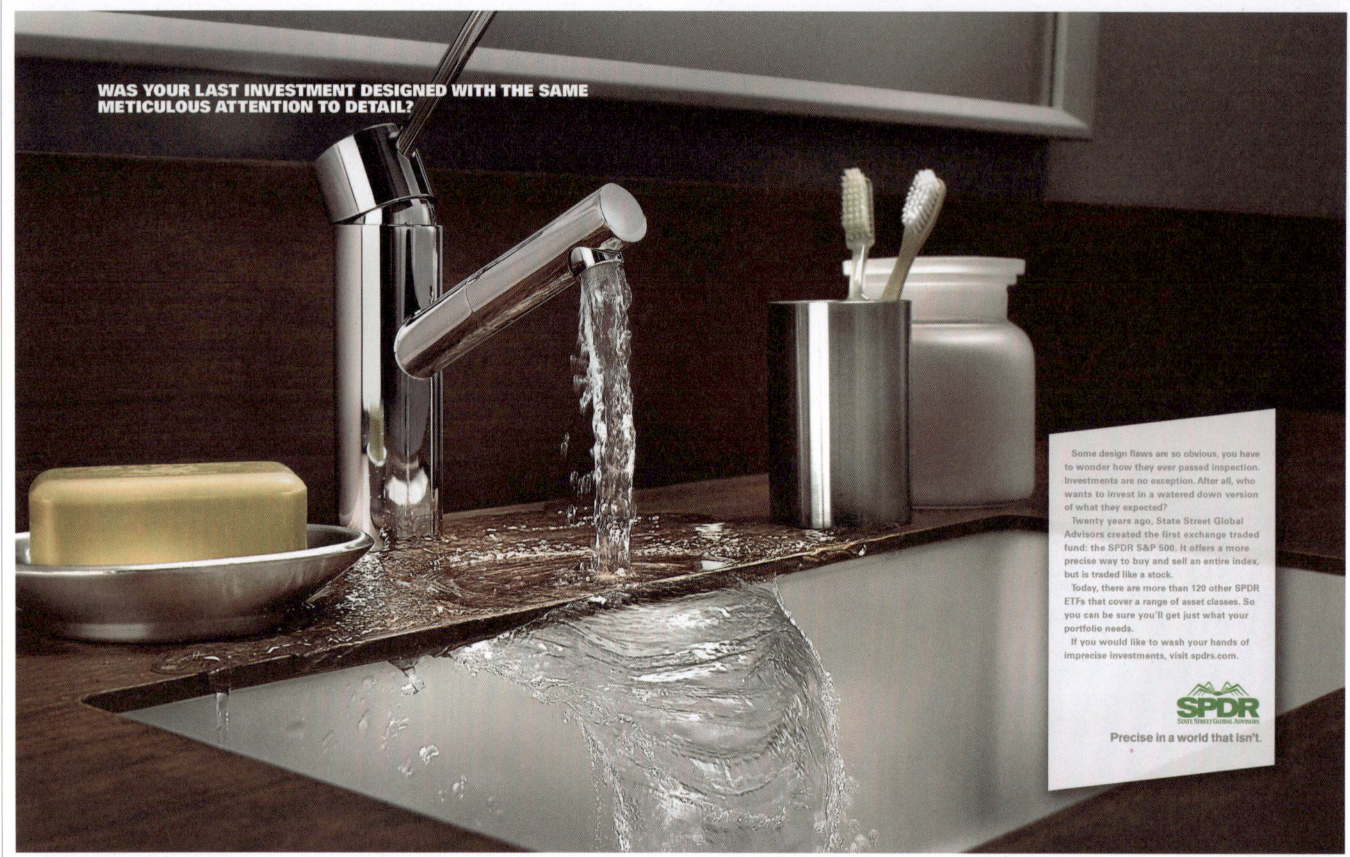

State Street Global Advisors; Copywriter: Mike Abadi; Art Director: Lily Kim

What is the greatest satisfaction you get from your work?
S.S.: I like solving problems, and I like challenges. I don't even mind working in a small box because the client has certain constraints. Being able to thread that needle is what excites me.
C.W.: Even after all these years, I still enjoy encountering work out in the world. Whether it's a print ad, TV spot, or even a banner ad, there's something about being able to step back and appreciate all the time and effort that went into something. It's especially satisfying to be able to hold the work in your hands or to come across it while flipping through channels.

What interests do you have outside of your work?
M.A.: My passion for vintage films and rare books has led to countless hours of intellectual and emotional bliss. I'm drawn to biographies of the weird and wonderful, the clever films of the silent-era comedians, and the treasures of New York's art galleries and museums.

How do you define success?
D.B.: Beyond getting your work in Graphis, the One Show, D&AD, and Cannes, success is doing work you're proud of; the kind of work you'd not only want to show your friends in the business, but your friends who aren't in the business.

Where do you seek inspiration?
D.B.: I like reading famous speeches. When the British evacu-ated Dunkirk, Churchill didn't apologize for the defeat or fall back on some hackneyed platitudes. He said, "We shall defend our island, whatever the cost may be. We shall fight on the beaches, we shall fight on the landing grounds, we shall fight in the fields and in the streets, we shall fight in the hills. We shall never surrender." Pretty inspiring words, even if you're not fighting for your life.
S.S.: Books, movies, music, popular culture, the Saturday Farmer's Market in Union Square, walking laps around Madison Square Park, and secretly listening into conversations while riding the subway. There's also sitting on my couch with a cup of coffee and saying to myself, "How in the hell am I going to solve this one?"
M.A.: A conversation, a sentence, a photo, or a lyric. Sometimes inspiration seeks me. More than once, a particularly vivid dream has triggered the left side of my brain.

What would you change if you had to do it all over again?
S.S.: I would have saved more for retirement.

Where do you see yourself in the future?
D.B.: In the future, I see myself reading this feature in Graphis and wondering why I didn't give you smarter answers.

The Gate www.thegateworldwide.com

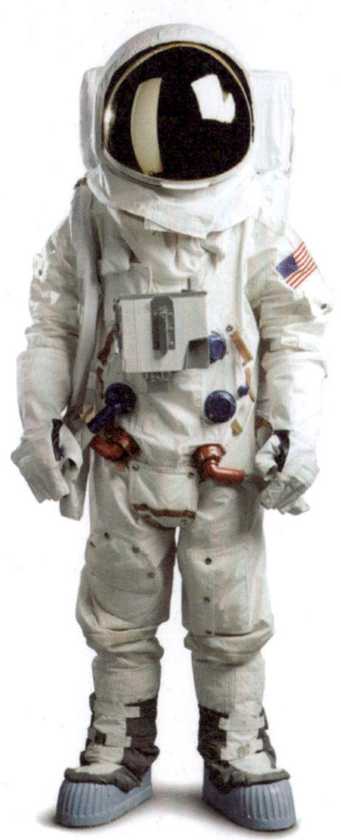

WHAT CAN YOU LEARN ABOUT INVESTMENTS FROM A SPACE SUIT?

Imagine the vision it took to build a suit fit for the rigors of space. FS Investments approaches investing with a similar devotion to thoughtful design. We go beyond traditional thinking, seeking to provide you access to alternative sources of income and growth you may need for the challenges ahead. Explore our philosophy at fsinvestments.com. And see how the right investments can take your portfolio to places it's never been before.

SMART NEVER SETTLES.

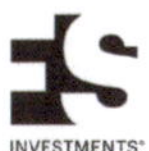

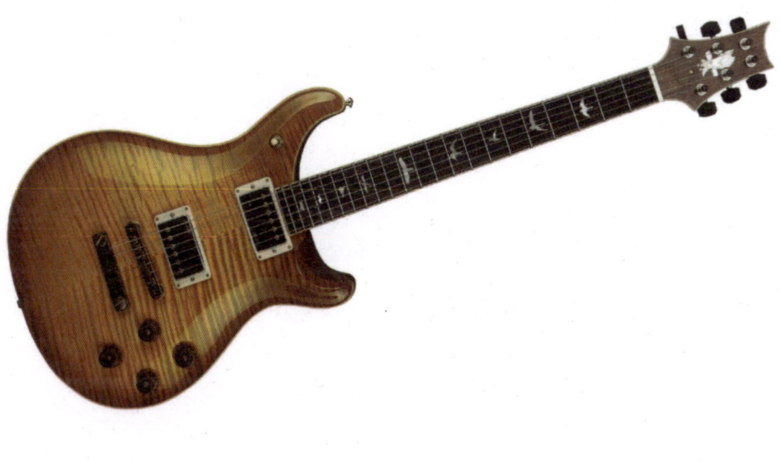

WHAT CAN AN ELECTRIC GUITAR TEACH YOU ABOUT PORTFOLIO DESIGN?

To craft a guitar good enough to be chosen by the world's finest musicians, every detail had to be considered. FS Investments approaches investing with a similar devotion to thoughtful design. We go beyond traditional thinking, seeking to provide you access to alternative sources of income and growth you may need for the challenges ahead. Explore our philosophy at fsinvestments.com. And see how the right investments can fine-tune your portfolio.

SMART NEVER SETTLES.

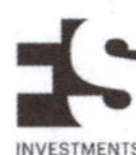

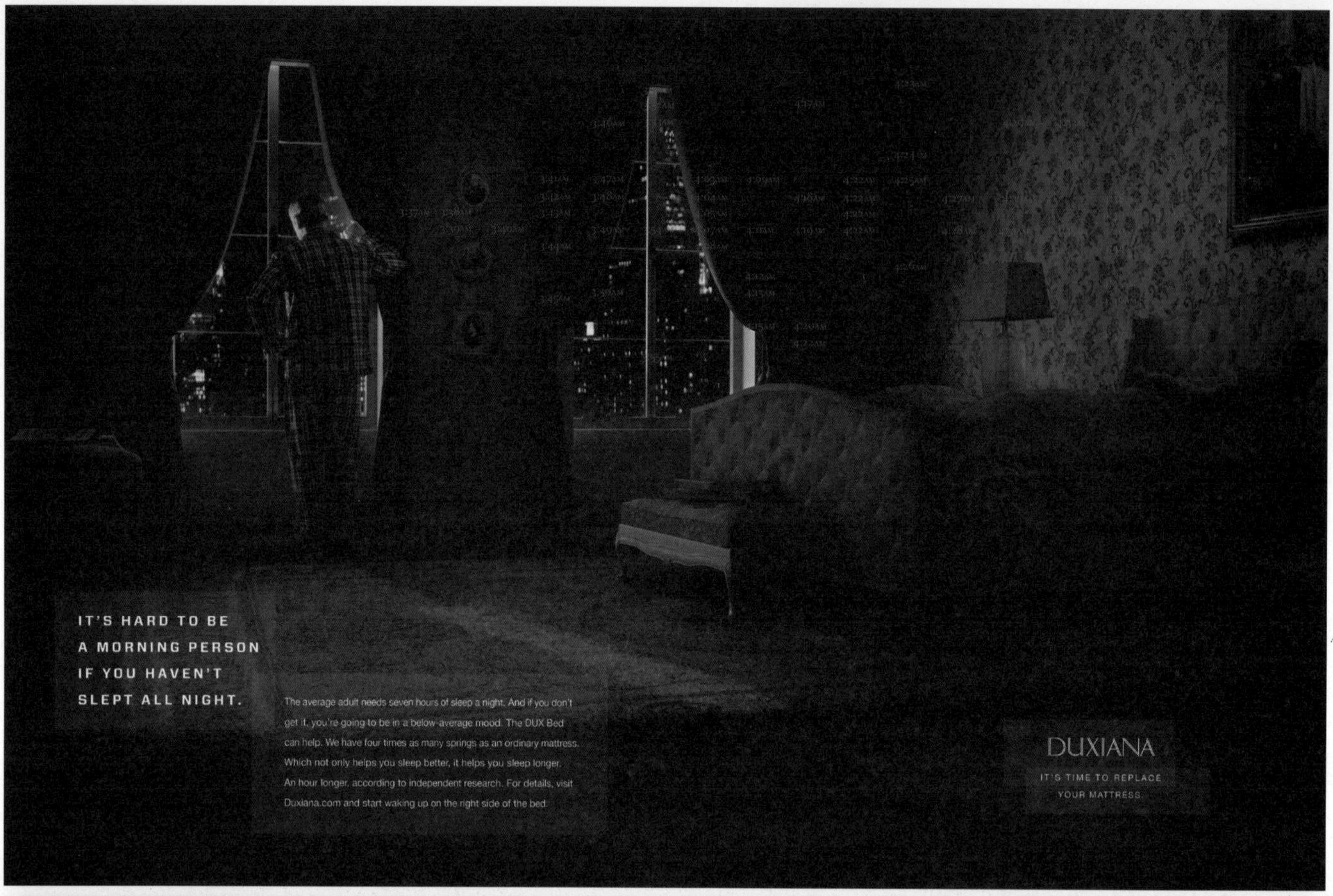

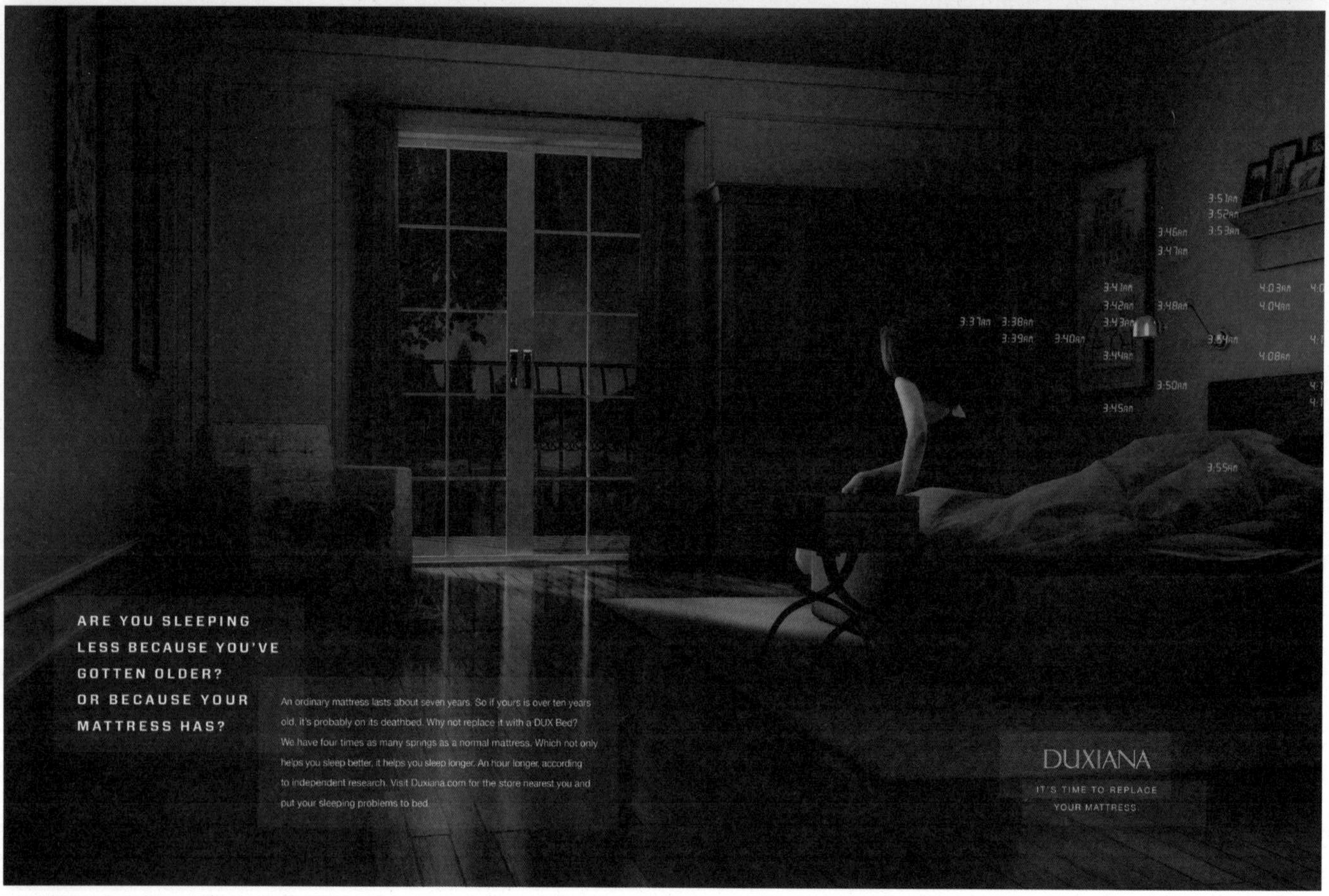

Duxiana; Copywriter: David Bernstein; Art Director: Alex Olmsted

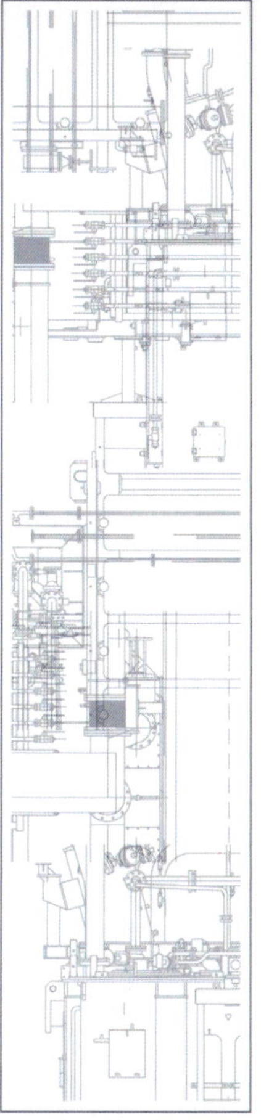

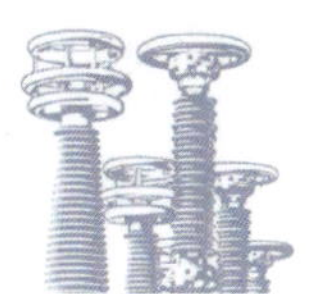

QUARTERS DON'T MAKE YOUR WASHING MACHINE WORK. ELECTRICITY DOES.

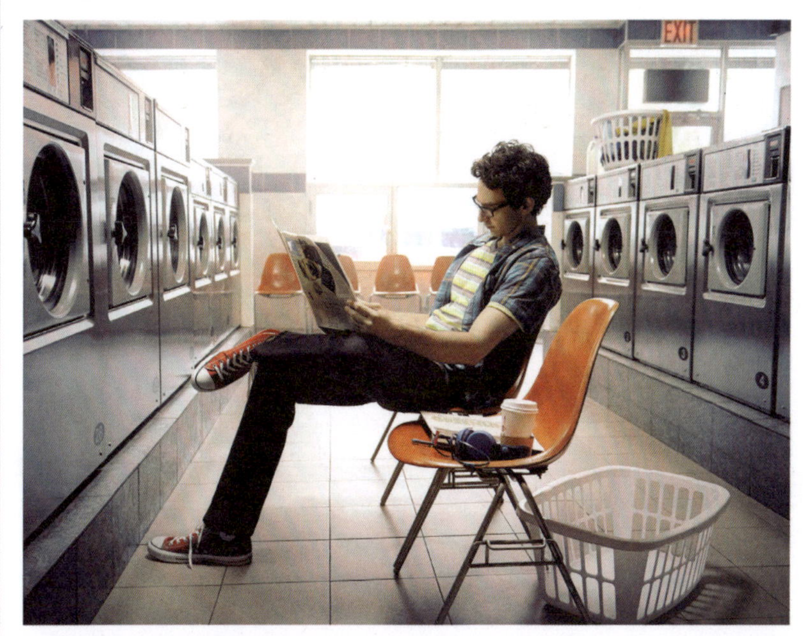

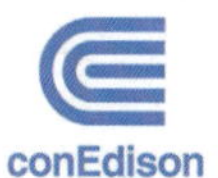

It's easy to forget how important electricity is to our daily lives. But rest assured, Con Edison never does. Of course, all that reliability doesn't come cheap. So we offer more than 100 money-saving tips on our website. Like washing your clothes with cold water and not over-drying them. After all, doing the laundry shouldn't clean out your wallet. For more tips, visit conEd.com and follow us on Facebook or Twitter.

conEdison

EVERYTHING
MATTERS

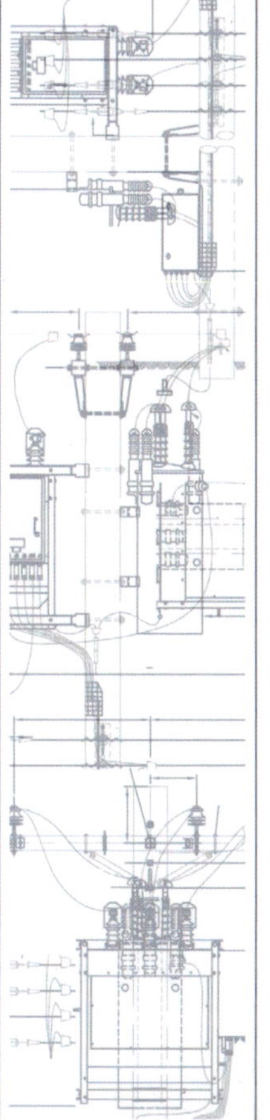

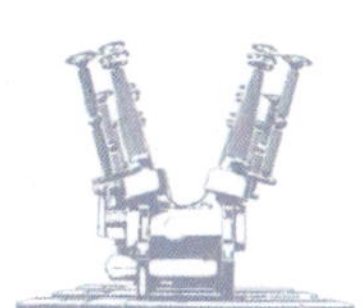

ARE LANDMARKS ANY MORE IMPORTANT THAN NIGHTLIGHTS?

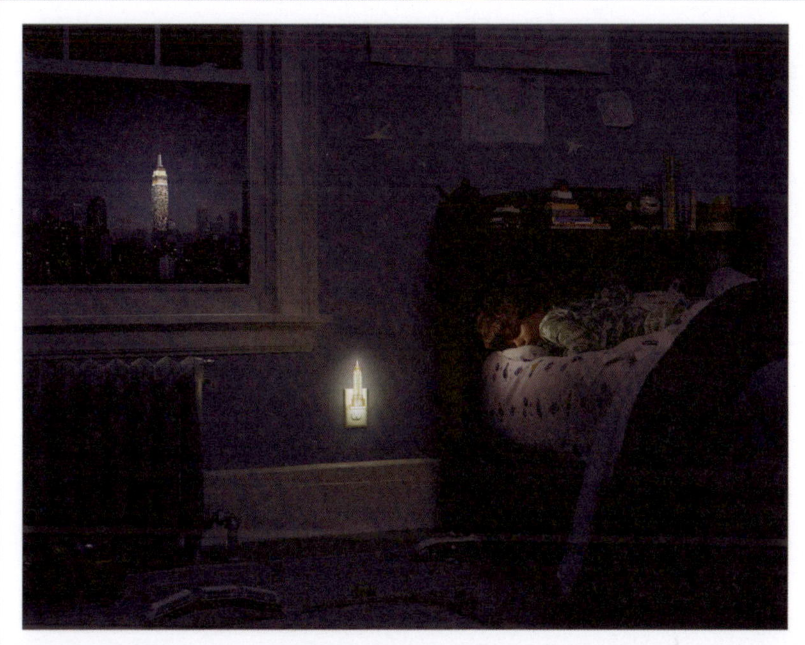

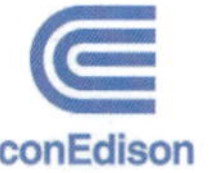

At Con Edison, we know everything that depends on power matters to someone. So everything matters to us. That's why we're spending more than $1 billion on storm-protection improvements: from higher flood barriers to submersible electrical equipment. Of course, if you ever do experience a problem with your power, please report it at conEd.com or by calling 1-800-75-CONED. And follow us on Facebook or Twitter. Rain or shine, we want everything to work. Or there are going to be a lot of cranky people in the morning.

conEdison

EVERYTHING
MATTERS

Page 7: Con Edison; Copywriter: David Bernstein; Art Directors: Alex Olmsted and Patrick Sutherland

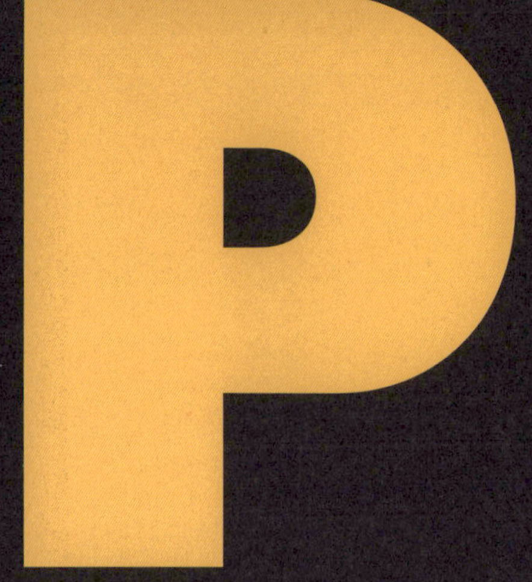

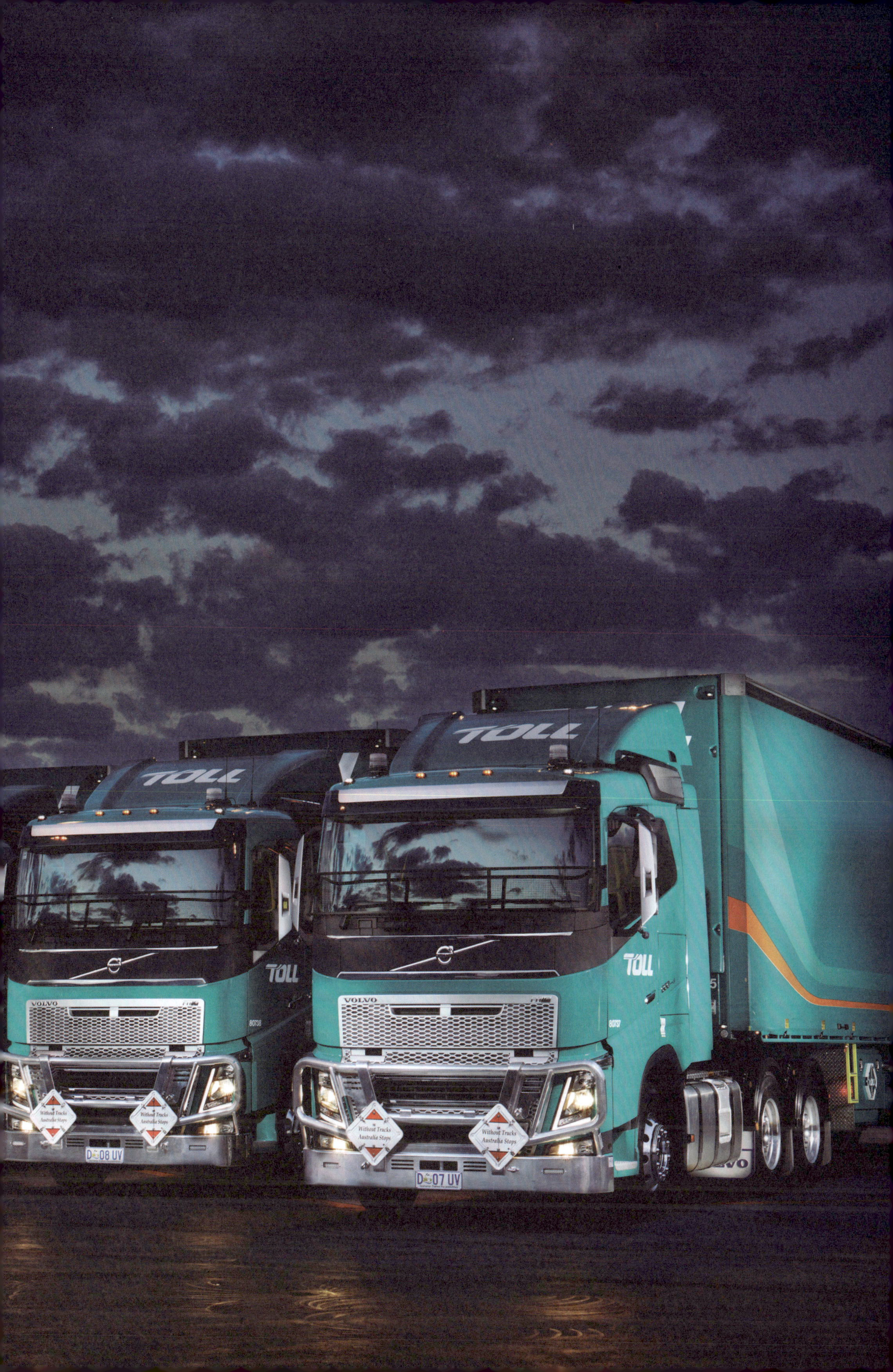

I'VE WORKED WITH PETER FOR THE PAST TEN YEARS. I TAKE HIS SUPERIOR TECHNICAL SKILLS FOR GRANTED, WHICH ARE OBVIOUS FROM HIS WIDE RANGE OF PHOTOGRAPHS.

HE CRAFTS A STRONG VISUAL SIGNATURE FOR MY JEWELRY. I TRUST HIM SO MUCH THAT I SOMETIMES DON'T THINK A PIECE IS WORKING UNTIL I'VE SEEN IT PHOTOGRAPHED BY HIM.

Linda van Niekerk, *Jewelry Designer, Linda van Niekerk Jewelry*

HE'S A MASTER OF FORM, CAPTURING CURVES AND CONTRAST WITH IMAGES THAT LEAVE YOU WANTING MORE. HIS PHOTOGRAPHY REVEALS A DEPTH OF MATERIAL AND SUBSTANCE WITH EXCEPTIONAL CLARITY AND COMPOSITION.

Brodie Neill, *Furniture Designer, Brodie Neill Studio*

HE'S PHOTOGRAPHED MANY OF OUR PROJECTS, BUT ONE EFFORT IS VERY SPECIAL; HE CREATED A UNIQUE PHOTOGRAPHIC COLLAGE WITH AN ALL ENCOMPASSING "FISH EYE" VIEW. IT'S TESTIMONY TO HOW HE CREATES A MEMORABLE IMAGE.

Robert Morris-Nunn, *Principal, Circa Morris-Nunn Chua Architects*

FOR OVER THIRTY YEARS, HE'S PHOTOGRAPHED OUR BUILDINGS AND CERAMICS I'VE EXHIBITED. HE CAPTURES DRAMATIC, EVOCATIVE MOODS AND LIGHTING THAT TRANSFORMS OBJECT DOCUMENTATION INTO MEMORABLE MOMENTS.

Yvette Breytenbach, *Director, Morrison & Breytenbach Architects*

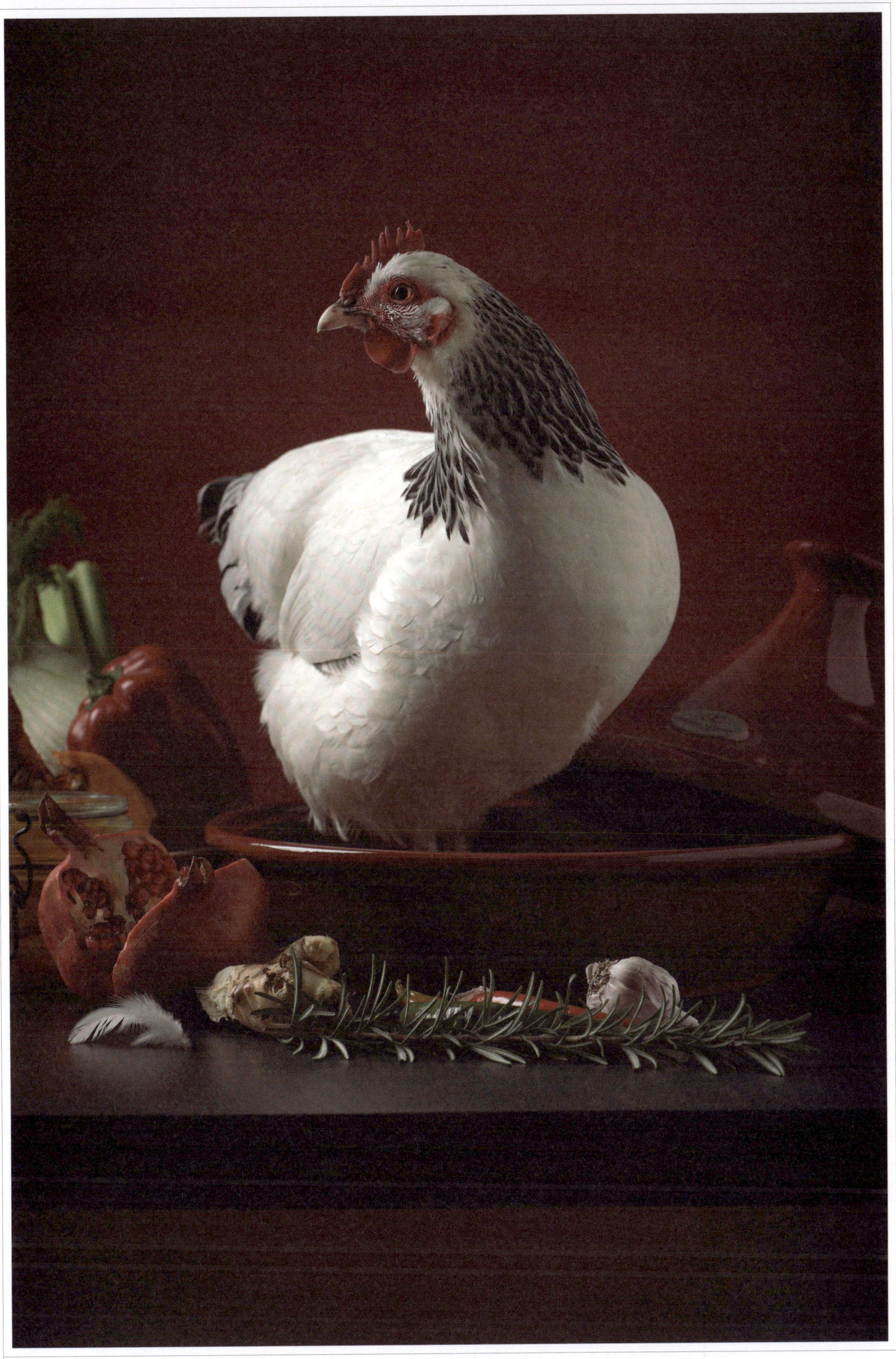

(Page 53) Title: 5 Volvo Trucks; Year: 2014; Client: "Volvo Trucks Australia. Toll IPEC Logistics"; Project: Toll promotion.
(Above) Title: Tagine Chicken; Year: 2012; Client: Norman & Dann; Project: Ongoing retail window campaign; Design, Art Direction, Styling: Peter Whyte

I have known and collaborated with Peter for over thirty years. We both arrived in Tasmania in the early 1980s when there was very little thought given to photography or design. But with time, and by consistently producing works of excellence, talent can't be ignored. Peter's imagery strongly reflects a sense of place, of "islandness" and wild beauty. Most importantly, the close rapport that he has with his subject, be it a person, a piece of art, a product, or a landscape, is the thing that sets him apart. This "intimate" connection beyond the lens is clearly evident in all of Peter's work as he seeks out the beauty in everything, and in doing so, he also makes us look deeply into our own world.

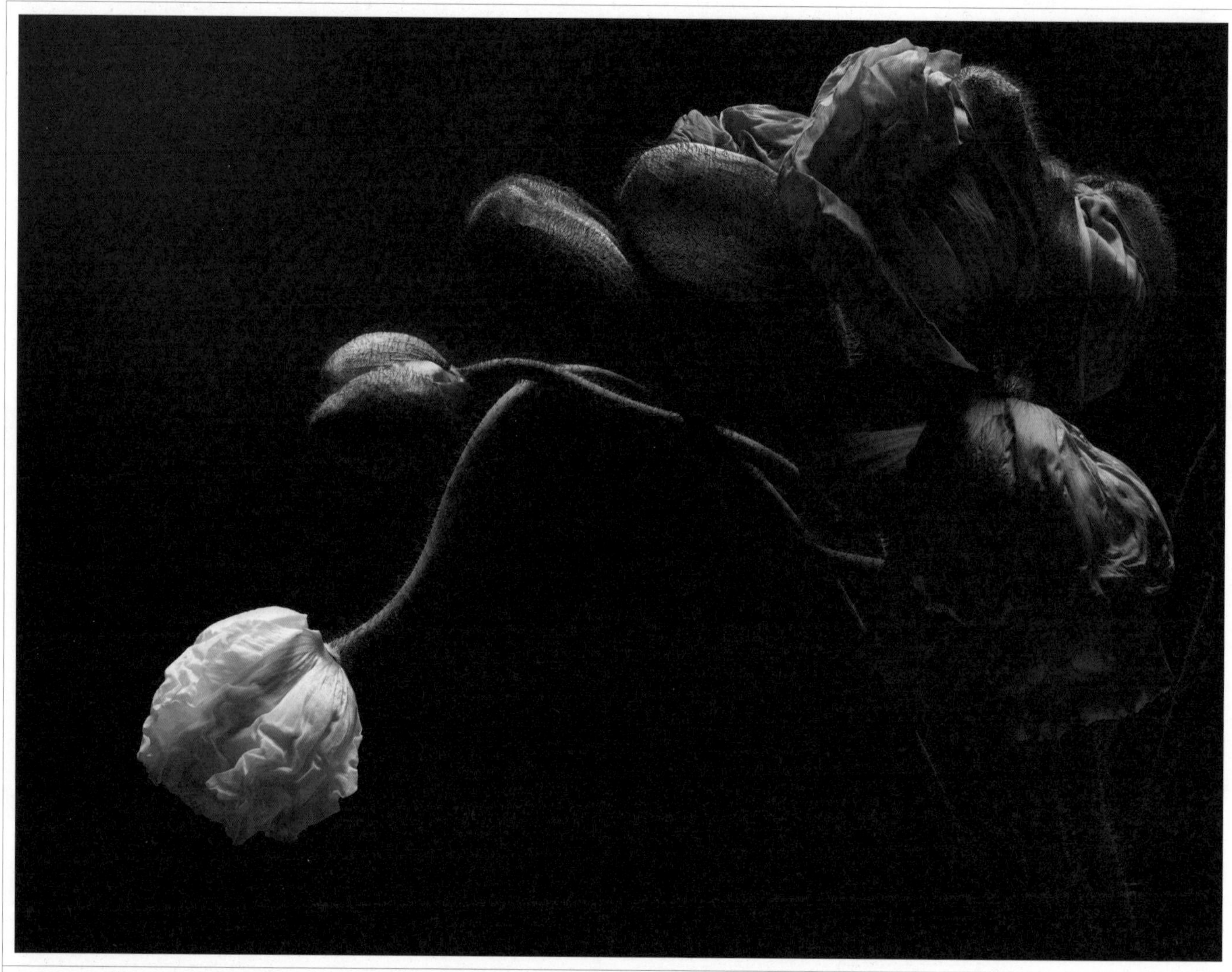

(Above) Title: Emerging Poppies 061; Year: 2014; Client: Self-initiated; Project: "Exhibition Emerging - Decaying Exhibition. Bett Gallery Hobart"; Design, Art Direction, Styling: Peter Whyte
(Opposite page) Title: The Art of Tea 002; Year: 2012; Client: Norman & Dann; Project: Ongoing retail window campaign; Design, Art Direction, Styling: Peter Whyte
(Following spread) Title: Yellowfin Tuna; Year: 2018; Client: "Institute of Maine & Antarctic Studies IMAS"; Project: Campaign promoting sustainable practices for recreational fishermen; Design, Art Direction, Styling: Peter Whyte

DO WHAT YOU LOVE. PRIORITIZE INTEREST OVER RETURN. BE PREPARED TO SAY NO.

Peter Whyte, *Photographer, Peter Whyte Photography*

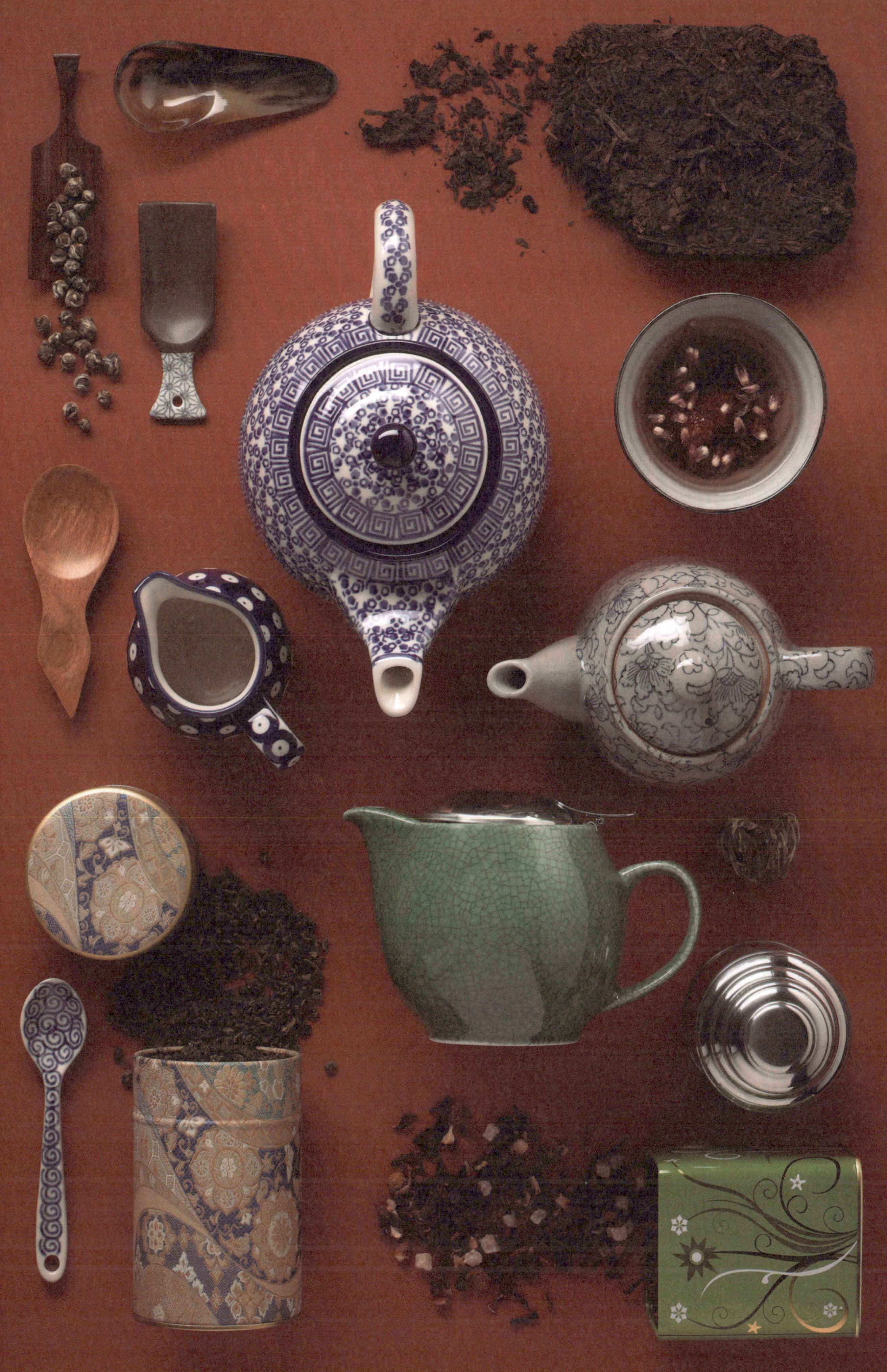

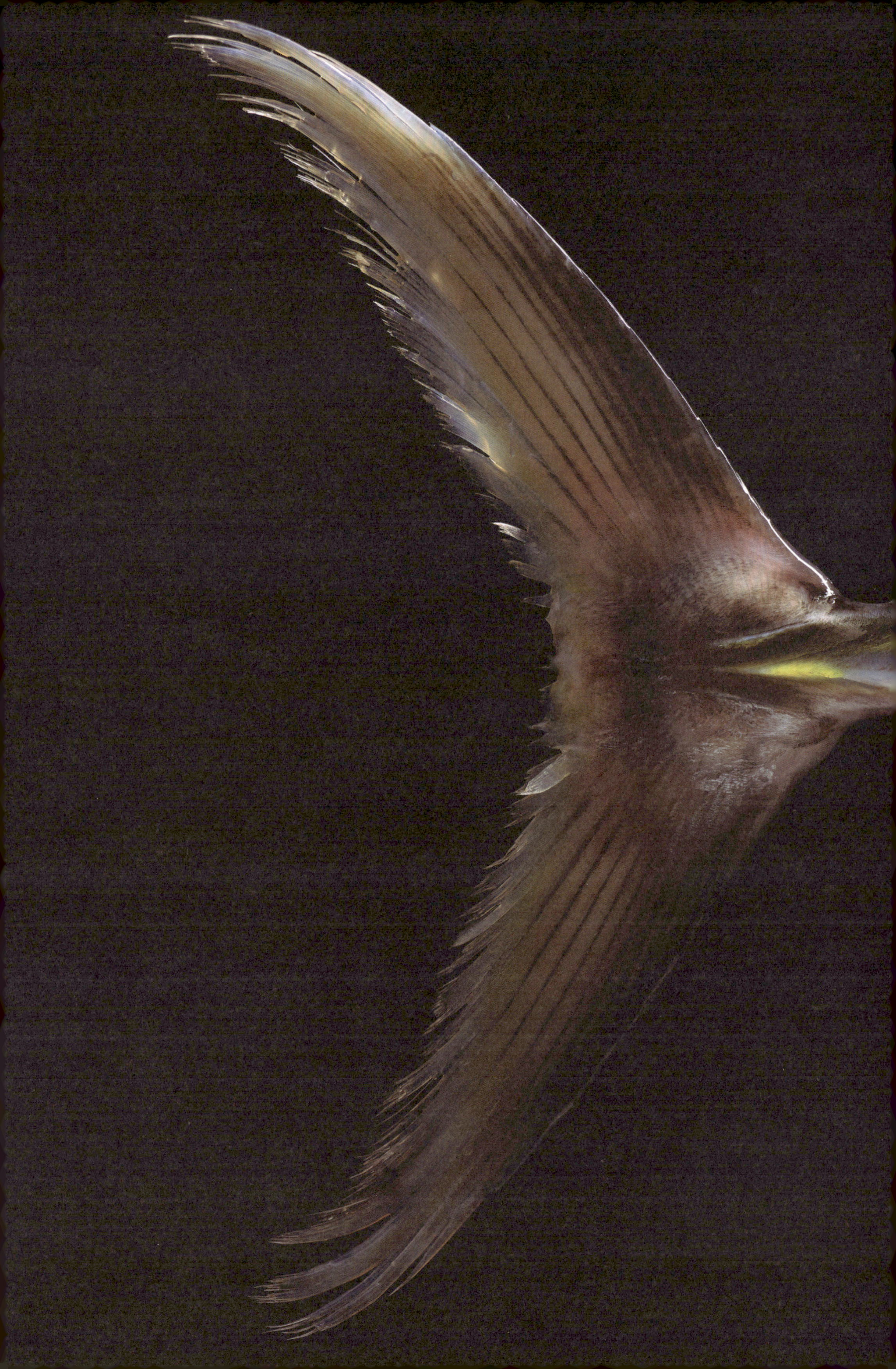

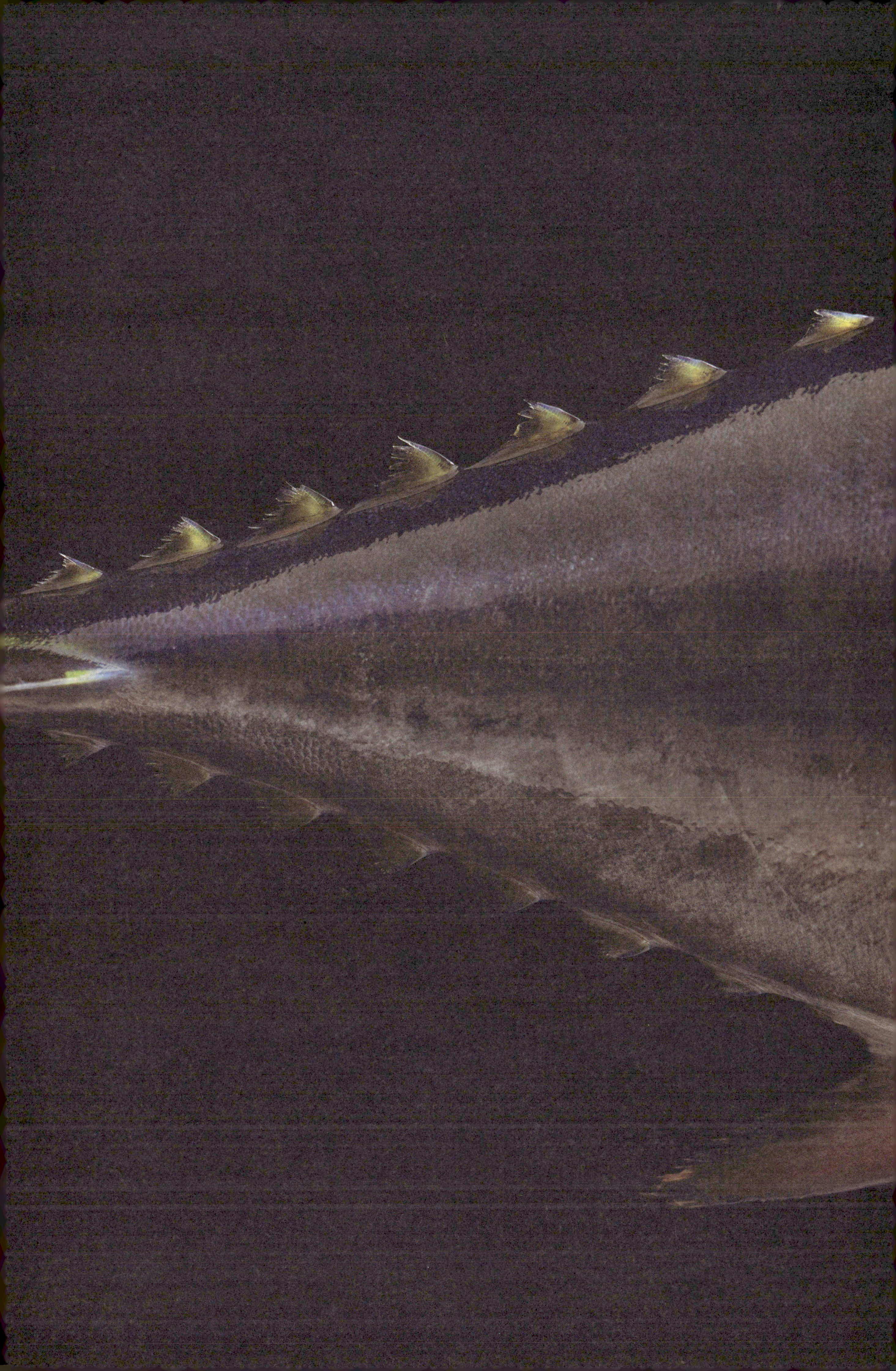

What inspired or motivated you into your career?
I grew up in a large, stimulating yet fairly visually illiterate farming family in rural Victoria and went to a high school with no art department. It was while studying graphic design at RMIT in Melbourne that my photography developed in conjunction with my design education. For me, these two disciplines are inseparable and the backbone of my practice.

What is your work philosophy?
Do what you love. Prioritize interest over return. Be prepared to say no.

Who is or was your greatest mentor?
My greatest mentor is master graphic designer Lynda Warner, who was recently inducted into the Australian Graphic Design Association Hall of Fame. Lynda is a friend and colleague with whom I've collaborated for more than three decades.

What is it about photography that you are most passionate about?
I'm passionate about lighting and, in particular, shadows. This isn't from a technical point of view, but more about the credibility, content, and intent of the image. Shadows hold mystery and give form to face and landscape. Shadows allow me to control what I wish to reveal or conceal. Shadows leave the viewer wanting a little more, having to imagine what they cannot clearly see.

What has been your most memorable project?
I spent four and a half years documenting the work at MONA, the Museum of Old and New Art in Hobart, Tasmania. Working closely with the creative director Leigh Carmichael, we developed a distinct visual style for the museum. It was a privilege to just quietly spend time with each of these sometimes challenging artworks.

Other memorable projects have been documenting the installation of solar-powered telecommunication systems in the Republic of Kiribati and documenting food tourism in Sicily and northern Italy.

What is your approach to fine art photography, and how does it differ from your approach to commercial photography?
The relationship between commercial and fine art work in my practice is symbiotic. Each feeds and is dependent upon the other. Experiments in personal work are incorporated into commercial work, while ideas and skills developed in commercial work feed my personal practice. My commercial work has a client and an external audience who need to be addressed, while my personal work ultimately has an audience of one.

Who were some of your greatest past influences?
Painters like Caravaggio, Vermeer, and Rembrandt, and photographers such as Karl Blossfeldt, Edward Weston, Imogen Cunningham, Olive Cotton, Max Dupain, David Moore, Irving Penn, Robert Mapplethorpe, and Peter Dombrovskis.

Who among your contemporaries today do you most admire?
Hiroshi Sugimoto, Ori Gersht, Tine Poppe, Albert Watson, and Adam Fuss.

You've worked on various genres of photography; do you have any specific favorites?
Still life photography would be my favorite genre. It beautifully combines design, composition, construction, attention to detail, and lighting. Swiss typographer Wolfgang Weingart said in an inspiring lecture in Hobart that graphic design is to make an empty space not empty. That is how I approach still life photography.

Who have been some of your favorite people or clients you have worked with?
My favorite group of clients are the myriad of artists whose work I document. Of these painters, ceramicists, jewlers, glass artists, sculptors, and furniture makers, most just eke out a living, but all are passionate. Photographing their work is often very challenging and extremely rewarding.

From this work came my ongoing personal project of artists' portraits. My only regret is that I didn't start it a couple of decades earlier.

What are the most important ingredients you require from a client to do successful work?
Come to me with a question, not a solution. I like a well articulated, open brief with clearly defined communication objectives, a target audience, and no firm preconceived visual outcome. But I do encourage input and thrive on collaboration.

What is your proudest professional achievement?
Surviving as a photographer for over four decades doing what I love.

What advice would you have for students starting out today?
From day one, do for yourself what you're being asked to do for others — promote yourself.

What interests do you have outside of your work?
Living on the beautiful island of Tasmania on the edge of the Southern Ocean, this ancient environment has an immense influence on how we live here — its power, beauty, and alarming fragility from human endeavors and climate change. Sea kayaking, bushwalking, mountain biking, and fly fishing all allow me to enjoy this place and recharge with family and friends.

Where do you seek inspiration?
As Pablo Picasso famously said, "Inspiration exists, but it has to find you working."

Ideally, I like to work alone when shooting in my studio, just with music. This enables me to think clearly and work decisively. Inspiration is there.

Unlike any other time in history, we literally have the world at our fingertips. The giants upon whose shoulders we stand have never been so easily accessible. From the work of master photographers past and present, endless movies, works of art, tutorials, troubleshooting, and what's happening socially and politically in the world — it's all instantly accessible.

Inspiration also comes from a lifetime of close observation of my everchanging environment and how light falls. Analysis and understanding of natural light enables me to create credible light in the studio and the confidence to break rules for incredible lighting.

Where do you see yourself in the future?
Continuing moving my emphasis from commercial to personal work.

Peter Whyte peterwhytephotography.com

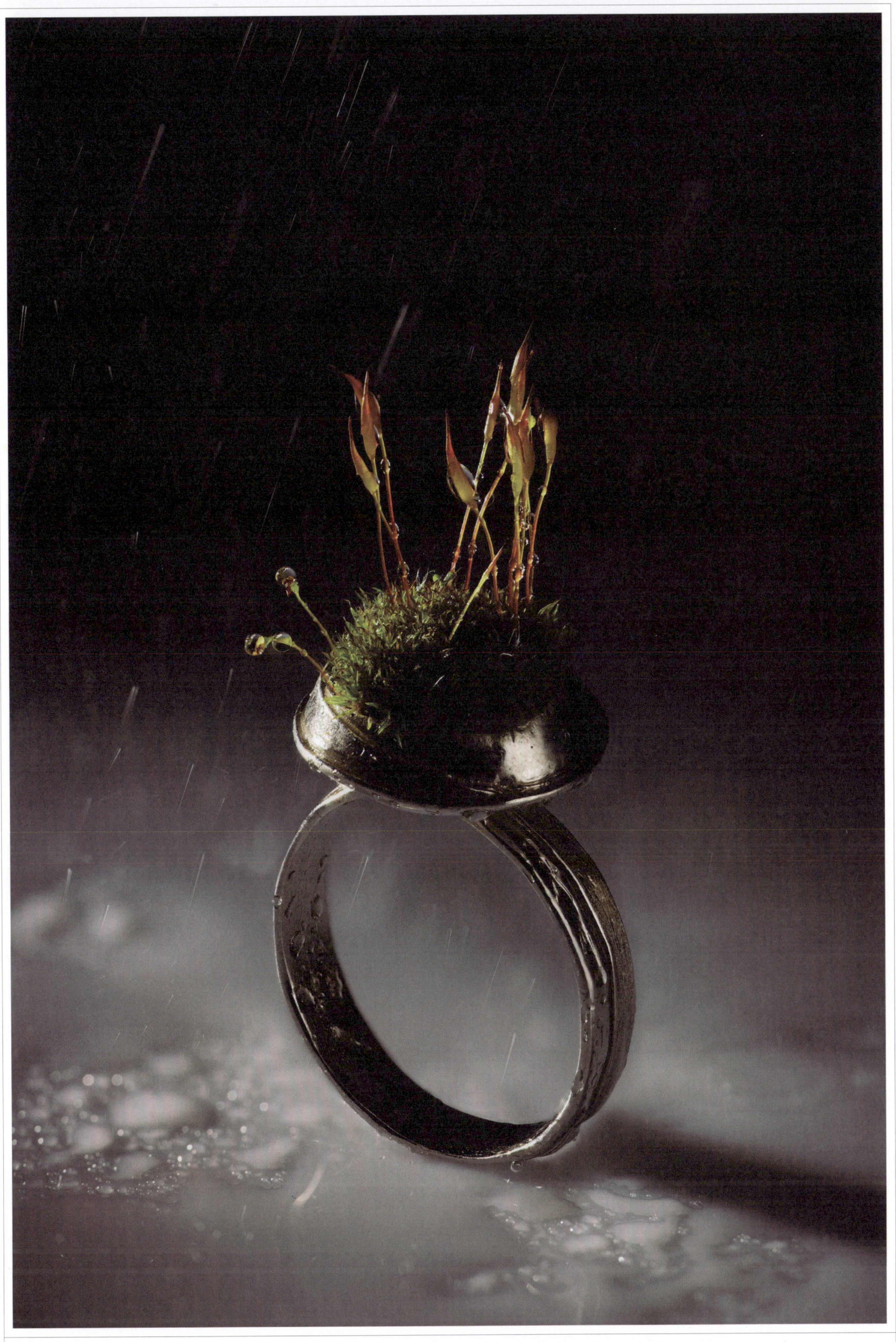

*Title: 'Care-Ring' by Anita Dineen; Year: 2018; Client: Anita Dineen, designer and jeweller. The 'Care-Ring' contains a living miniature moss garden.
Project: Designed object documentation; Design, Art Direction, Styling: Peter Whyte*

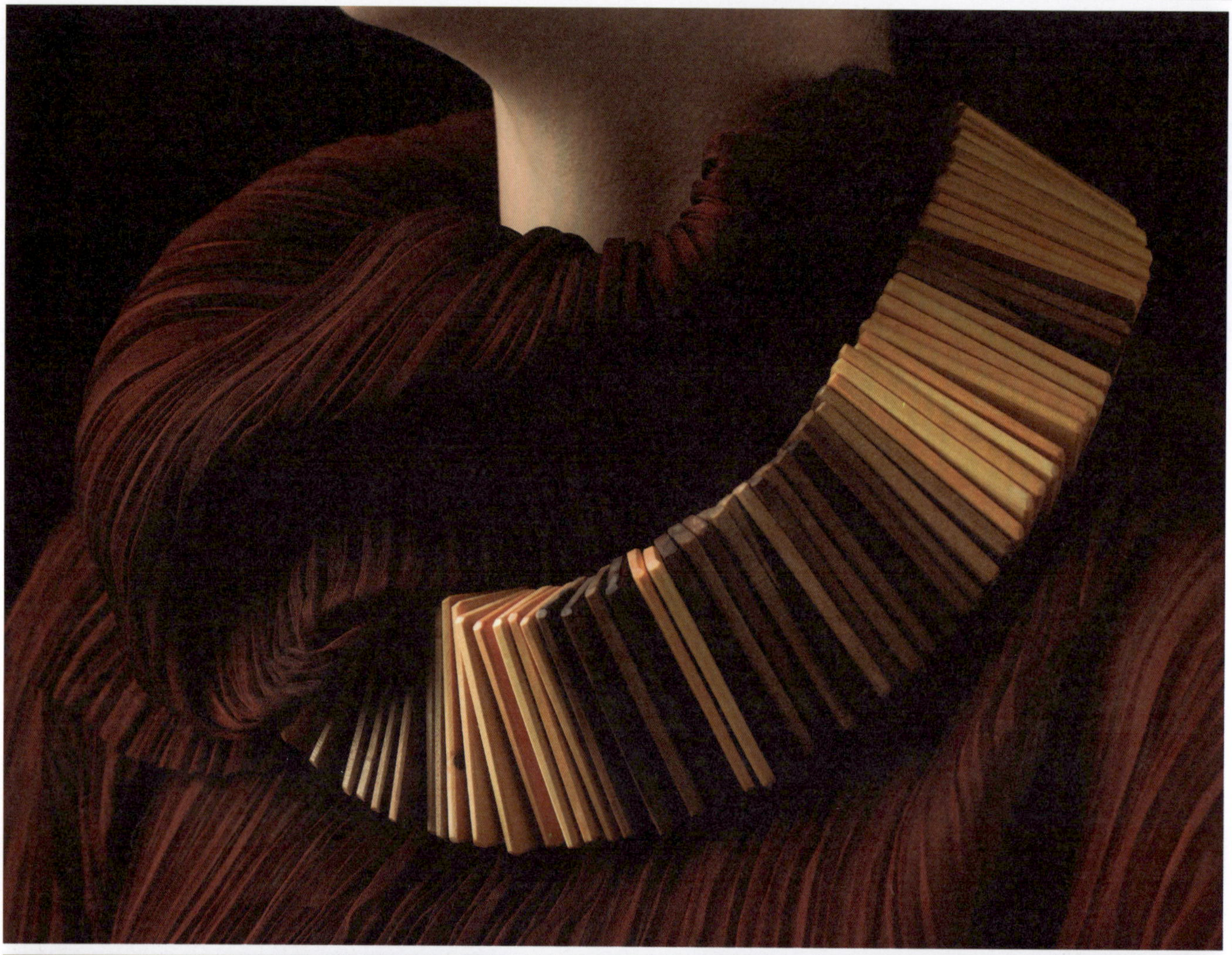

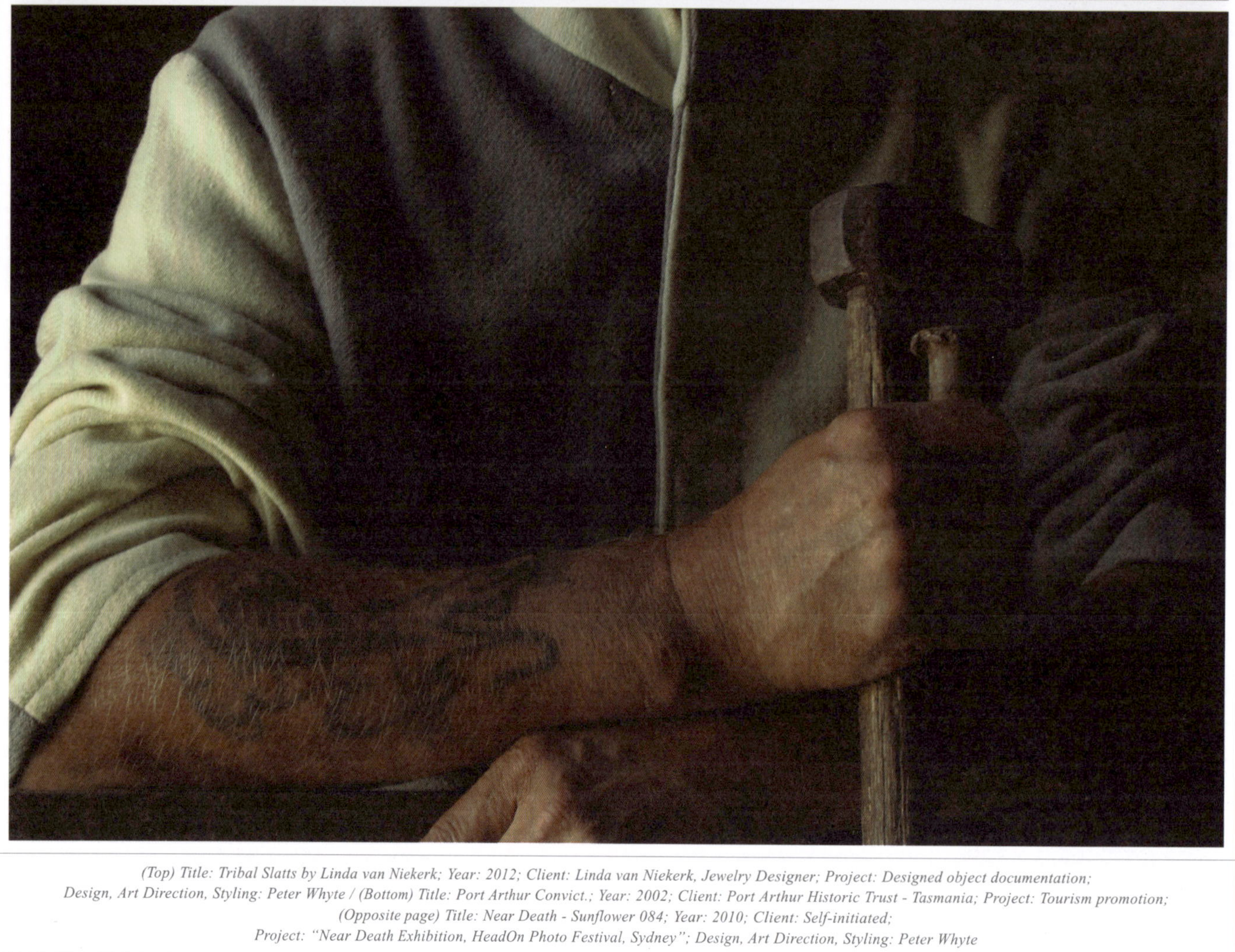

(Top) Title: Tribal Slatts by Linda van Niekerk; Year: 2012; Client: Linda van Niekerk, Jewelry Designer; Project: Designed object documentation; Design, Art Direction, Styling: Peter Whyte / (Bottom) Title: Port Arthur Convict.; Year: 2002; Client: Port Arthur Historic Trust - Tasmania; Project: Tourism promotion; (Opposite page) Title: Near Death - Sunflower 084; Year: 2010; Client: Self-initiated; Project: "Near Death Exhibition, HeadOn Photo Festival, Sydney"; Design, Art Direction, Styling: Peter Whyte

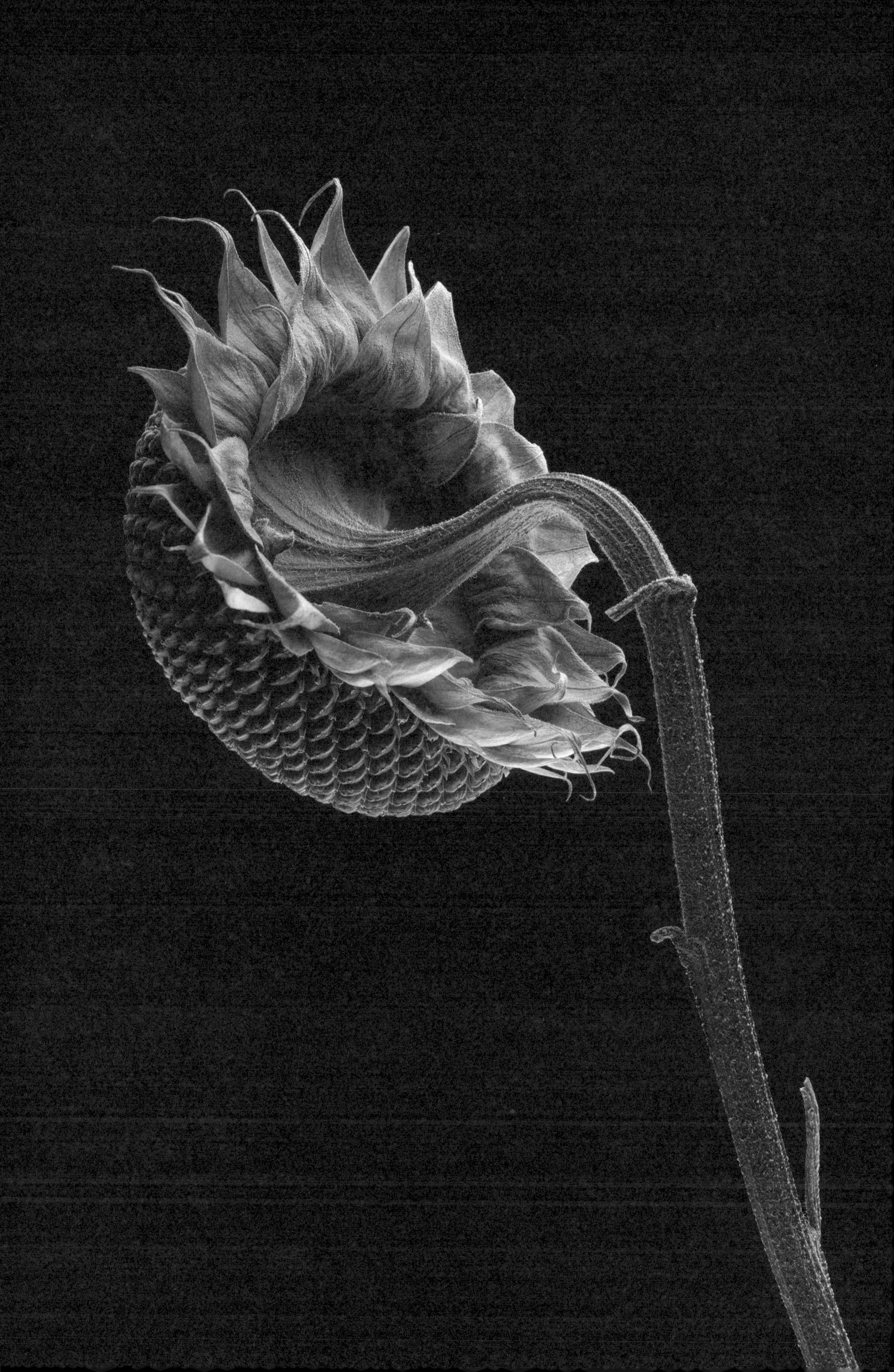

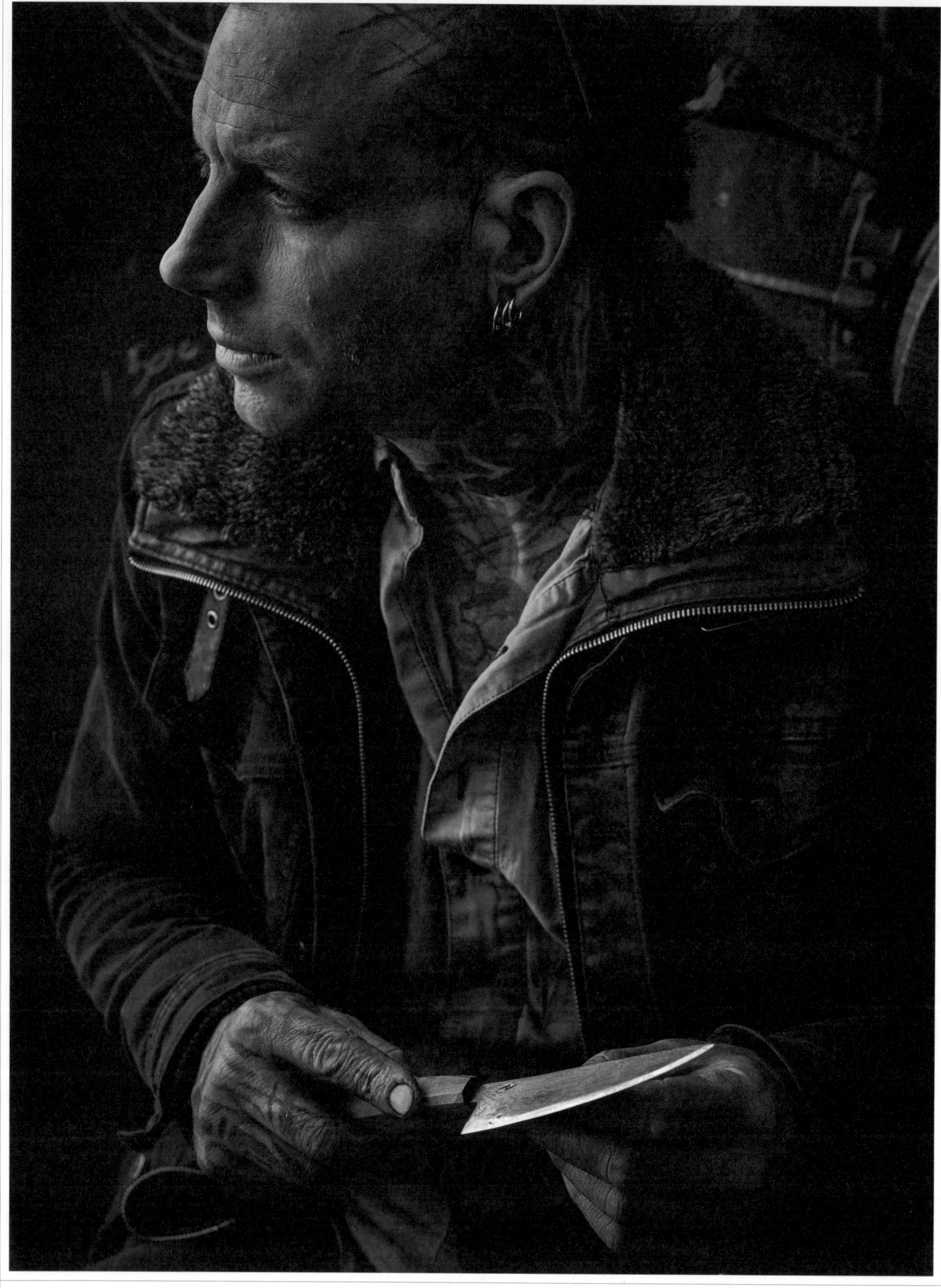

Title: Portrait of Pete Mattila, Blacksmith and Sculptor; Year: 2019; Client: Self-initiated; Project: Ongoing personal project of artist portraits

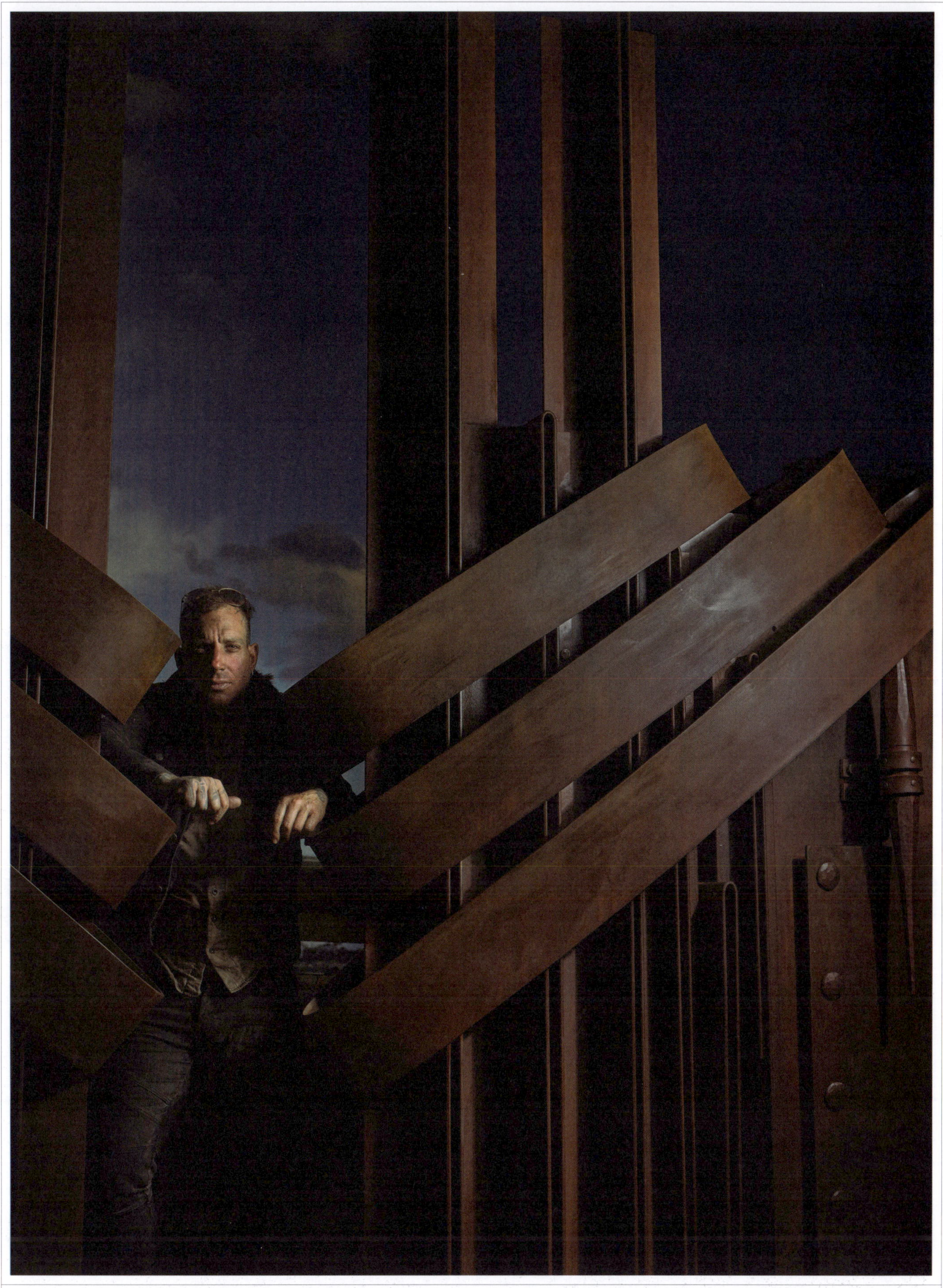

Title: Portrait of Pete Mattila, Blacksmith and Sculptor; Year: 2019; Client: Self-initiated; Project: Ongoing personal project of artist portraits

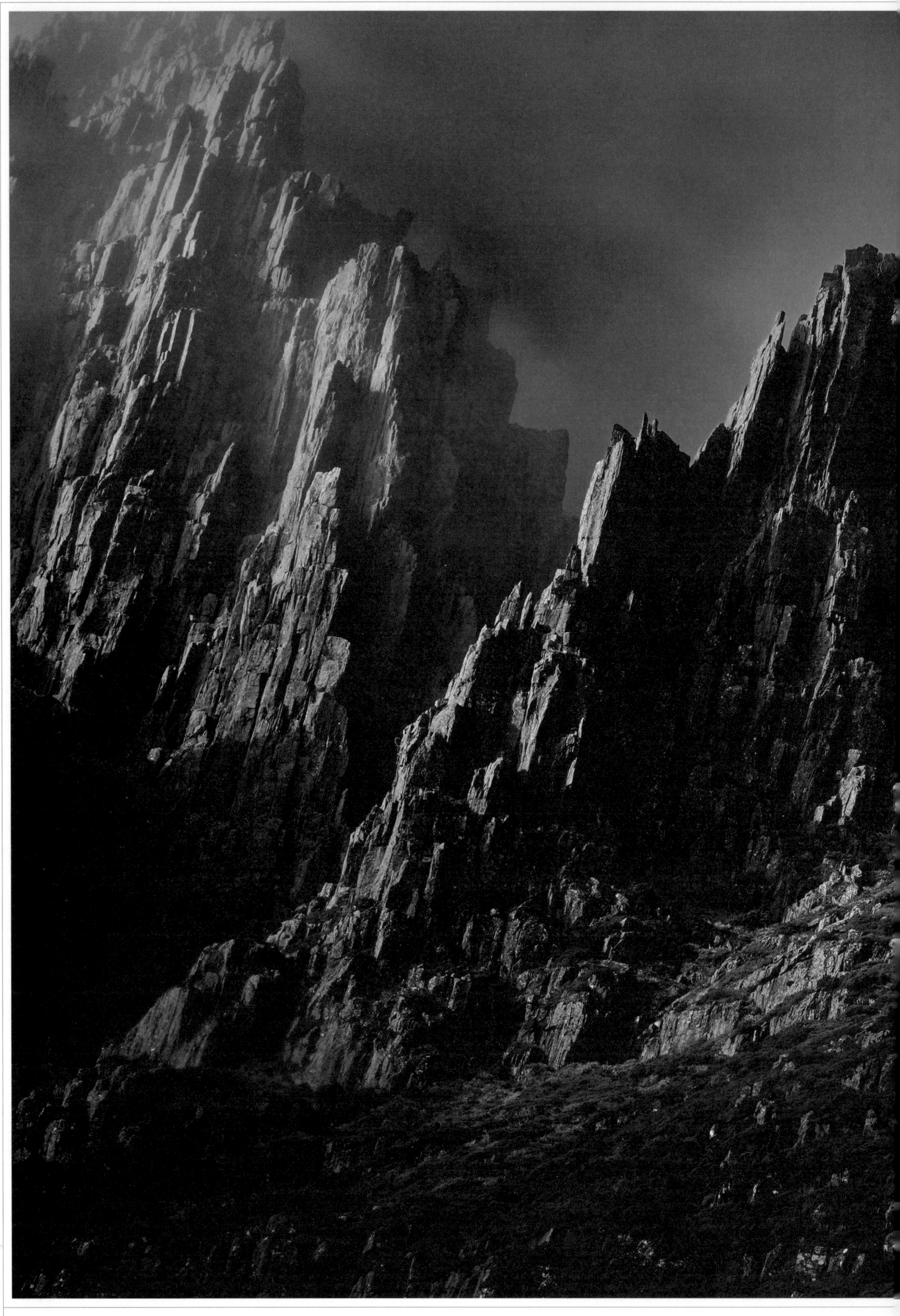

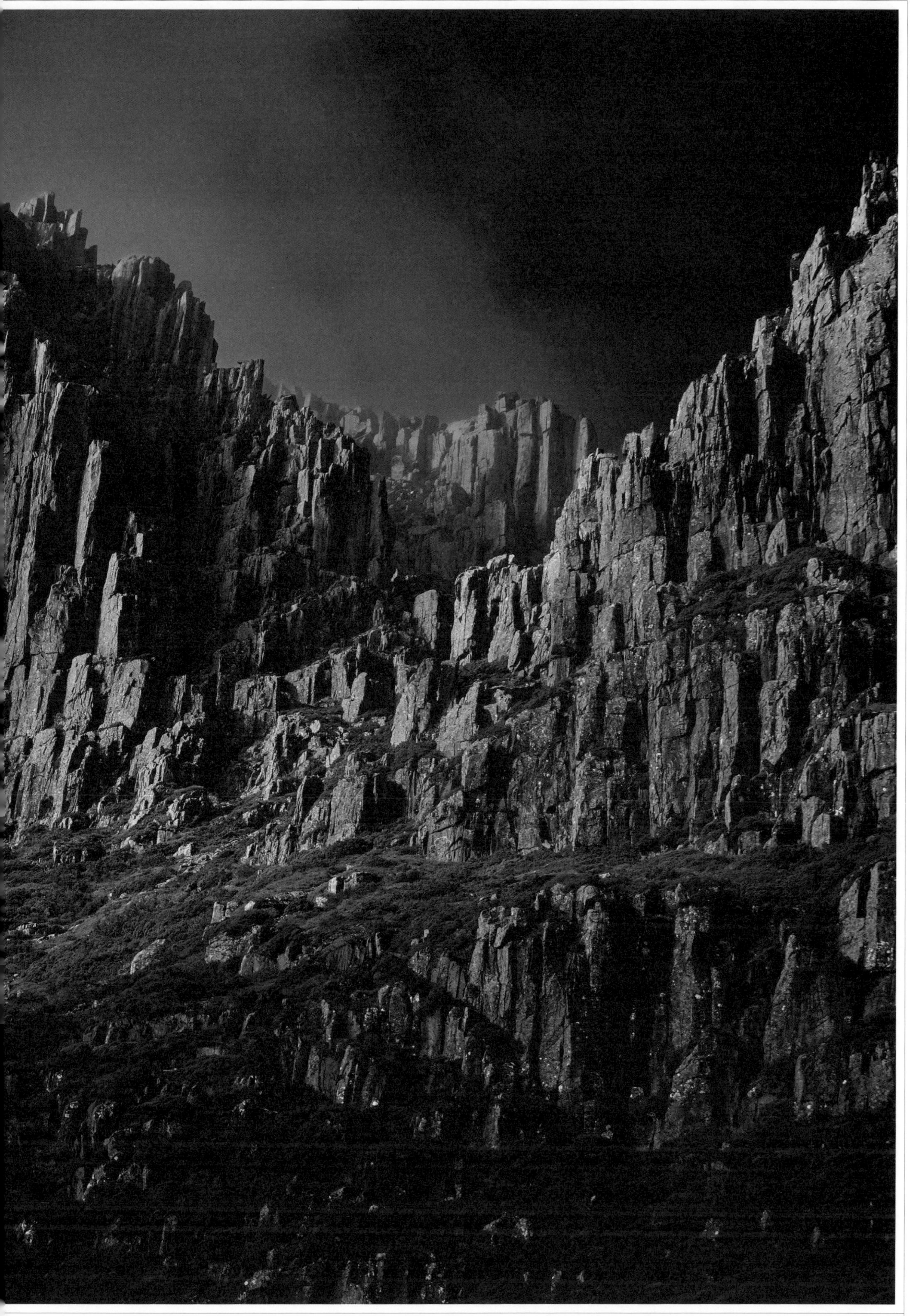

Title: Cradle Mountain - Lake St. Clair National Park, Tasmania; Year: 2010; Client: Self-initiated; Project: Personal work documenting living on the island of Tasmania

LOCATION, STUDIO PORTRAIT, STILL-LIFE, EDITORIAL —MICHAEL HAS TACKLED THEM ALL. I CAN'T THINK OF ANYONE MORE SKILLED AT POST-PRODUCTION DIGITAL WORK. HE'S CONSISTENTLY EXPLORING NEW TECHNIQUES AND STYLISTIC IDEAS.

Scott Eggers, *Founder & Graphic Designer, Eggers Design*

HAVING WORKED WITH MICHAEL FOR NEARLY THIRTY YEARS, I'VE WATCHED HIM WORK ON HUNDREDS OF PROJECTS. HE APPROACHES EVERY ASSIGNMENT WITH THE SAME ENERGY AND PASSION, REGARDLESS OF THE SIZE OR SCOPE.

HE SEES EVERY PHOTO AS AN OPPORTUNITY TO TELL A STORY. HE DOESN'T GET DISTRACTED BY TRENDS OR GET LOCKED INTO A PARTICULAR STYLE. HE CRAFTS AND PUSHES IMAGES THAT RESONATE WITH HIS AUDIENCE.

Richard Oliver, *Chief Creative Officer & Partner, Faktory*

I'VE WORKED WITH SEVERAL GIFTED CREATIVES; VERY FEW ARE LIKE HIM. AGENCIES OFTEN HIRE OUTSIDE TALENT, AND IN DOING SO, WE EXPOSE OURSELVES TO VARIABLES WE CAN'T CONTROL.

WORKING WITH HIM RELIEVES THIS VULNERABILITY. GENUINE CREATIVITY, HONEST PROFESSIONALISM, AND A REAL "KNOCK IT OUT OF THE PARK" MENTALITY SEEM TO BE HIS GO-TO.

Ben Craner, *Creative Director, Good Better Bestest*

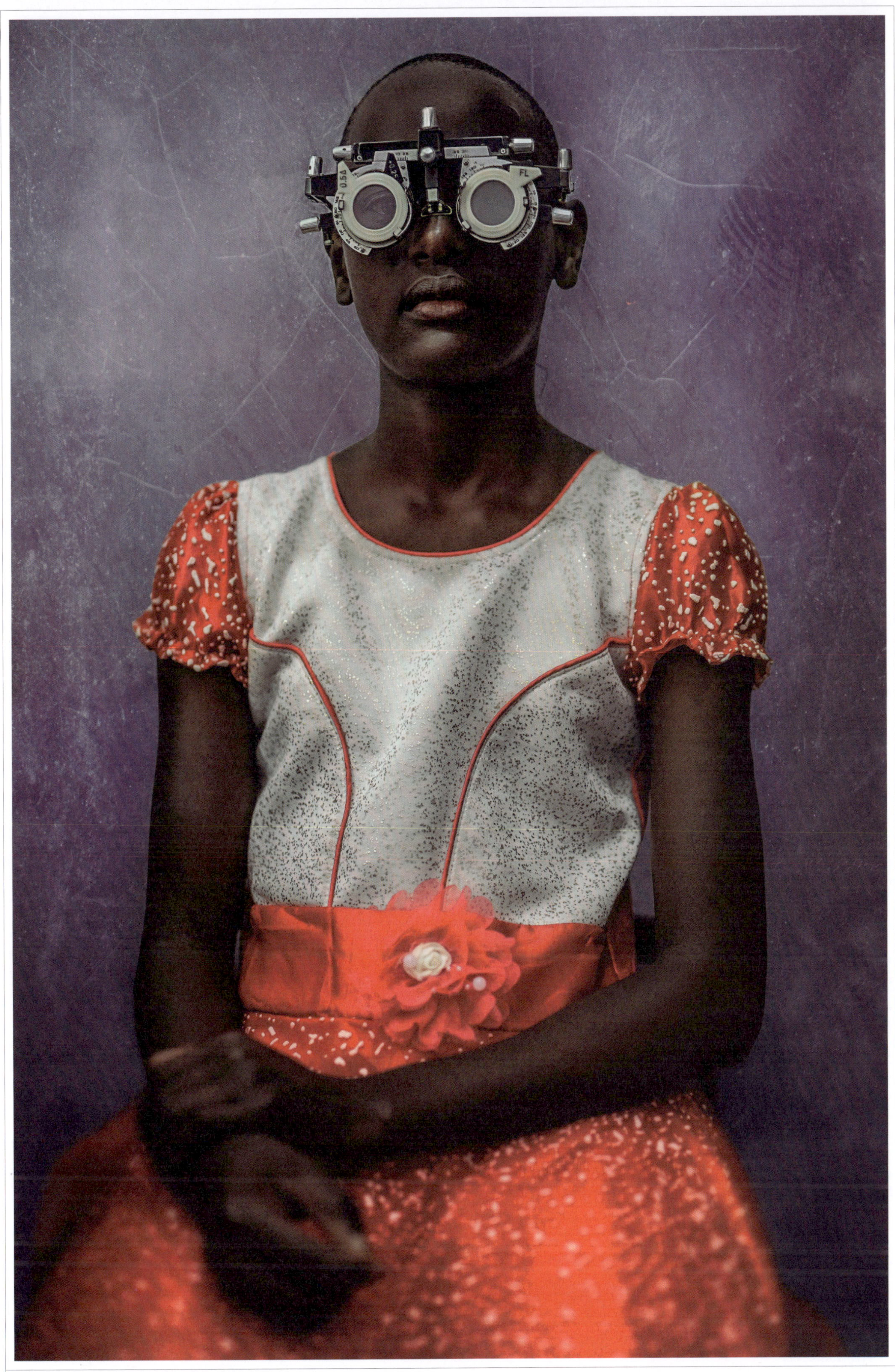

I had an amazing worldwide adventure with Michael; we started in Toronto, then off to Berlin, Tokyo, and Mumbai. What I love most about Michael is that he can look at a person and see their true self, and that's because he is always his true self. He is an amazing human, full of thoughtfulness and love. Because of this, his work is also thoughtful, loving, beautiful, and amazing. We were shooting IT professionals (not models), but he was able to find the model within each person and the images were authentic and amazing. Working with Michael was an adventure of a lifetime.

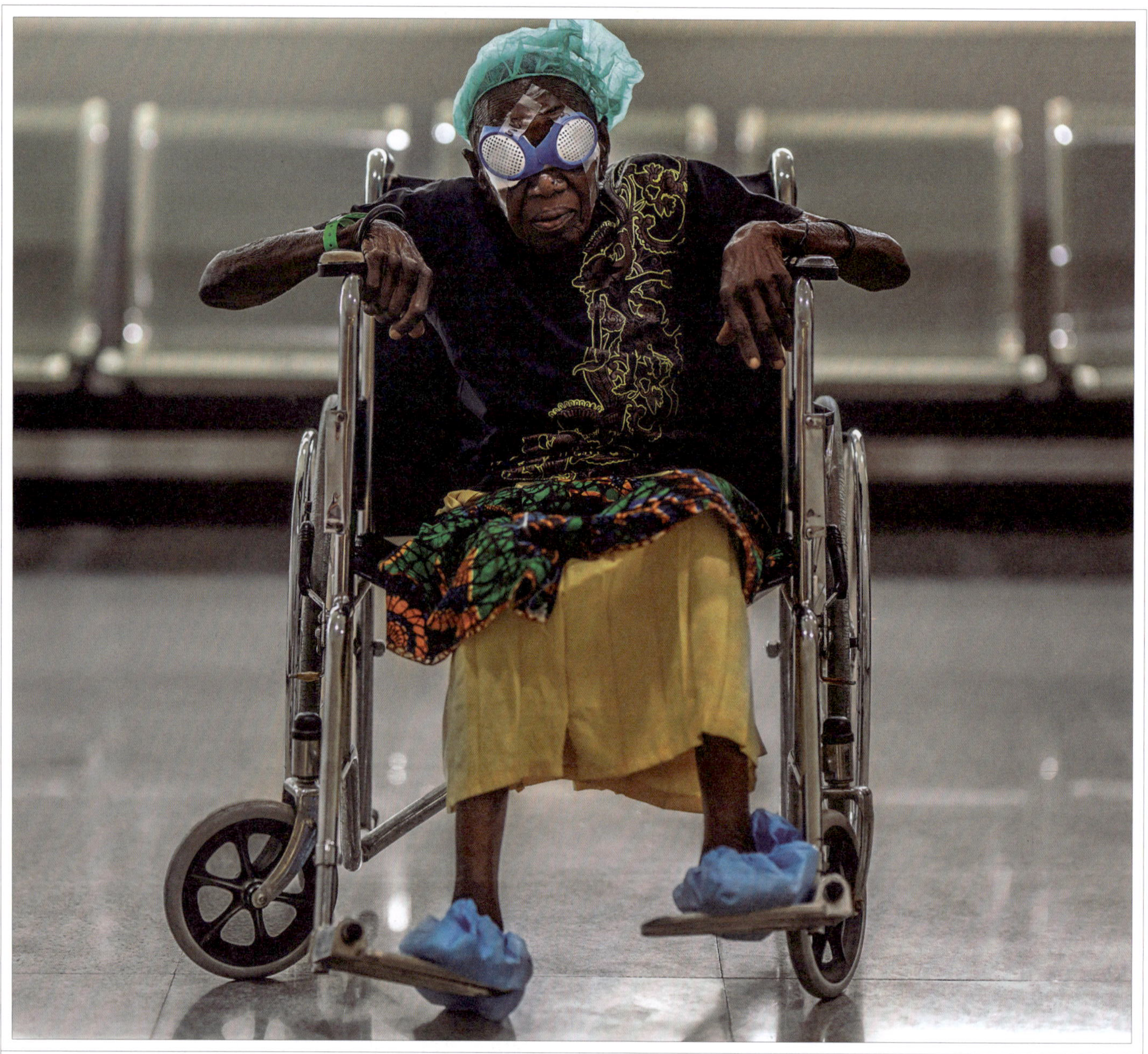

This lady has just received double cataract surgery, which is quite rare. Her prognosis and outcome were excellent. I have had unfettered access to the entire medical process on all of my humanitarian missions to date. It puts quite a responsibility on one's shoulders to find a new way to capture something going on in front of you, without repeating yourself.
Clients: Moran Eye Global Outreach and Eye-corps

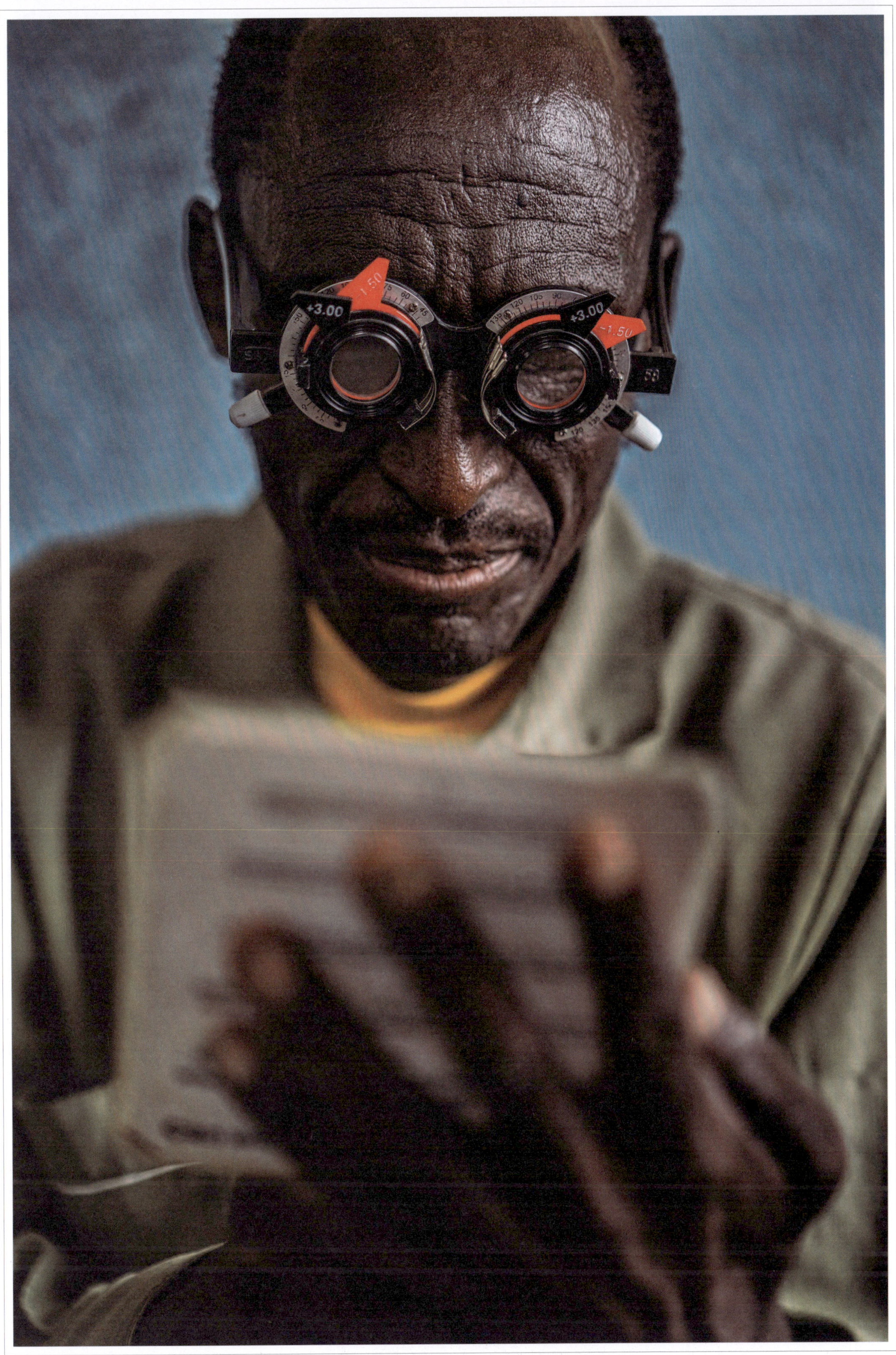

Some of the most precious, enjoyable, mind-expanding experiences I've had were in Africa, Guatemala, and the South Pacific as a photographer for various humanitarian missions.
Clients: Moran Eye Global Outreach and Eye-corps

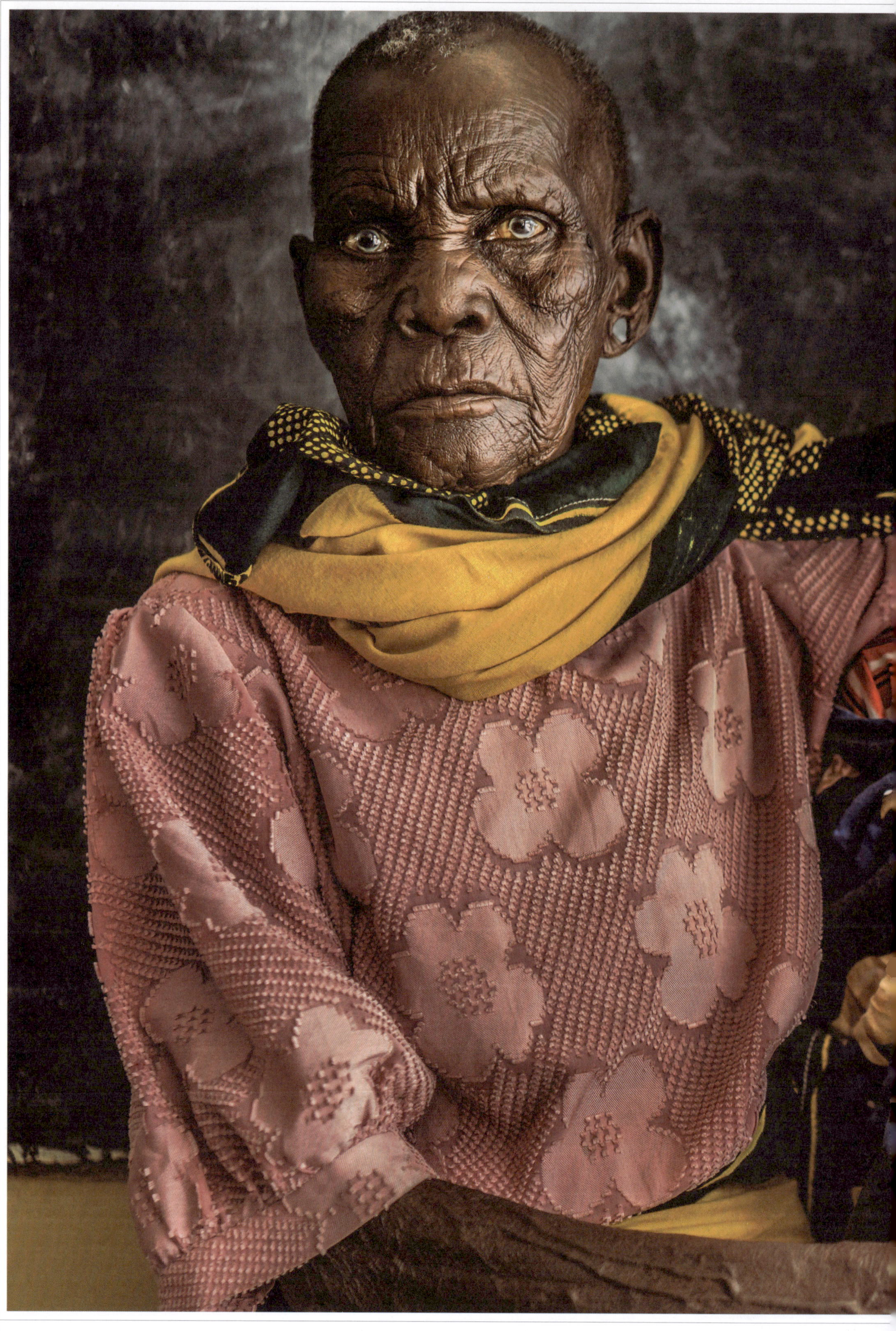

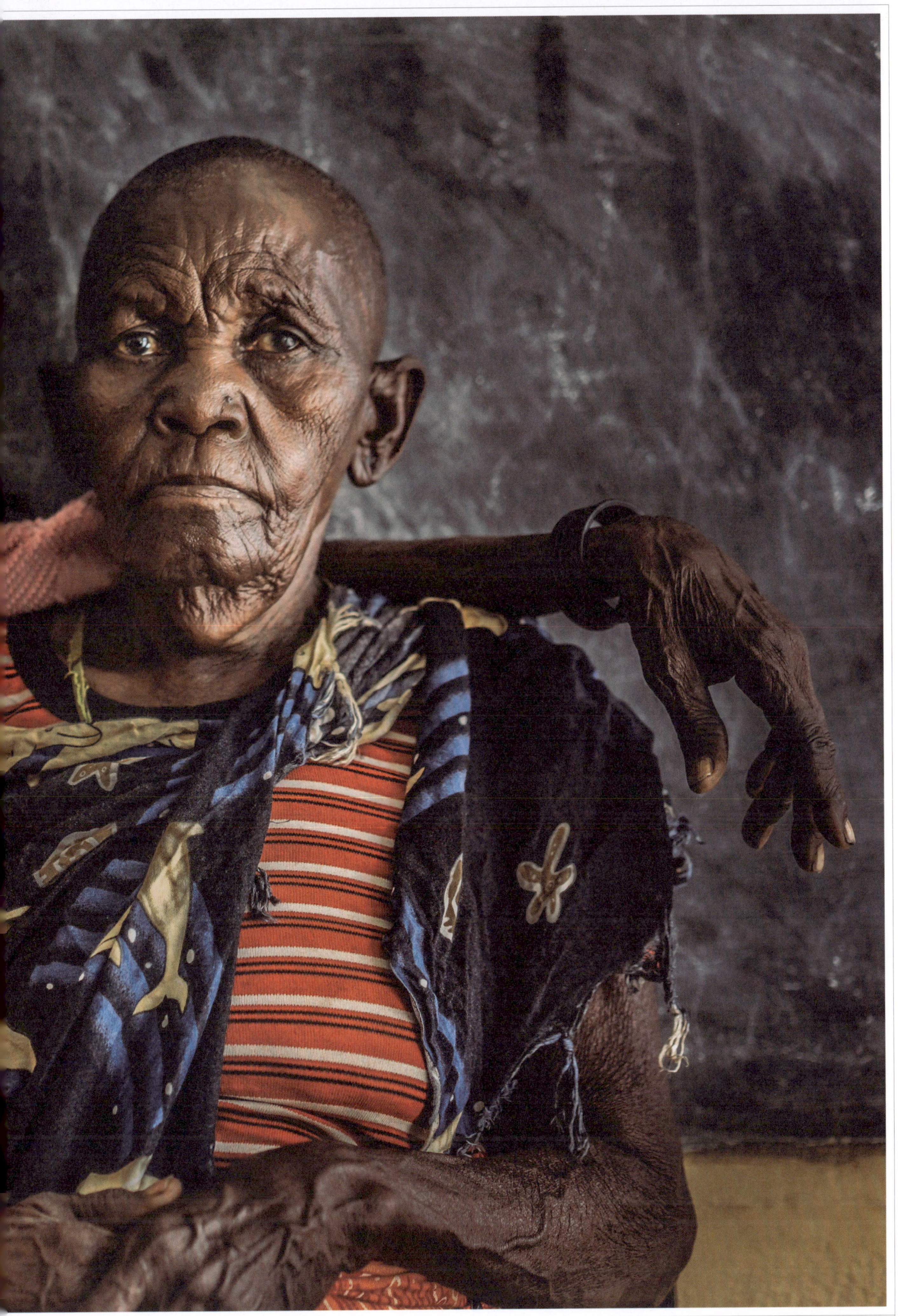

These two ladies in Tanzania are sisters, and received cataract surgeries during one of my medical missions to Africa.; Clients: Moran Eye Global Outreach and Eye-corps

What inspired or motivated you into your career?
I was an aspiring musician, and after spending a little over a year on the road nonstop, I decided I wanted a more grounded life. My father, after hearing my pitch for photography, was equally disappointed in my second choice for a career.

What is your work philosophy?
Work hard and smart. Learn the technical language, and then commit it to muscle memory so it doesn't get in your way. Try and see the world with fresh eyes. You miss less when you set aside your biases, which you're always available to return to if you choose.

Who is or was your greatest mentor?
When I attended university, the campus photographer was a sociology graduate who was so passionate about photo-journalism. He instilled passion and dedication in my work. Thank you, John Shupe.

What is it about photography that you are most passionate about?
While I believe the craft and technology of image-making are the essential language you must speak to achieve intentional results, once I could speak it with fluency, I started relying on my emotions. That's brought me the greatest joy.

What is the most difficult challenge you've had to overcome to reach your current position?
At the beginning of my career, balancing the work/life paradigm (being a father, friend, paying the mortgage) was daunting. It left precious little time to ponder the bigger artistic questions that are necessary to create maturity in an artist's work. Now I have time and few excuses.

What's your favorite type of photography? What's your favorite thing to photograph?
I've always loved photographing faces; it's not quite right to just refer to my images as "portraits" because I want to discover everything behind the face, especially a sense of intimacy. But because of my chosen life constraints, I decided to base my career in Salt Lake City, and it was virtually impossible to build a viable/financially successful business around one type of work. As such, I adore still lives almost as much as people.

Much of your work involves education, healthcare, and humanitarian subjects. What drew you to these subject matters?
As I began to understand my affinity for "intimacy" as a core component of my work, it dove-tailed perfectly into those three areas. In 2015, I was invited to document the work of an NGO which did medical work in equatorial agrarian countries suffering from a high incidence of cataracts. I fell deeply in love with that organization and the people of those countries. Guatemala, Micronesia, the Navajo reservation, and five trips to Tanzania confirmed that love. I can't wait to get back into the field.

Educational institutions (mostly involving children) and healthcare organizations are rich visual subject areas, and I'm indebted to the clients who give me opportunities to work for them. Thank you.

You also make short films. How did you get into filmmaking? How does it influence your photography or vice versa?
How did I get into filmmaking? Fourteen years ago, I convened a meeting of friends and associates and prematurely proclaimed the "inflection point" of convergence between photography and filmmaking had finally arrived. I've since discovered that I was off by a few years. I believe that time

is now, and I spent my time during the COVID lockdown deep diving into the technology required to fully capitalize on today's real inflection point. Heady times, and much to my delight, I have zero pressure to make profit in my film work. That opens up such wonderful opportunities for more heart-felt work.

Who were some of your greatest past influences?
Irving Penn, Richard Avedon, Sebastião Salgado, Diane Arbus, August Sanders, Arnold Newman, Henri Cartier-Bresson, Elliott Erwitt, Albert Watson ... I could go on. Meeting Arnold Newman and his delightful wife many years ago was a treat I'll never forget.

Who among your contemporaries today do you most admire?
Anyone who is still punching "above their weight" as a personal and professional artist. I don't need to mention how difficult it is to remain relevant. I guess I just did.

What would be your dream assignment?
Working for more major publications (I'm looking at you, *New York Times*) and having the outlined brief require both photographs and motion.

Who has been some of your favorite people or clients you have worked with?
Ron Crump from Intel was such a delight; traveling to Canada, Germany, and China with folks who rapidly became friends — pure joy. Richard Oliver, partner at a creative firm called Faktory: our careers have paralleled each other, and to have such a long-term collaborative friendship has meant a lot to me. Annette Gaddis, creative director for YESCO, an international sign company: only Annette can fully understand the opportunity that traveling to almost every state and many countries has provided me in the development of my portrait work. The Las Vegas strip is almost exclusively YESCO signs, or at least all the great ones. Enough said.

What are the most important ingredients you require from a client to do successful work?
Respect (mutually shown) and a sense of trust between us. If that's present, magic will happen.

What are some of the most memorable awards you have won?
Best of Show at the Utah State Fair; it set my imagination in motion at an early age. PDN, APA, New York Art Director's Club, One Eyeland, and, of course, Graphis. It's more than I could have imagined when I began. Thank you.

What is your greatest professional achievement?
Paying my bills with a profession that I intensely enjoy every day.

What are the benefits of having your own studio?
Twenty years ago, I would've answered differently. It was a necessity then, and now it's not so much. Smaller markets required it. I guess the best answer is owning real estate in a major U.S. city is an obvious benefit.

What is the greatest satisfaction you get from your work?
I would have to say that making a living doing something I love brings me daily joy and gratitude.

What part of your work do you find most demanding, considering your position?
Marketing has become increasingly complicated. I respect that

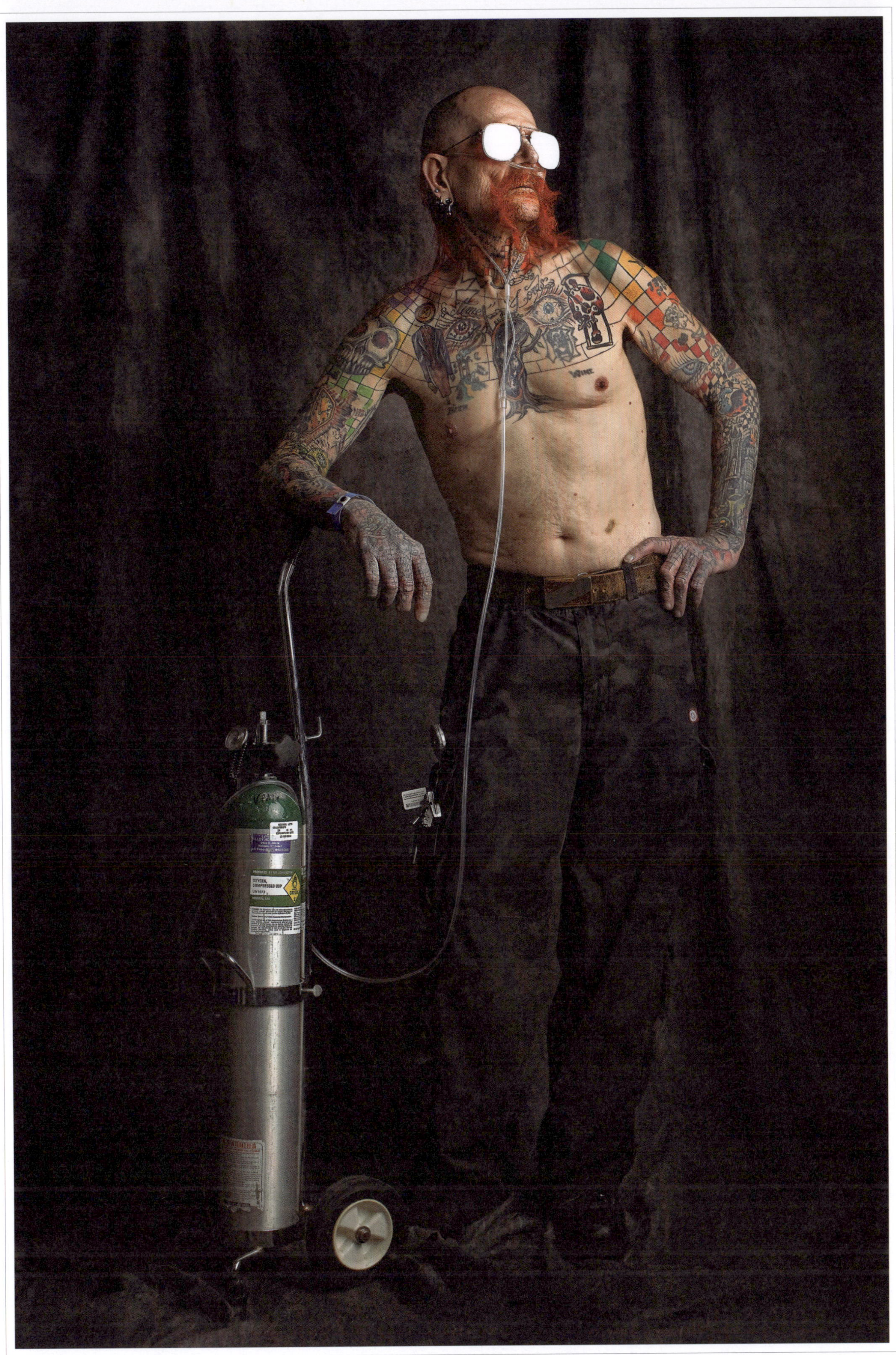

I became fascinated about ten years ago with the idea that all people have an inner self and an outer costume that masks that inner self. This was part of a series of images I created at a tattoo convention, one of many self-initiated projects on that idea. Much to my surprise, the subjects, amidst the craziness of a convention floor, were completely willing to disrobe for a photograph.

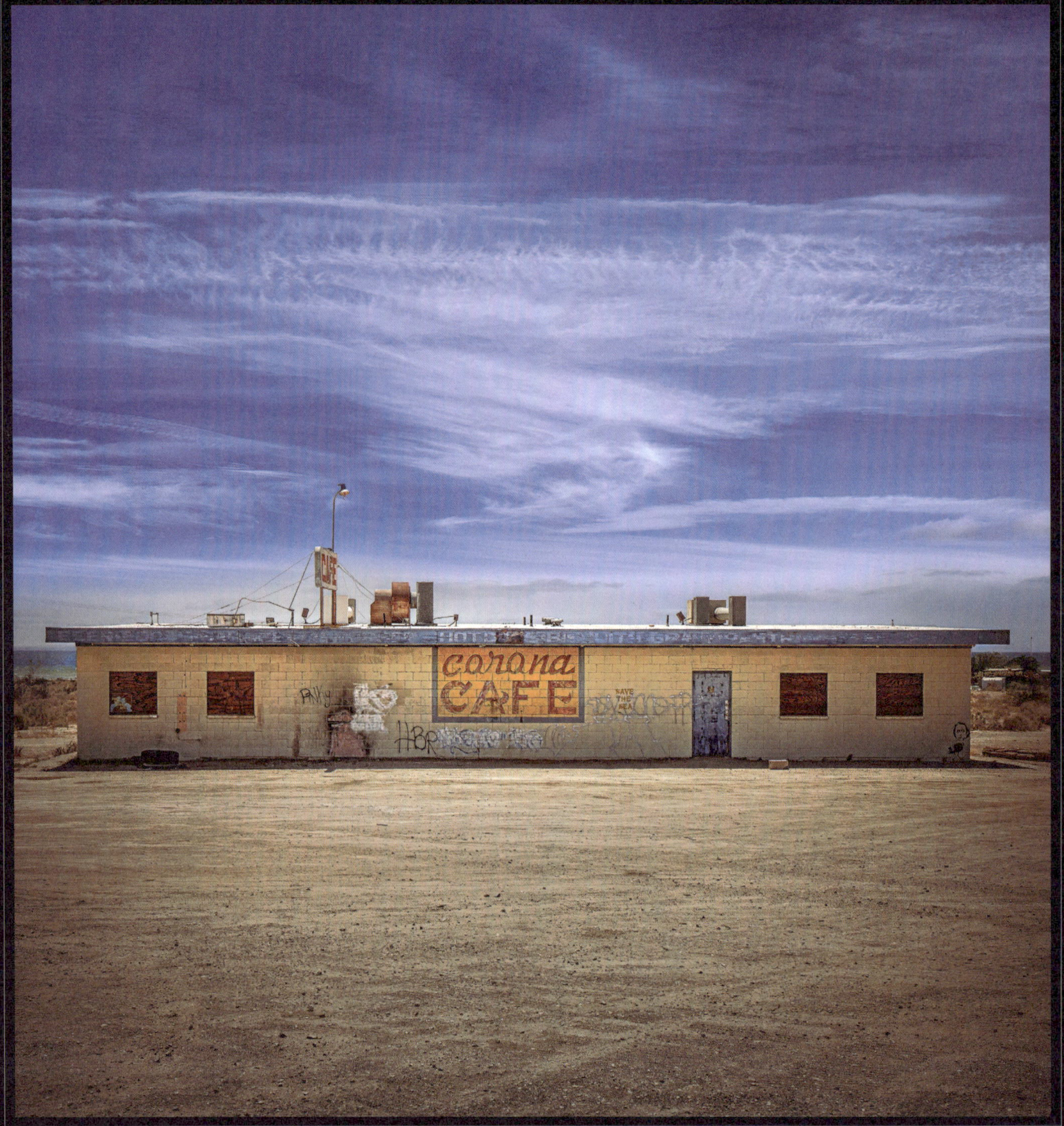

This image was created during a trip to the Salton Sea and the Palm Springs area of California.

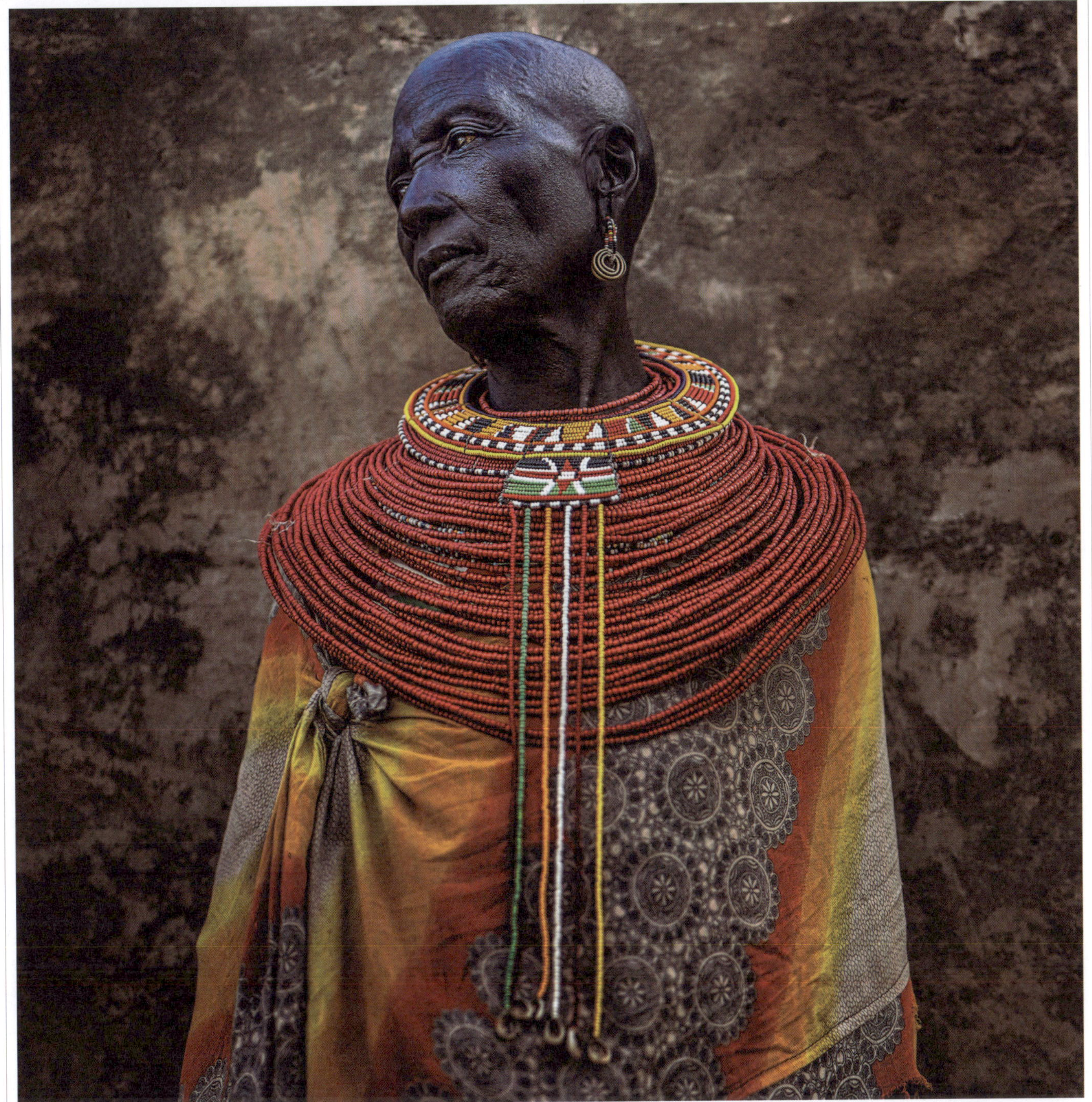

Serendipity has played an outsized role in my work. A friend of mine mentioned a village in northern Kenya, the UMOJA women's village, near the grasslands of the Samburu desert. After completing my assignment with the medical mission, I made arrangements to travel to this village and photograph twenty of the women and some children who live there. Men are not allowed to stay in the village at night. They are some of the strongest women I have ever met in my life.

clients are inundated with new material, and that alone creates a greater "signal to noise" ratio, which must be daunting.

What advice would you have for students starting out today?
Work hard, make time every day to pursue your personal vision, and buy some real estate while you're young.

What interests do you have outside of your work?
I still play music, write songs, and dream of running away and joining the circus. Hiking with my partner every day; real head clearing with that. I don't bring a camera when hiking (usually).

How do you define success?
Loving a piece of work (almost) as much as I love my family and partner. Having my daughter (Lucy Schoenfeld) decide that photography was her passion and that it was a life worth pursuing. My son (Max Schoenfeld) getting signed to an indie

label with his band (I warned him that the life of a musician is like running away and joining the circus, but he seems okay with that). Being a little less self-absorbed every day. Knowing I'm good enough as I am — no more validation required.

Where do you seek inspiration?
I really find inspiration in living my life as authentically as I can. No bullshit allowed.

Where do you see yourself in the future?
Not dead. Spending more time with my partner (we currently live in different places, and that's getting old). And still creating art. Albert Watson is my hero here.

Michael Schoenfeld www.michaelschoenfeld.com
See his Graphis Master Portfolio on graphis.com.

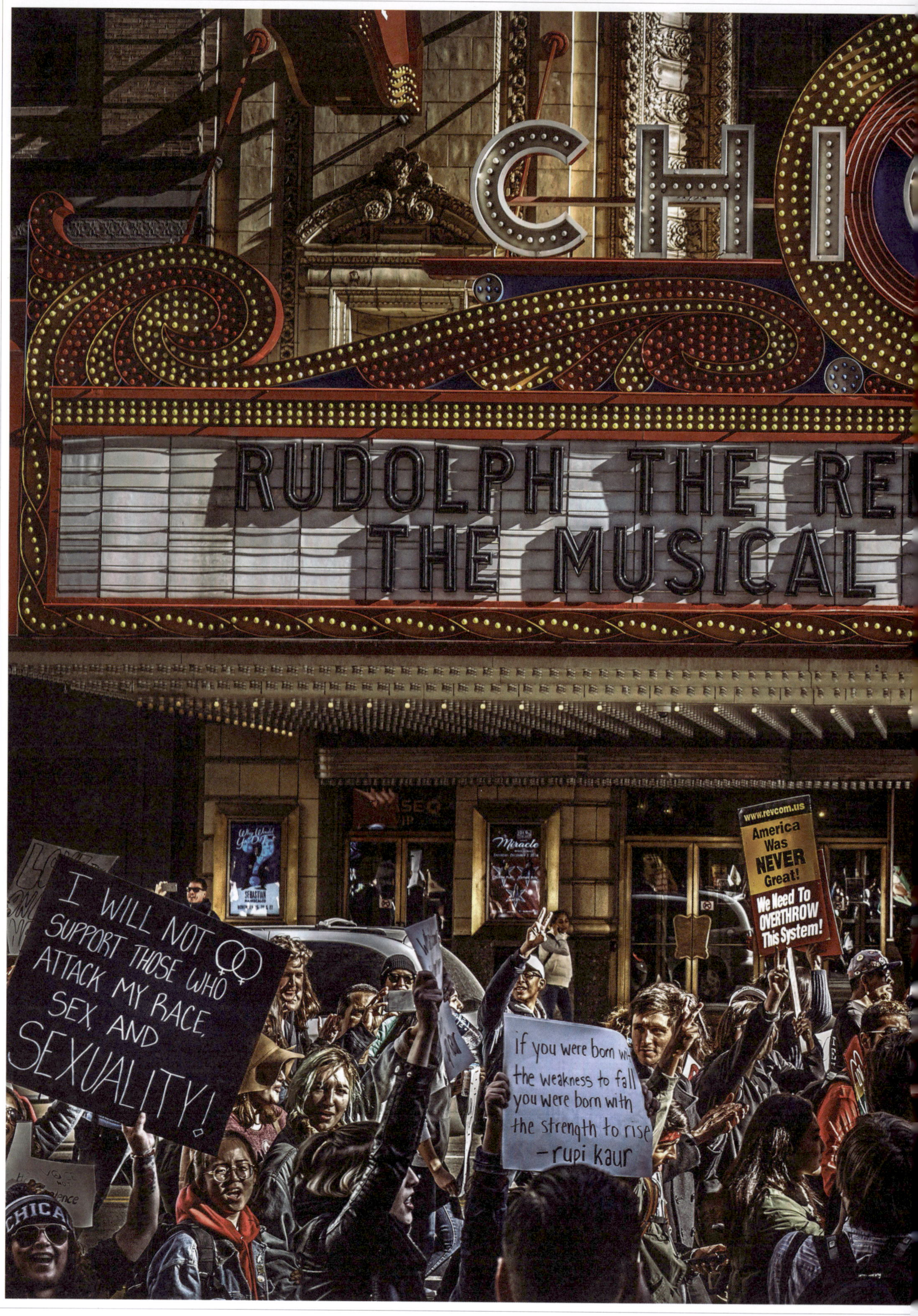

CHI
RUDOLPH THE RE
THE MUSICAL
I WILL NOT
SUPPORT THOSE WHO
ATTACK MY RACE,
SEX, AND
SEXUALITY!
www.revcom.us
America
Was
NEVER
Great!
We Need To
OVERTHROW
This System!
if you were born with
the weakness to fall
you were born with
the strength to rise
- rupi kaur
CHICA

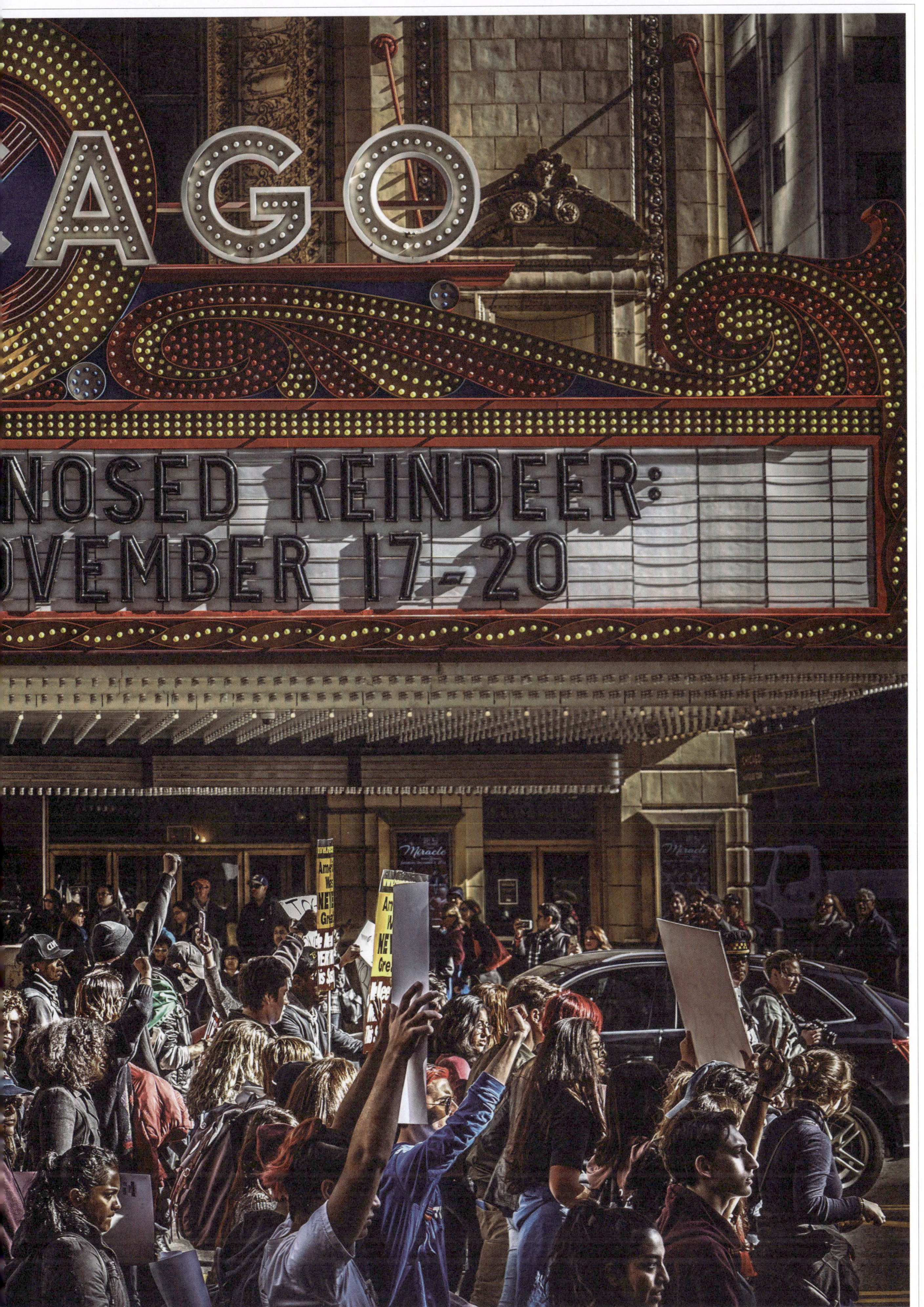

I attended a rally in Chicago six days after Donald Trump was elected president. The protesters marched past this theater, and two hours later I realized they would march past it again. On their second pass, I ran ahead three blocks and positioned myself, hoping something like this moment would occur.

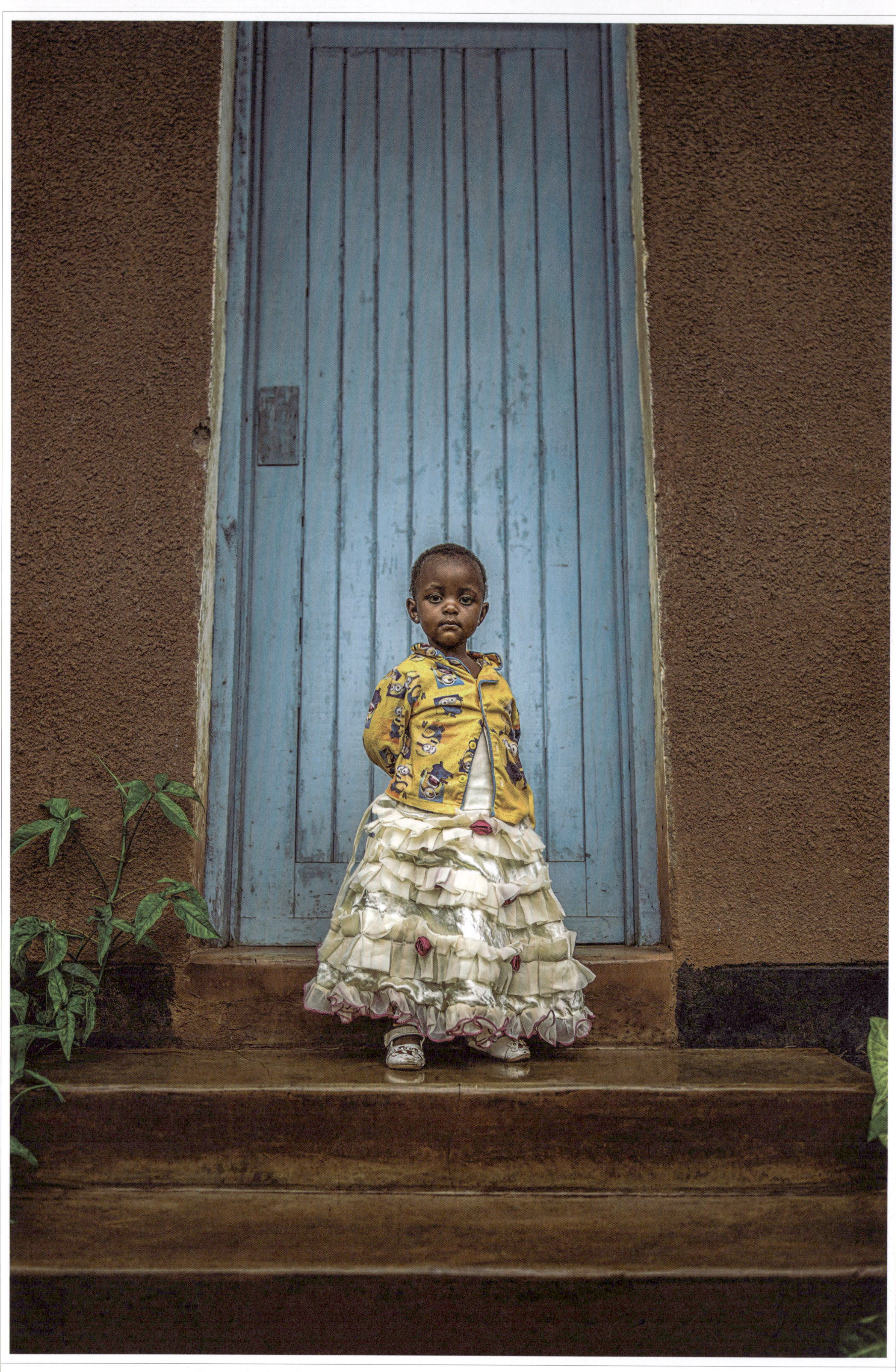

The young daughter of a cataract patient in northern Tanzania waiting for her mother to come out of surgery.

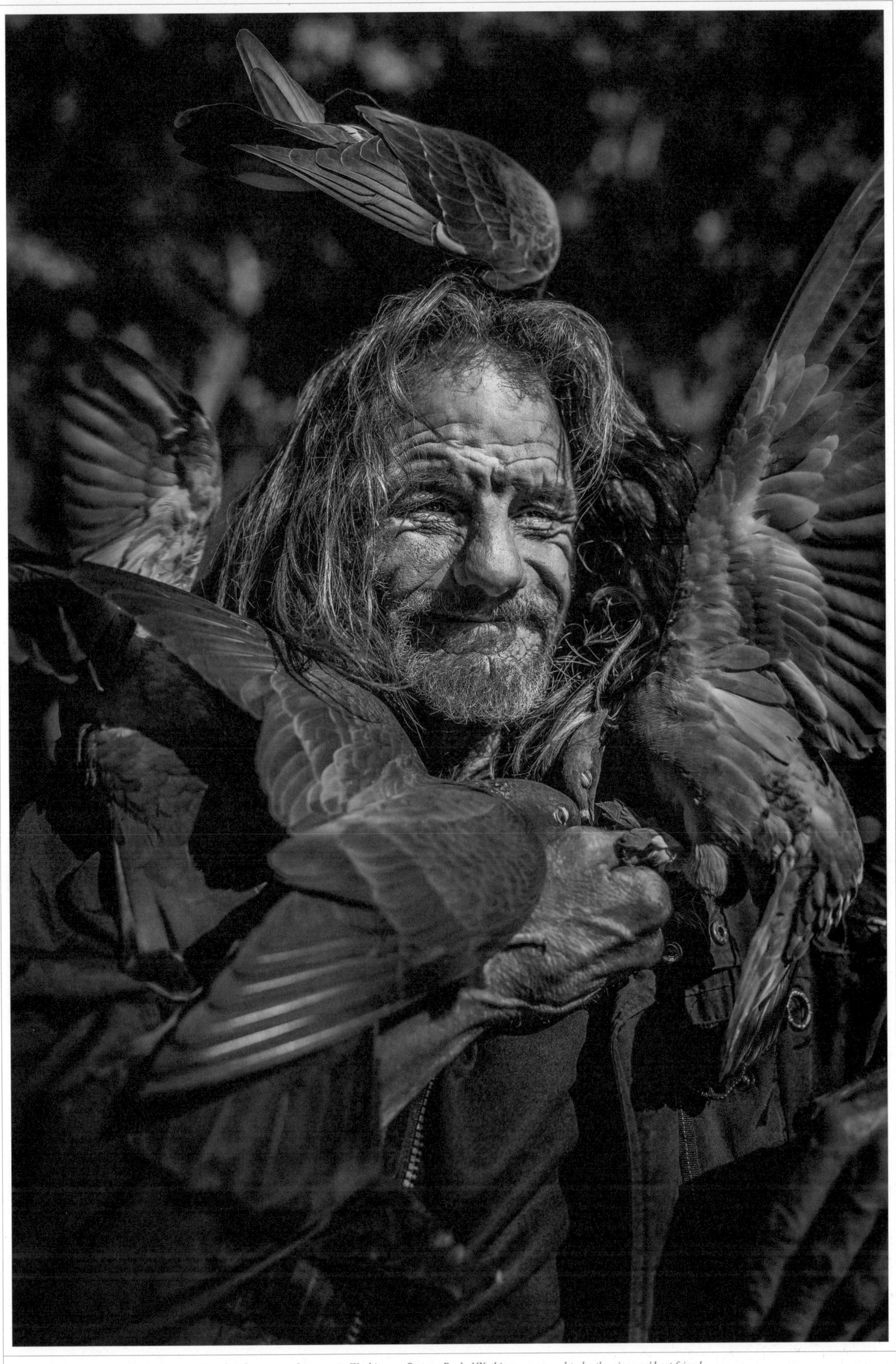

On a lovely spring afternoon in Washington Square Park, NY, this man seemed to be the pigeons' best friend.

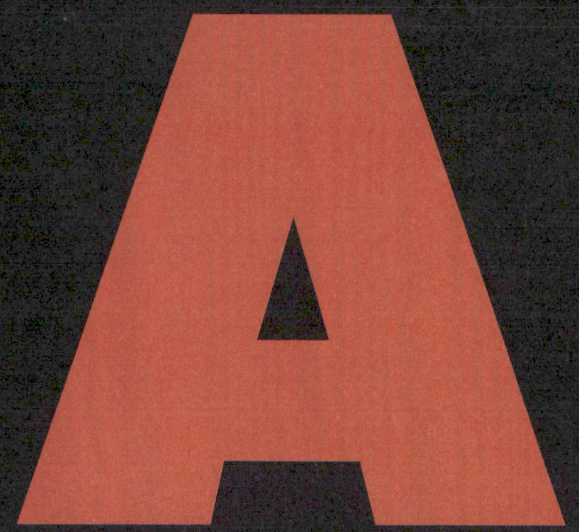

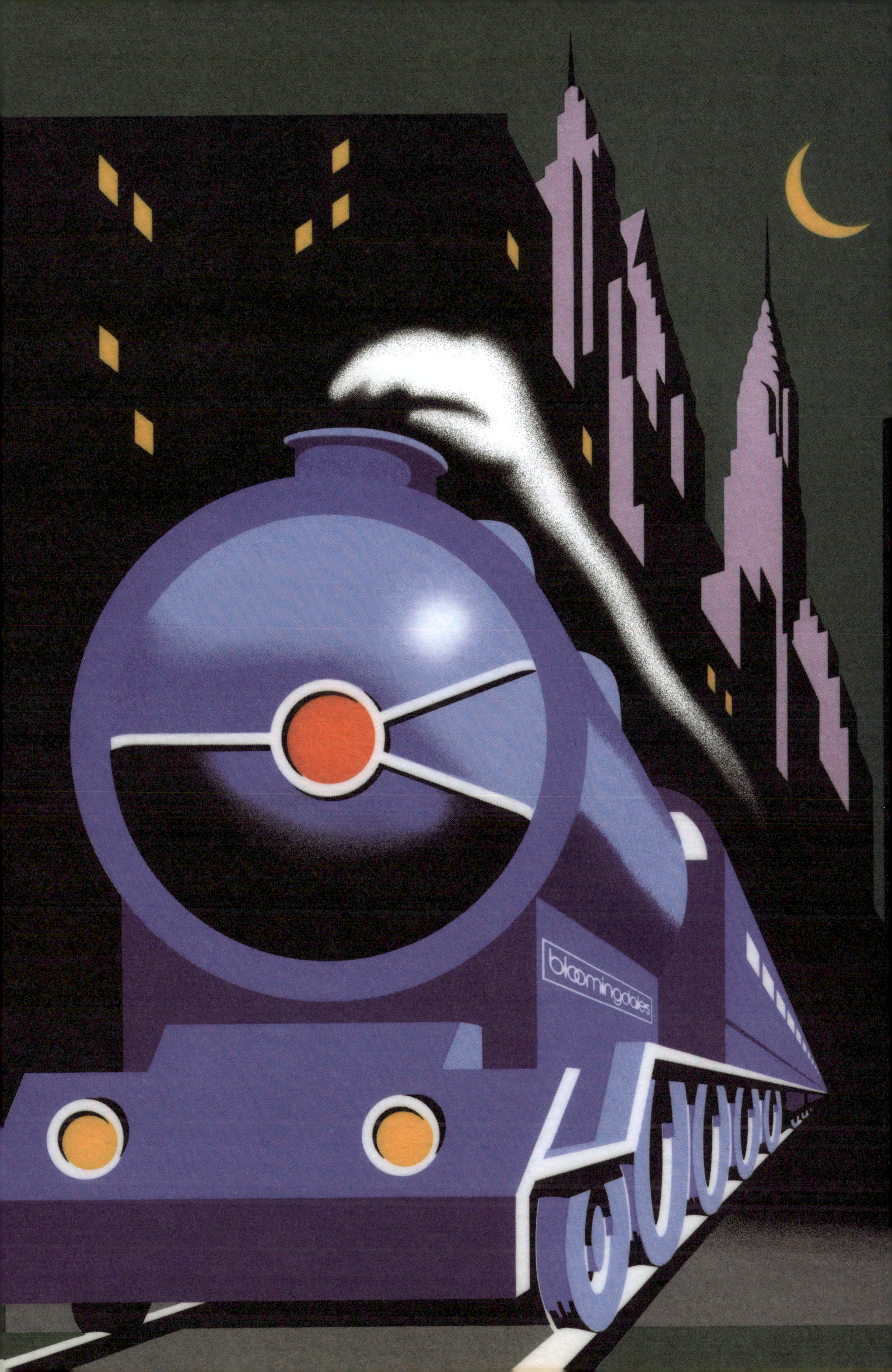

bloomingdales

WHEN MAKING A REDESIGN PROPOSAL TO *TIME* MAGAZINE IN 1977, I INCLUDED COVER DESIGNS I THOUGHT COULD CONTRIBUTE TO A FRESH NEW LOOK. MICHAEL'S "GAMBLING GOES LEGIT" COVER HELPED WIN THE DAY.

HIS SUBSEQUENT COVERS WERE ALWAYS UNIQUE, COMBINING A DYNAMIC USE OF LETTERFORMS WITH A CLEAN, PRECISE ILLUSTRATION STYLE. HE'S A DESIGNER WHO ALWAYS BROUGHT INTELLIGENT SOLUTIONS TO COMPLEX SUBJECTS.

Walter Bernard, *Creative Director, Walter Bernard Consultancy*

DESIGN, ILLUSTRATION, TYPOGRAPHY; WORTHY PURSUITS ALL, BUT EVEN COMBINED, FALL SHORT OF EMBRACING HIS SUBLIME OEUVRE. HIS WORK DEFIES CLASSIFICATION BUT IS BOUND TOGETHER BY ITS UNIQUE BRILLIANCE.

Daniel Pelavin, *Illustration & Typographic Designer*

THE LOGO HE CREATED FOR US IS BOTH HISTORIC AND TIMELESS. IT'S A DISTINCTIVE, ELEGANT MONOGRAM THAT HEARKENS BACK TO OUR HISTORY AS A LABOR ORGANIZATION AND PAYS HOMAGE TO THE CRAFT OF GUILD MEMBERS.

OVER THE MANY DECADES WE'VE USED THE LOGO, HE'S BEEN A SOURCE OF HONEST ADVICE AND A REMINDER THAT WE STAY TRUE TO OUR ROOTS. IT'S A REFLECTION OF HIS GENEROSITY TO OUR COMMUNITY, FOR WHICH WE ARE GRATEFUL.

Lara Kisielewska, *President, The Graphic Artists Guild*

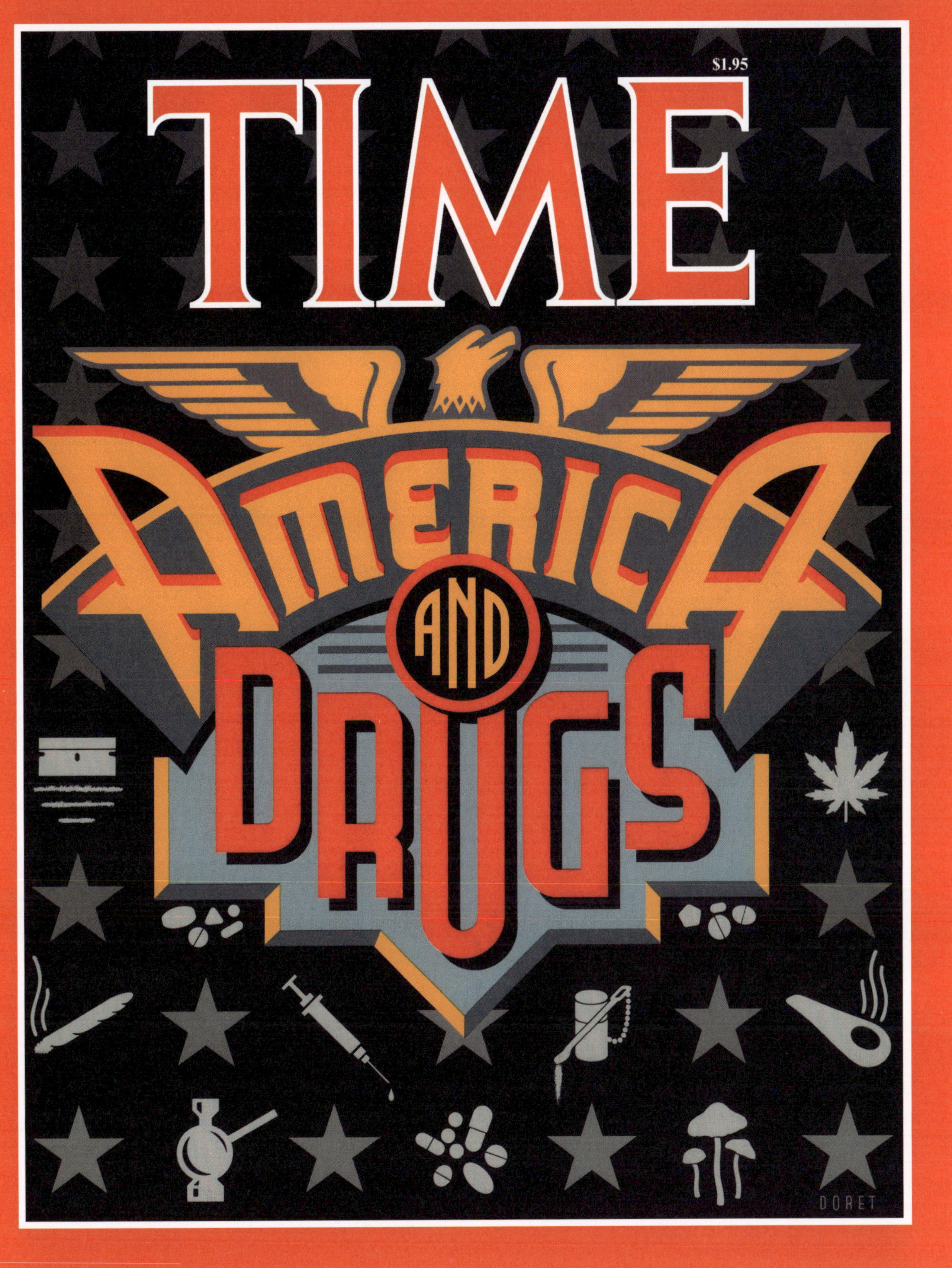

(Page 83) Le Train Bleu Menu Cover; 1979 – Bloomingdale's – John Jay, AD / (Above) America and Drugs TIME Cover; 1986 – TIME magazine – Rudy Hoglund, AD

Some images make a lasting impression: they just line up somehow perfectly with what appeals to you at the time. I'll never forget my first two encounters with the work of Michael Doret. Both images were on the cover of *Time* magazine. One was on "The Colombian Connection," the war on drug smuggling, and the other was on "The Oil Game." These images still resurface in my consciousness every once in a while and show their influence. When I was working for Disney, a project came along that was perfect for Michael. I called, knowing that he was quite busy, and I didn't know if this project would even interest him. Thankfully he took on the project, and two days later he presented sketches for the icon and title treatment for Disney's *Wreck-It Ralph*. His imagery did exactly what I was hoping for. The movie was hugely successful, and I'm sure, well, almost positive, that the unforgettable branding that Michael created played a huge part!

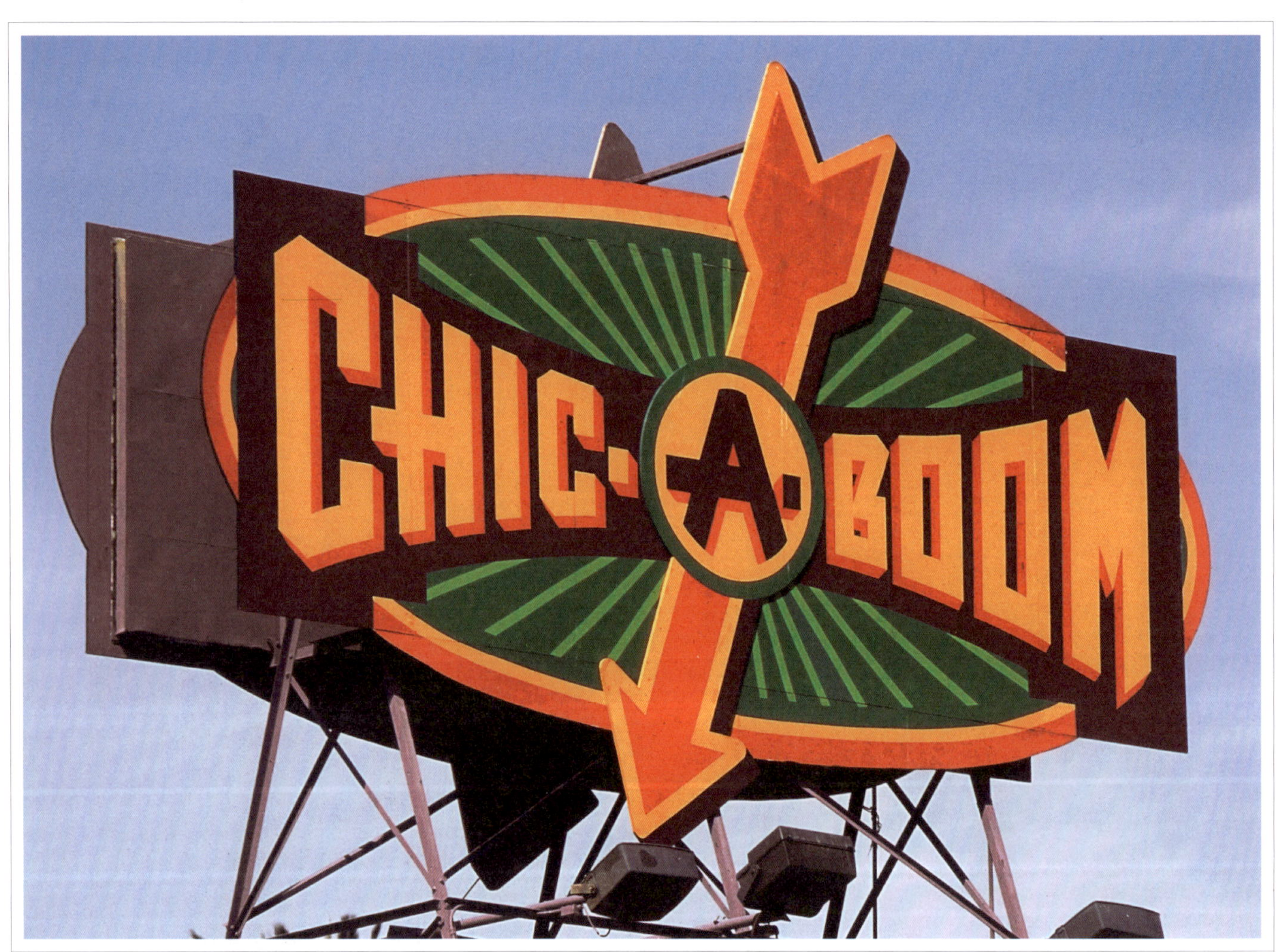

Chic-A-Boom Store Signage; 1993 – Chic-A-Boom Ephemera – Paul Scharfman, AD

DON'T BE SEDUCED BY THE COMPUTER, LEARN TO USE PENCIL AND PAPER (NOT A TABLET), STUDY DESIGN AND DESIGN HISTORY, AND IF SOMETHING'S NOT WORKING, DON'T HESITATE TO START OVER FROM SCRATCH. **Michael Doret,** *Illustrator & Lettering Artist, Michael Doret Graphic Design*

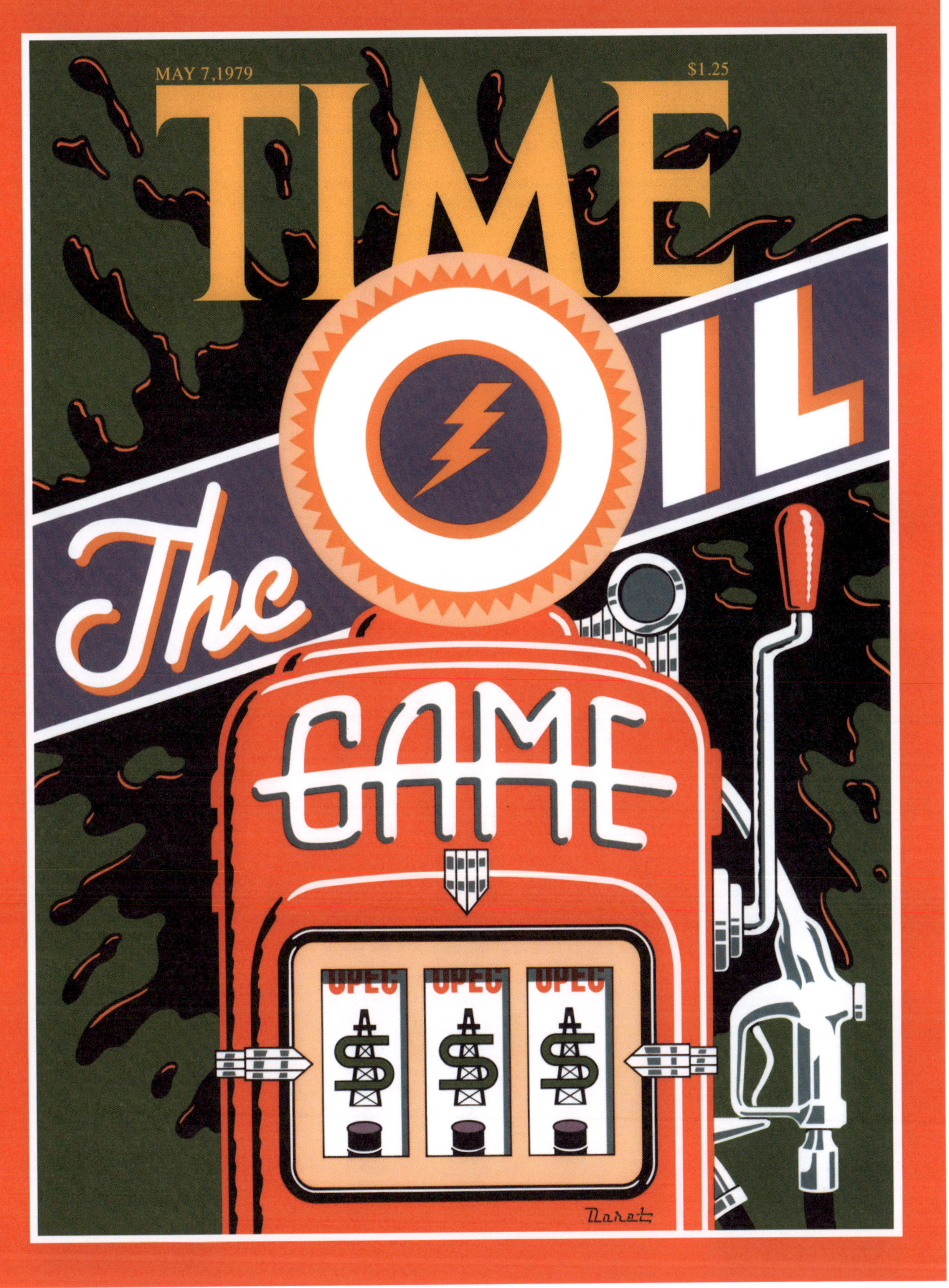

The Oil Game TIME Cover; 1979 – TIME magazine – Walter Bernard, AD

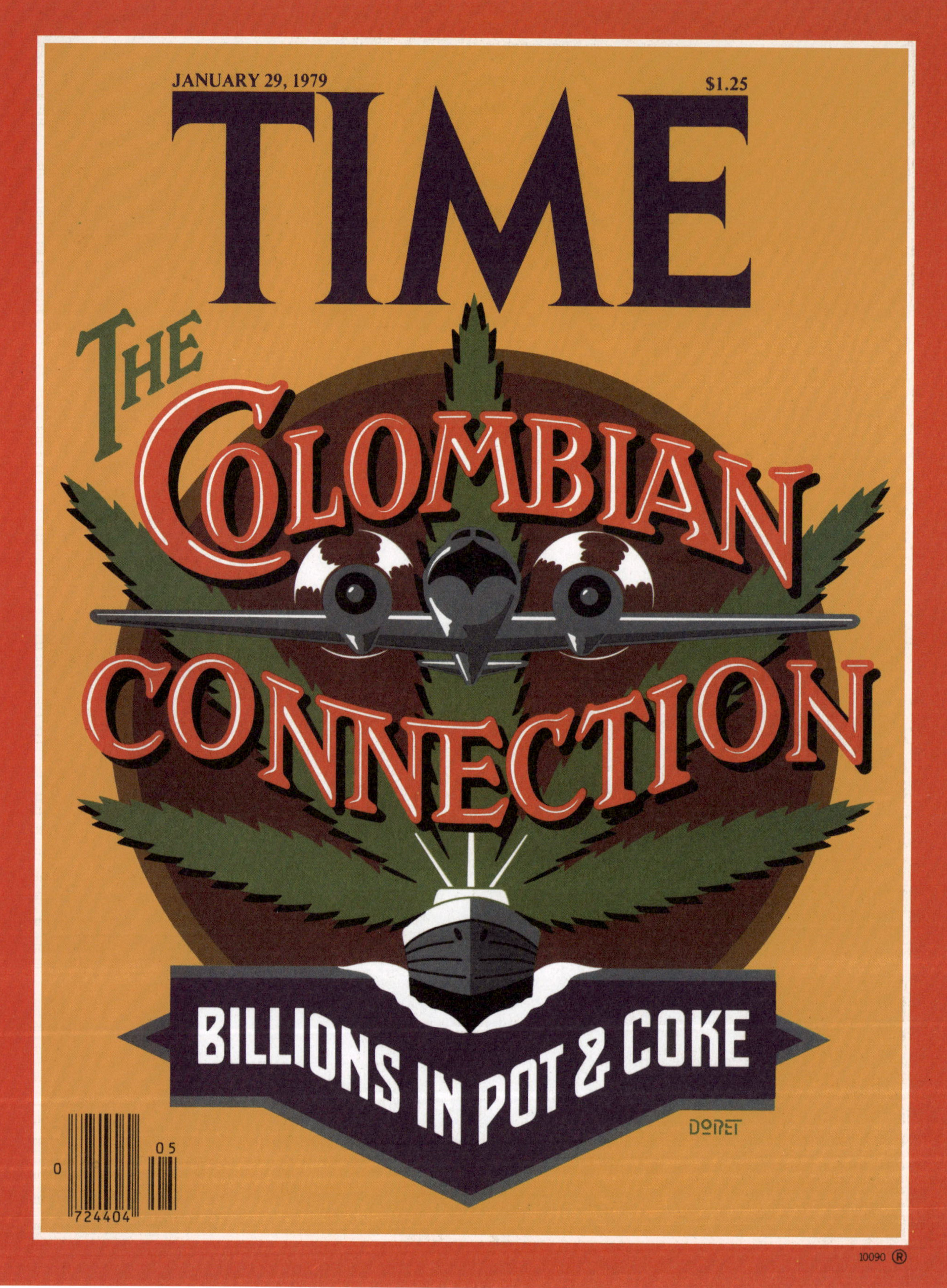

The Colombian Connection TIME Cover; 1979 – TIME magazine – Walter Bernard, AD

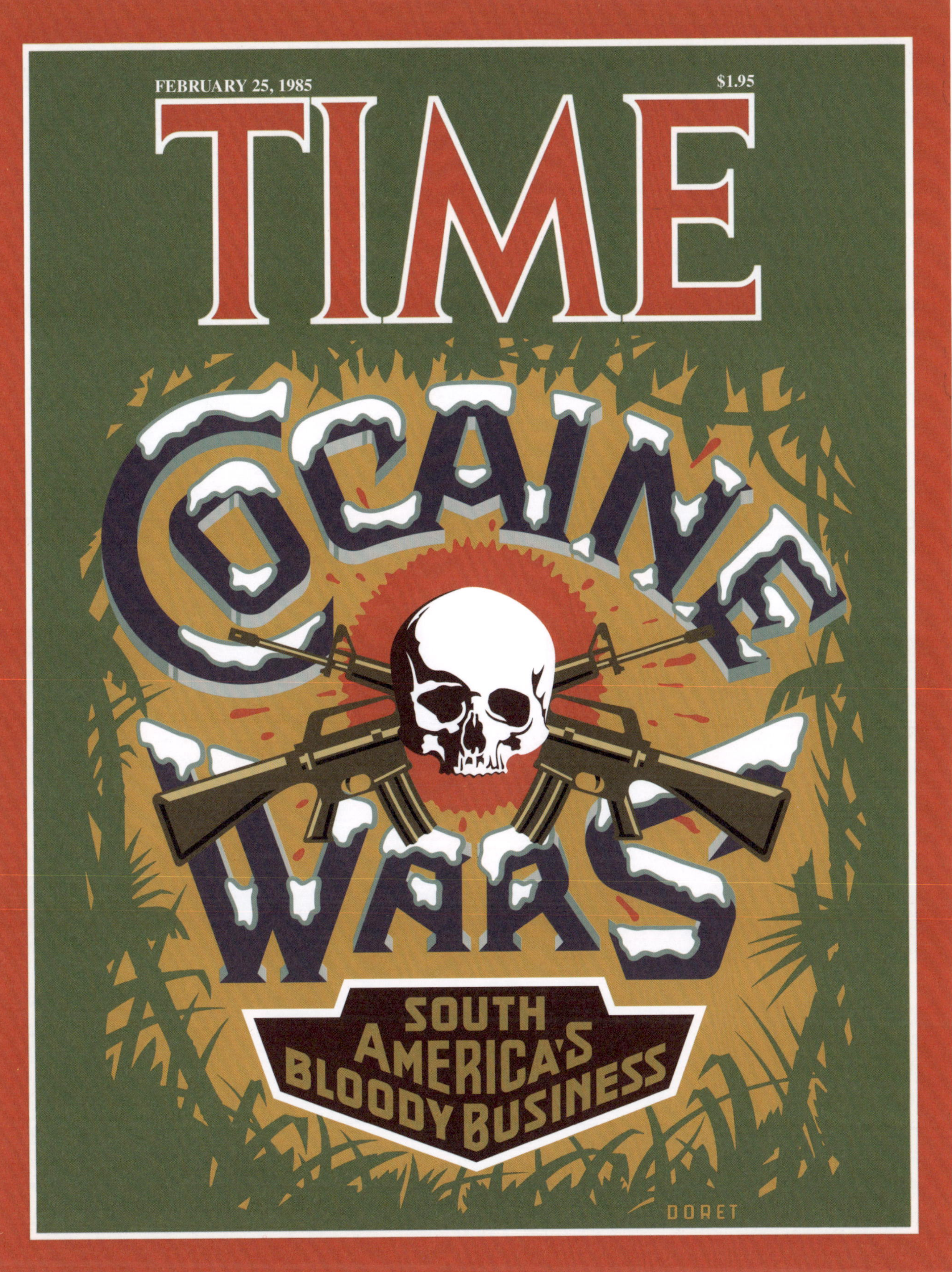

Cocaine Wars TIME Cover; 1985 – TIME magazine – Rudy Hoglund, AD

Who is or was your greatest mentor?
I've had many people over the years help guide and encourage me. My high school art teacher, Sol Schwartz, was probably the biggest and most influential mentor I've had. If he hadn't seen something in me and strongly encouraged me to follow my path towards a career in art, I probably would've ended up being an attorney. In college (Cooper Union), two of my professors were wonderful mentors: George Salter, my calligraphy teacher, and Robert Haas, my typography teacher, at whose print shop I interned at on school nights. After Cooper, my first real job was as Ed Benguiat's assistant. I learned almost everything I know about letterforms from him.

Who were some of your greatest past influences?
I can't really name anyone in particular as an influence. I'm most attracted to work from the past that was done by nameless designers and sign painters who may have had some training, but mostly did creative lettering work that didn't belong to any particular school of design or movement. Much of their work seemed to "break the rules" of accepted design practice — they didn't know all the rules, and didn't realize they were breaking them. It's this work by people who designed matchbooks, neon signs, film posters, pulp covers, comic books, cigar box labels, car badges, etc. that I look up to and admire.

Who have been some of your favorite people
or clients that you have worked with?
I've worked with many terrific ADs. Among the best of the best, I would count Walter Bernard, who I worked with when he was at *TIME* magazine, and John Sabel, when he was at Disney.

You have a distinct style that combines different elements
of lettering and illustration. How did you develop that style?
What influenced it?
If I developed a "style," it was on a completely subconscious level. I believe that the way my work appears evolved naturally, influenced by everything that surrounded me as I grew up in mid-century Brooklyn. I didn't ever try to give my work a style, or make my work look like anything in particular. I've always been solving problems in the work that I do, and, to me, the look of the work has evolved naturally from the type of solutions that I came up with.

You created a digital type foundry called Alphabet Soup. Would
you tell us more about it? What was the motive behind creating it?
Alphabet Soup was more of an experiment on my part than anything else. Creating fonts seemed like a natural outgrowth of the lettering work I'd been doing for decades. I thought that creating fonts would be an easy transition for me, but that's not exactly how it worked out. It turns out that although creating fonts has a lot in common with lettering, it's also quite different in many ways, and requires a different skill set. So, it didn't turn out to be something I could slide right into. As I quickly found out, creating fonts is very technical in nature, requires a lot of patience and, for me, was not as fulfilling as creating my lettering work. In the end, I created ten fonts that I'm very proud of, but I'm not sure I'll delve back into font creation again any time soon.

You have given many interviews and been featured in
many articles and books. Which ones are your favorites
and would recommend reading and watching?
Here are a few of the better articles about my work:
- "12 Years in the Making: Fruit & Vegetable Stamps for the USPS — Part 1 of 2"
- "12 Years in the Making: Fruit & Vegetable Stamps for the USPS — Part 2 of 2"
- "Michael Doret Advances "Wreck-It Ralph" To The Next Level"
- "ART IMITATING LIFE . . . IMITATING ART by Michael Doret" (Article for AIGA/Los Angeles)
- *It Began In Brooklyn: From A to Z & Beyond with Michael Doret* (Vimeo of my Cooper Union Talk)
- "Creative Characters" (from MyFonts)
- "Behind the Knicks Logo with Michael Doret: Part 1 of 2"
- "Behind the Knicks Logo with Michael Doret: Part 2 of 2"

You've also given lectures and made guest appearances at
different organizations. Which one was the most memorable?
I've given talks to many different organizations, including the Herb Lubalin Lecture Series at the Cooper Union (see the third entry above), TypeCon, the School of Visual Arts, the Art Institute of California, California College of the Arts, Pratt Institute, Syracuse University, the DSVC, the Envision Conference, the Society of Illustrators, the Type Directors Club, the Graphic Artists Guild, Deutsch Inc., and Grey Advertising.

What are the most important ingredients you require
from a client to do successful work?
That would differ from project to project and client to client. Generally, I'd ask for as much information from a client as possible regarding what they're looking for and why they think I'd be right for the job.

What is your greatest professional achievement?
I have several projects of which I'm very proud. I would include among them the covers I designed for *TIME* magazine, the logos I created for the Graphic Artists Guild and the New York Knicks, the title treatments for *Wreck-It Ralph* and *Zardoz*, the album jackets I created for The Squirrel Nut Zippers and Kiss, and the poster I designed for Simon and Garfunkel.

What would you change if you had to do it all over again?
I would've probably worked less and enjoyed life more.

What advice would you have for students starting out today?
Don't be seduced by the computer, learn to use a pencil and paper (not a tablet), study design and design history, and if something's not working, don't hesitate to start over from scratch.

How do you define success?
Success for me has been being able to be true to my own vision in my work while at the same time being able to satisfy my clients' needs.

Michael Doret www.michaeldoret.com
See his Graphis Master Portfolio on graphis.com.

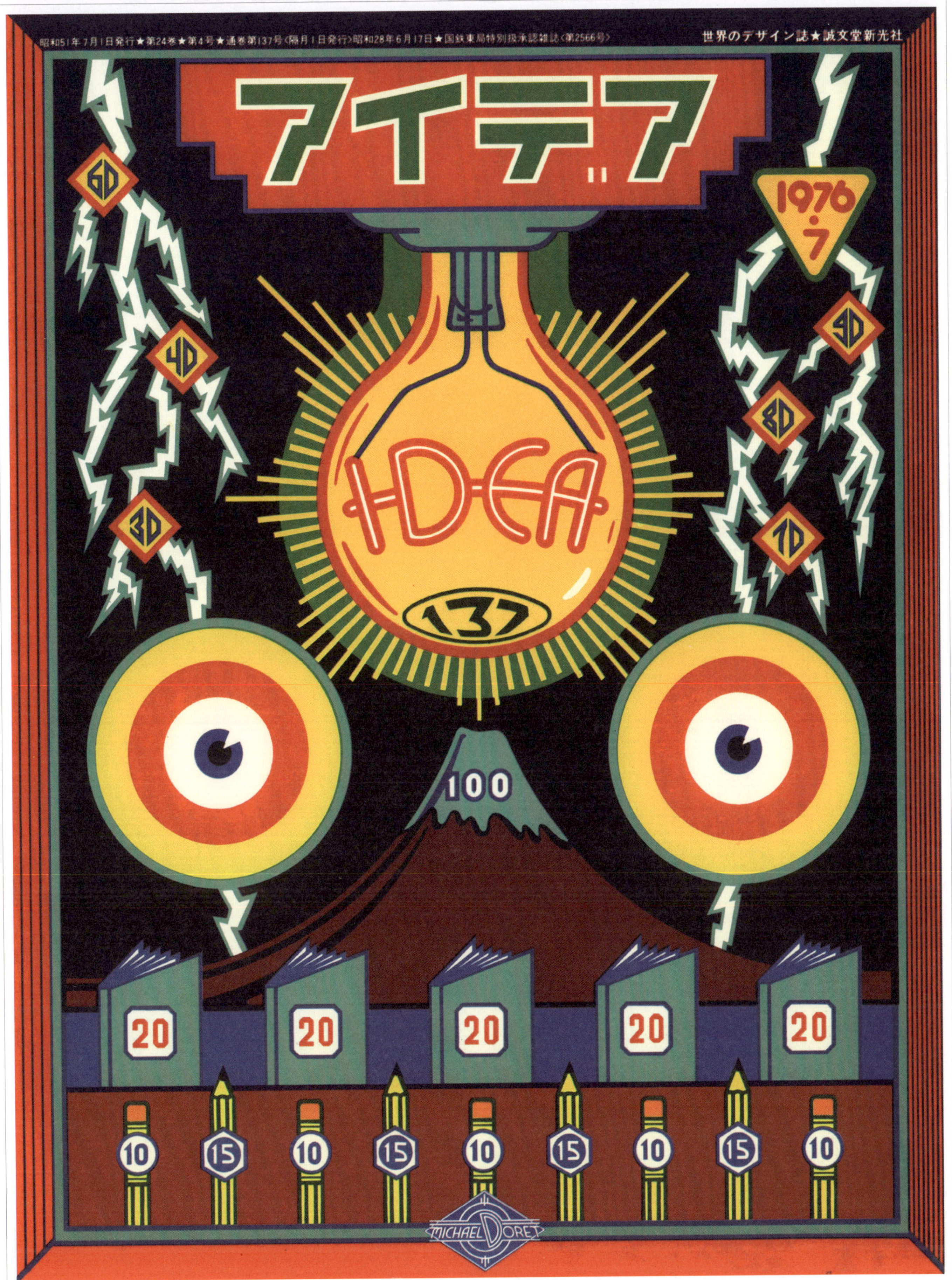

Idea Cover; 1976 – IDEA magazine – Michael Doret, AD

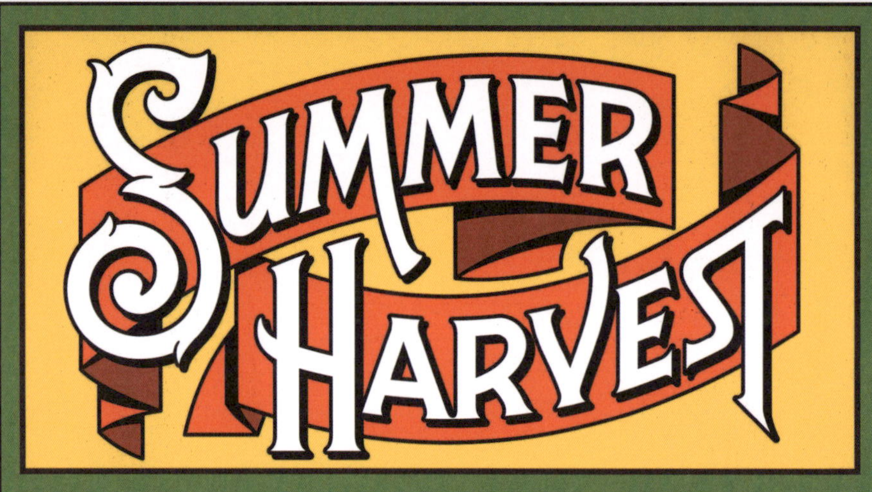

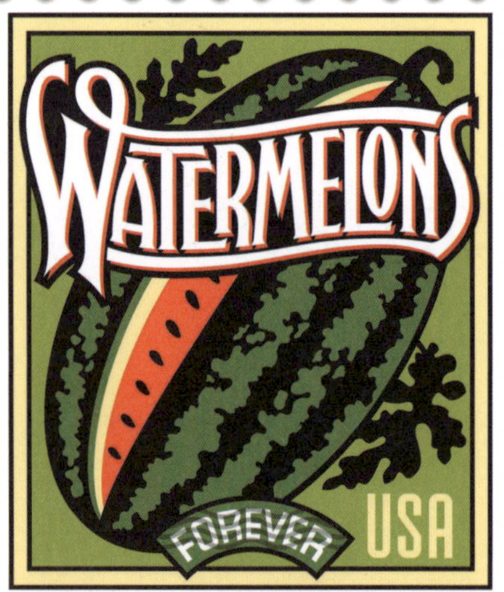

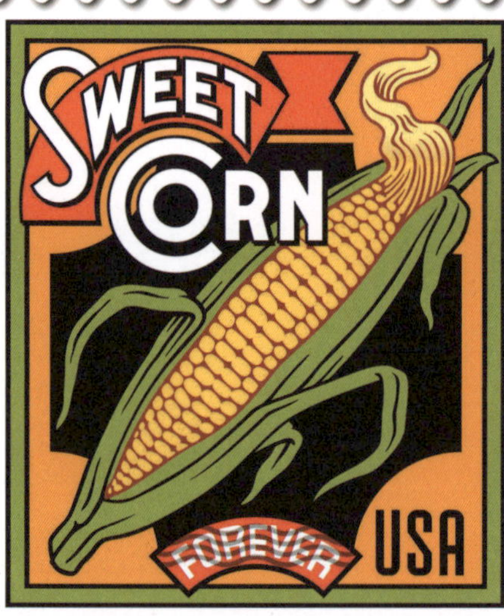

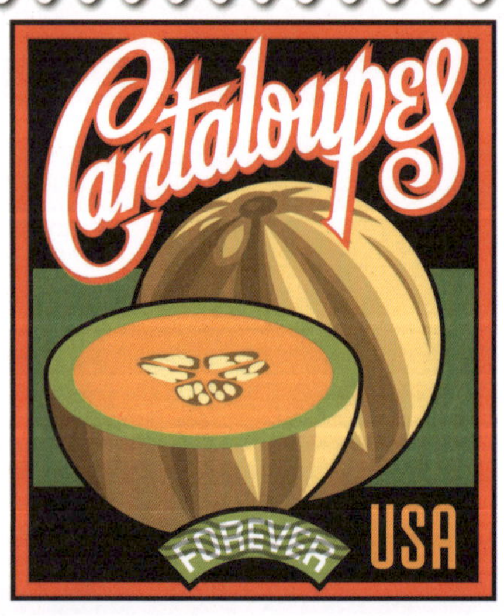

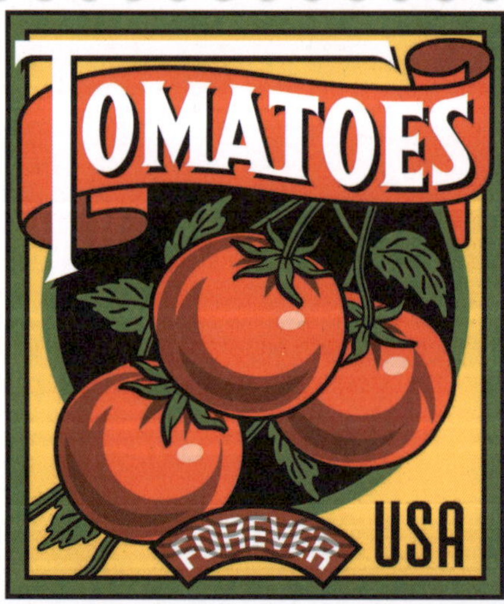

Summer Harvest Postage Stamps; 2013 – United States Postal Service – Antonio Alcalá, AD

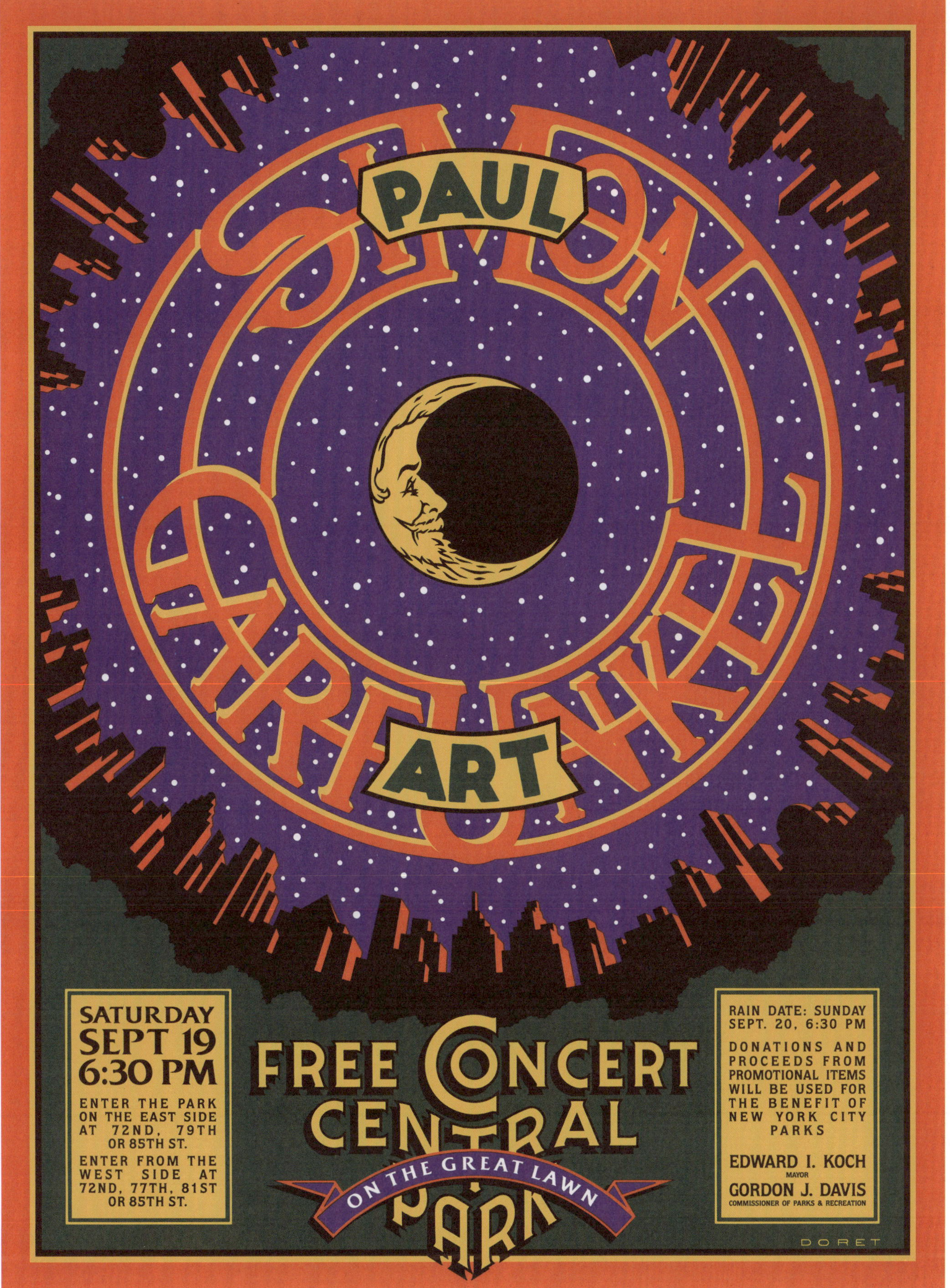

Simon and Garfunkel Concert Poster; 1981 – Irene Ramp, AD

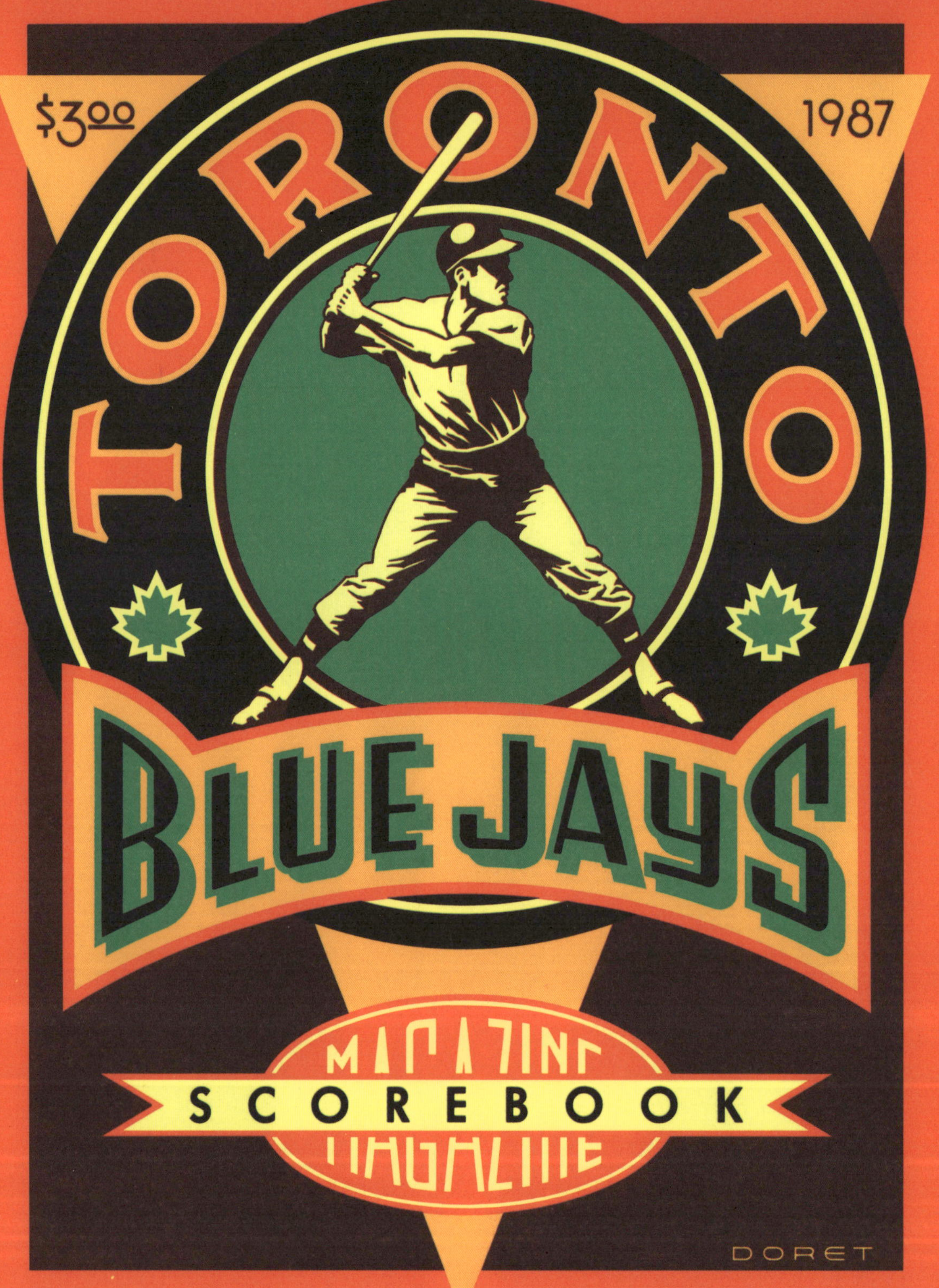

Toronto Blue Jays Scorebook Cover; 1987 – Reactor Art & Design – Shari Spier, AD

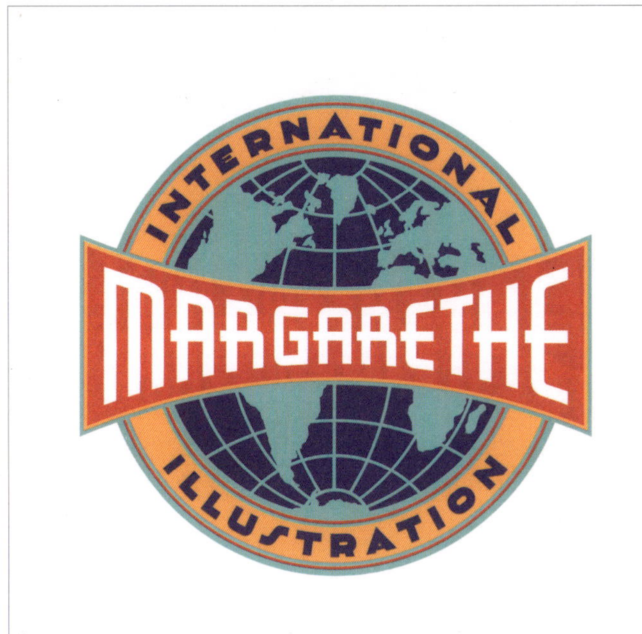

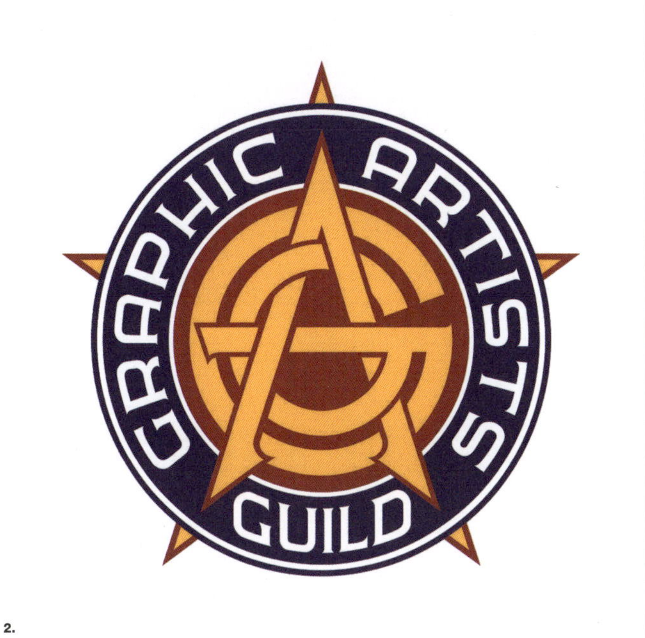

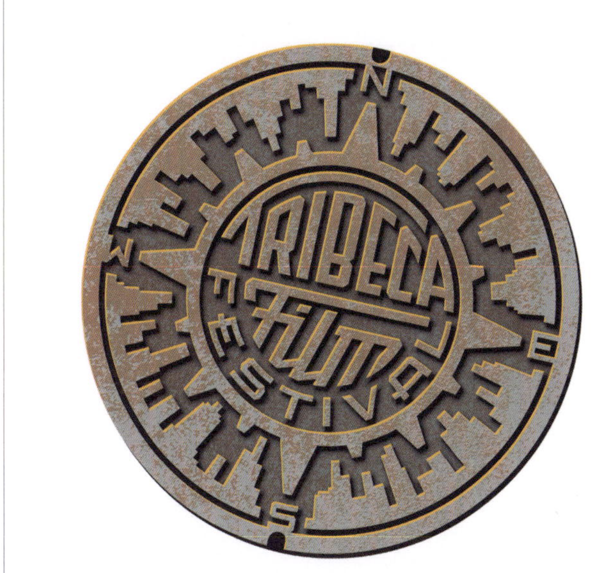

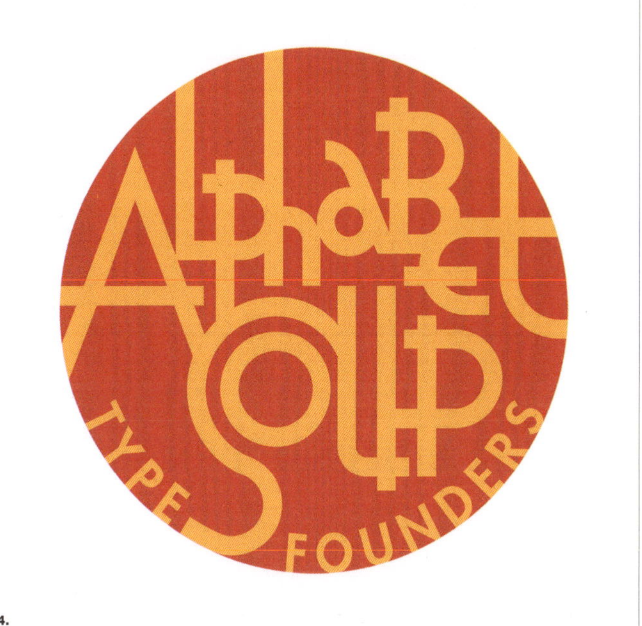

1.

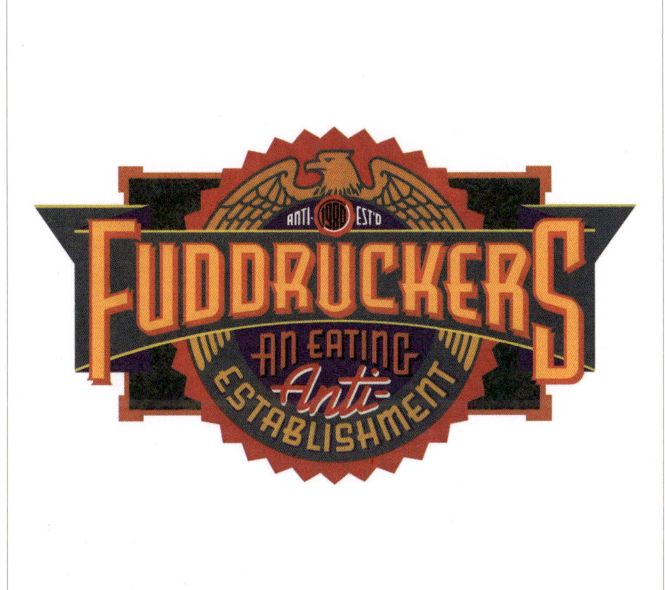

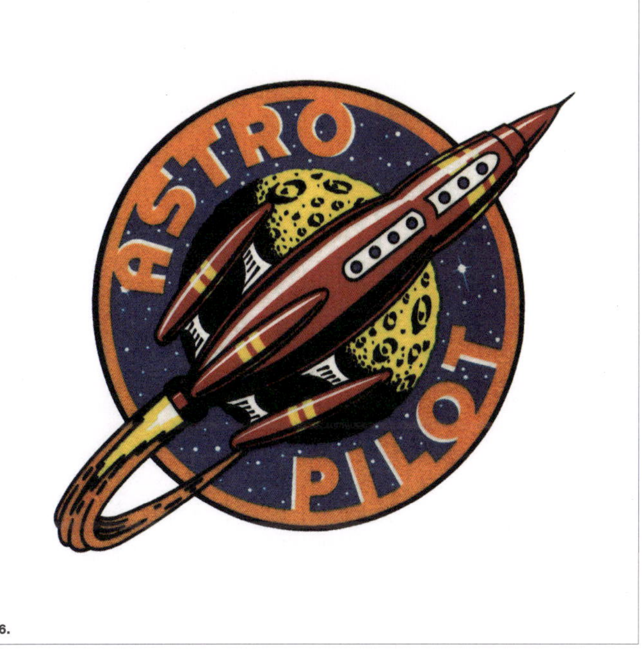

5.

6.

1. *Margarethe Logo; 1978 – Margarethe International Illustration – Margarethe Hubauer, AD* / 2. *Graphic Artists Guild Logo; 1979 – Graphic Artists Guild – Simms Taback & Debbie Holland, ADs*/ 3. *Tribeca Film Festival; 2006 – The New York Times – Richard Aloisio, AD* / 4. *Alphabet Soup Type Founders Logo; 2006 – Alphabet Soup Type Founders – Michael Doret, AD* 5. *Fuddruckers Logo; 1989 – Campbell Mithun Esty Advertising – Jerry Vaglio, AD* / 6. *Astro Pilot PJ Graphics; 1977 – Tom & Jerry – Jerry Ackerman, AD*

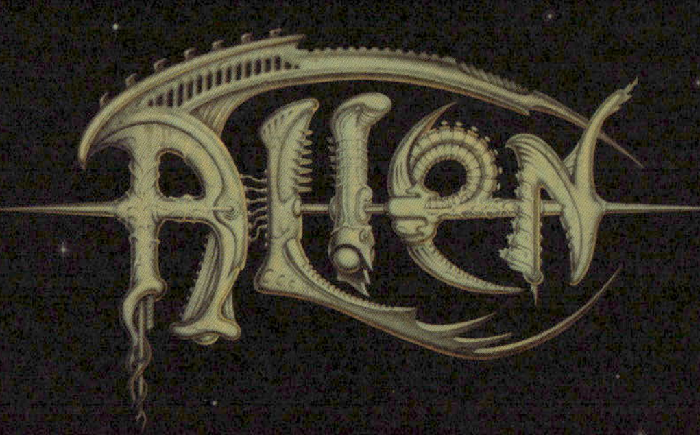

1.

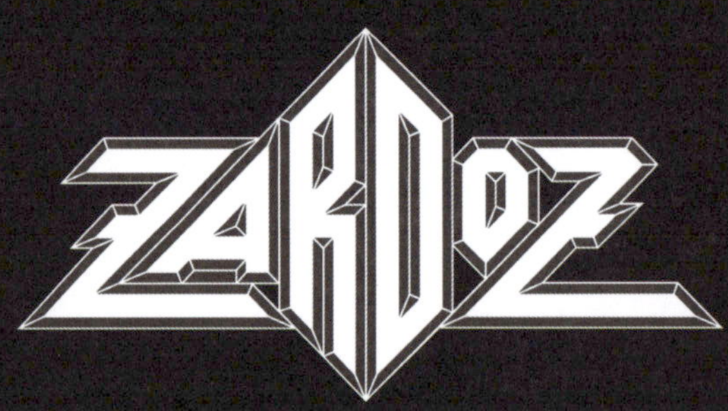

2.

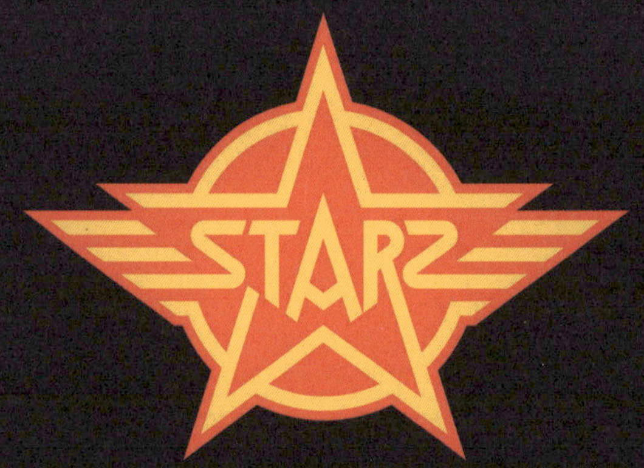

3.

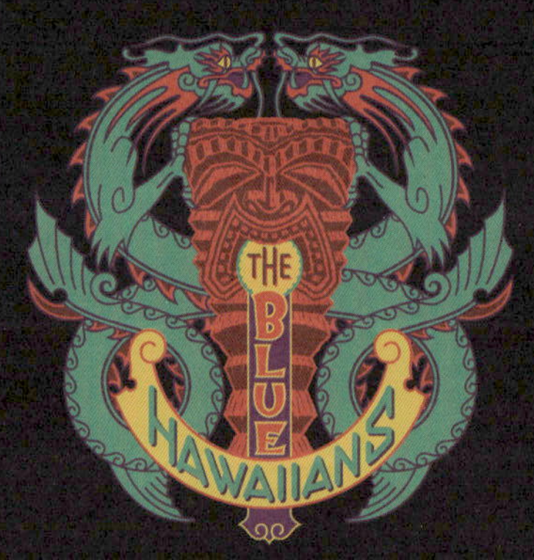

4.

5.

1. *Alien Title Treatment; 1979 – Smolen Smith & Connelly – Murray Smith, AD – Todd Schorr, Illustration* / **2.** *Zardoz Title Treatment; 1973 – Jon & Murray – Murray Smith, AD* / **3.** *Starz Logo; 1975 – Howard Marks Advertising – Dennis Woloch, AD* / **4.** *The Blue Hawaiians Logo; 1999 – The Blue Hawaiians – Brad Benedict, AD* / **5.** *Dracula Logo; 2011 – Acme Studios – Adrian Olabuenaga, AD*

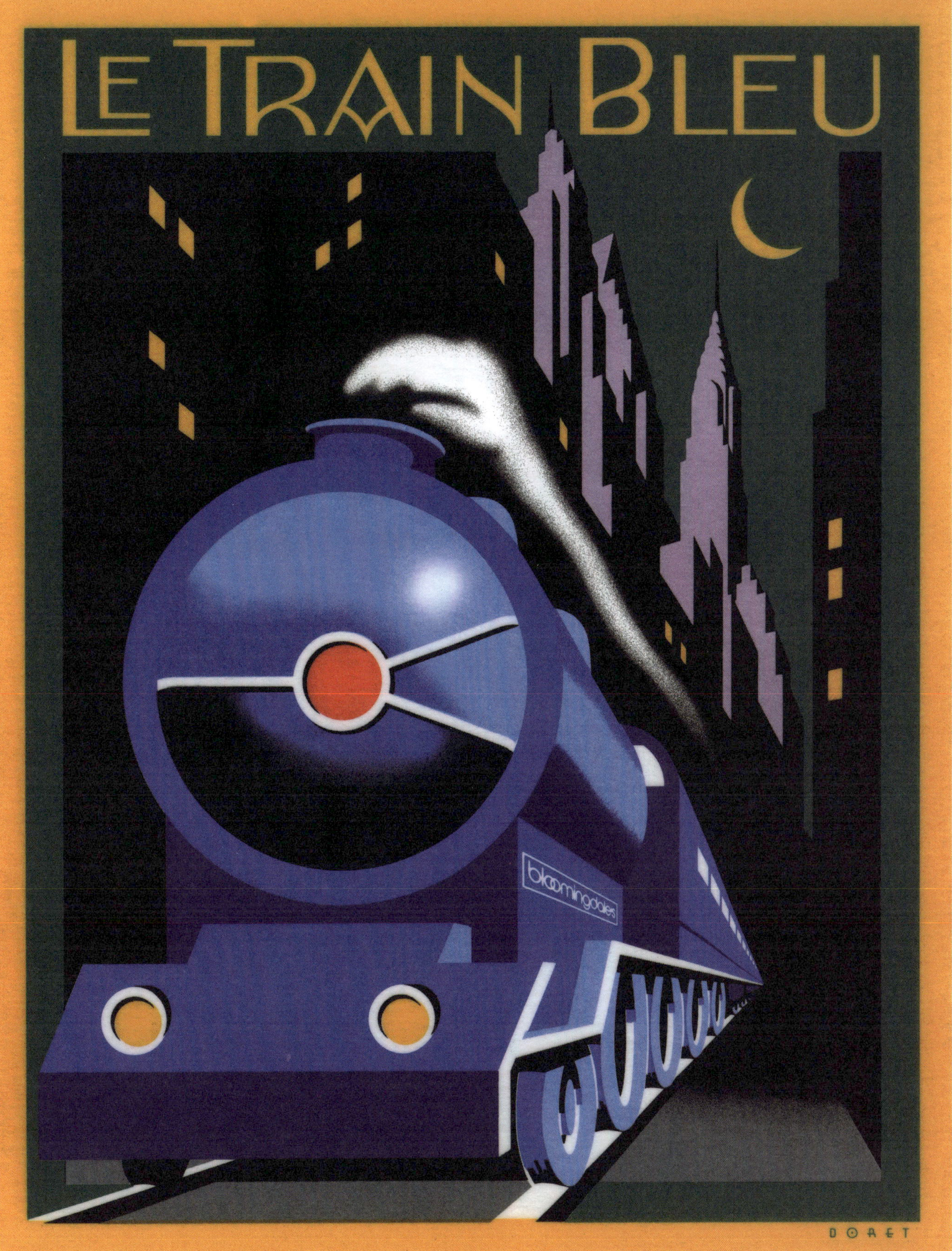

Le Train Bleu Menu Cover; 1979 – Bloomingdale's – John Jay, AD

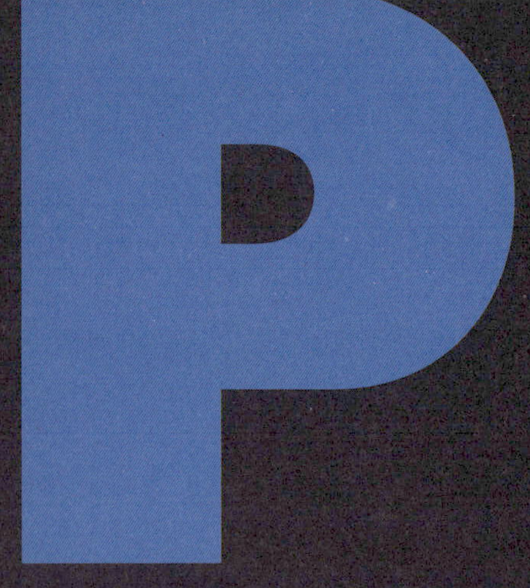

P

PRODUCT & INDUSTRIAL DESIGN

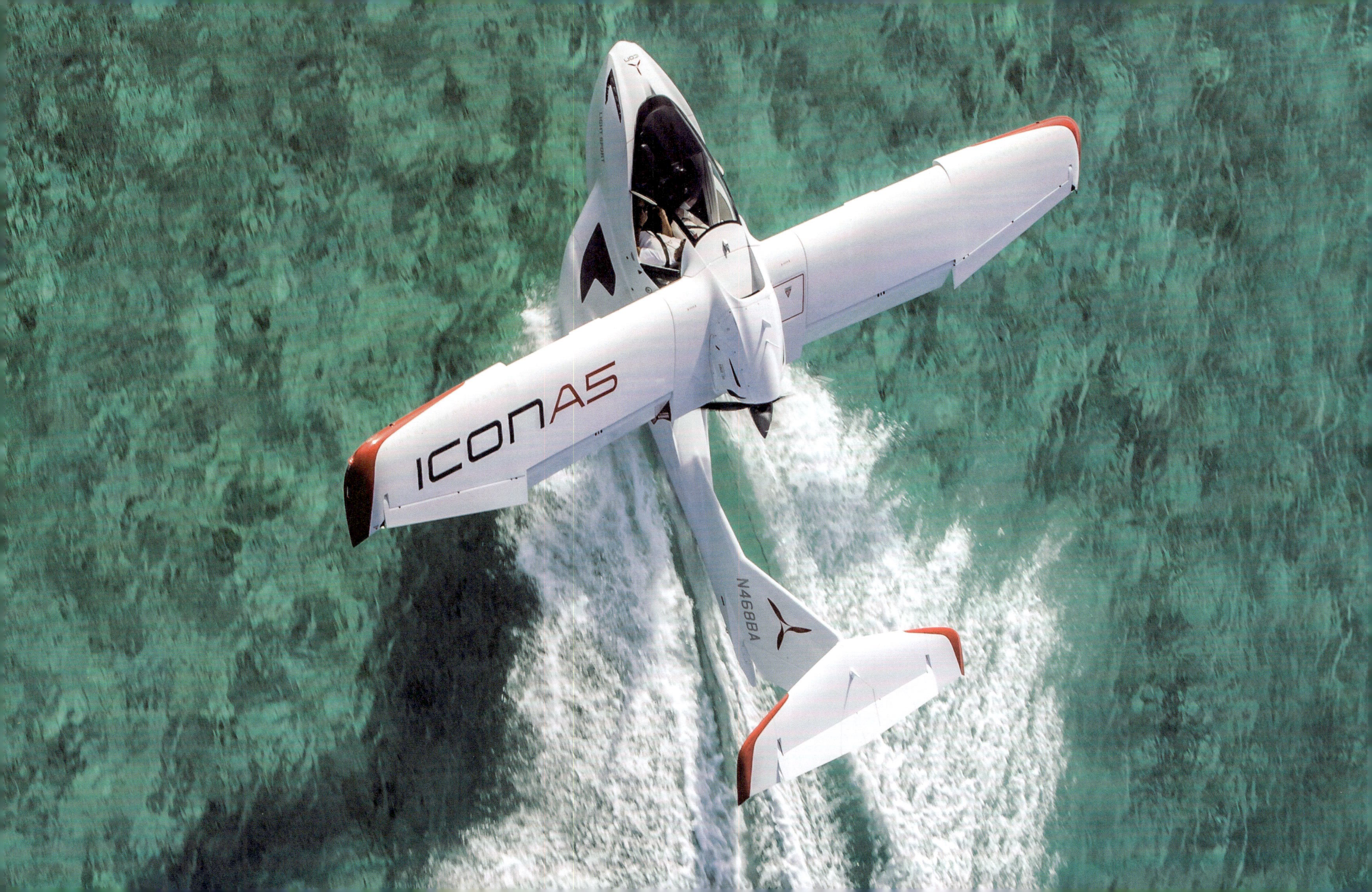

ICON A5
LIGHT SPORT
N468BA

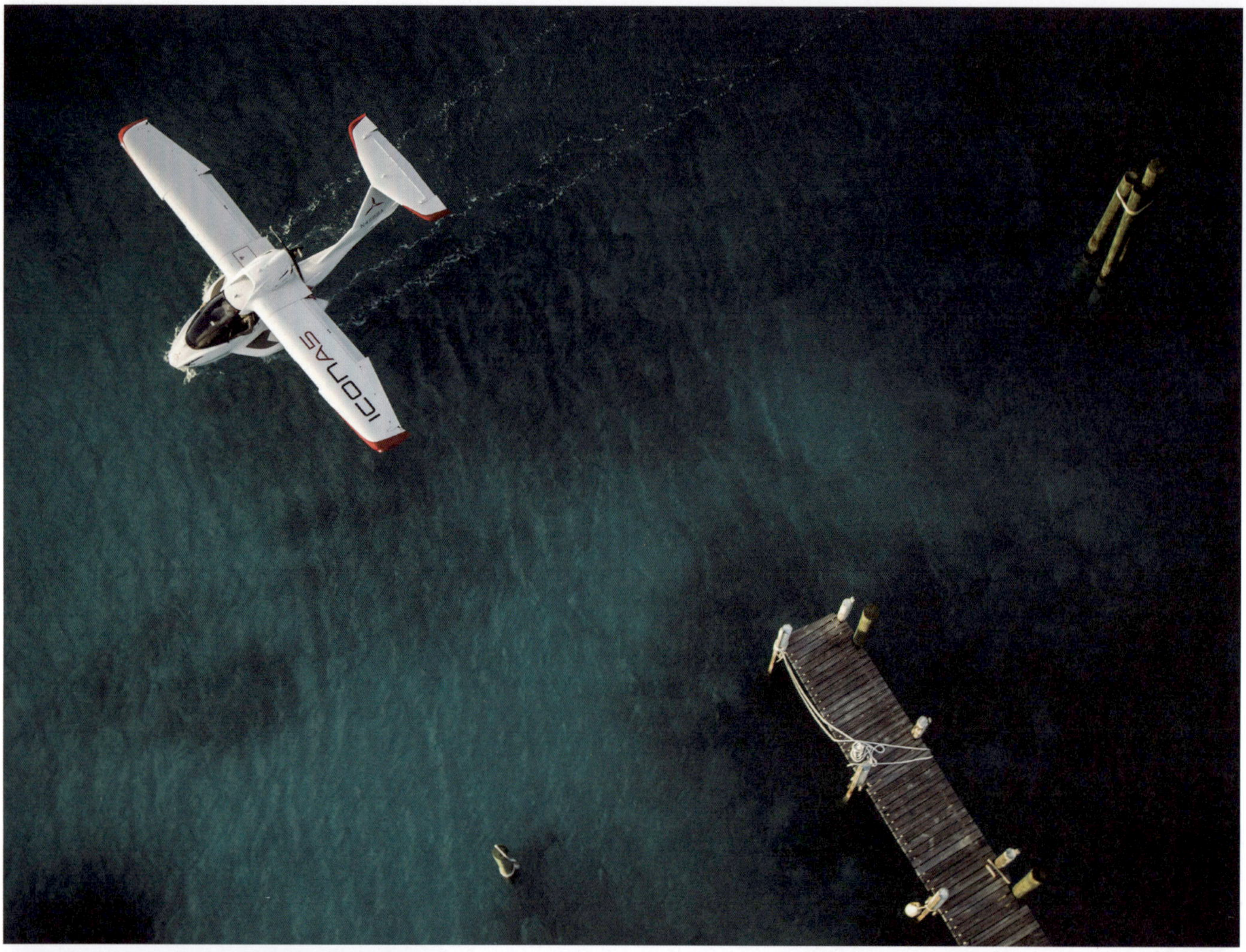

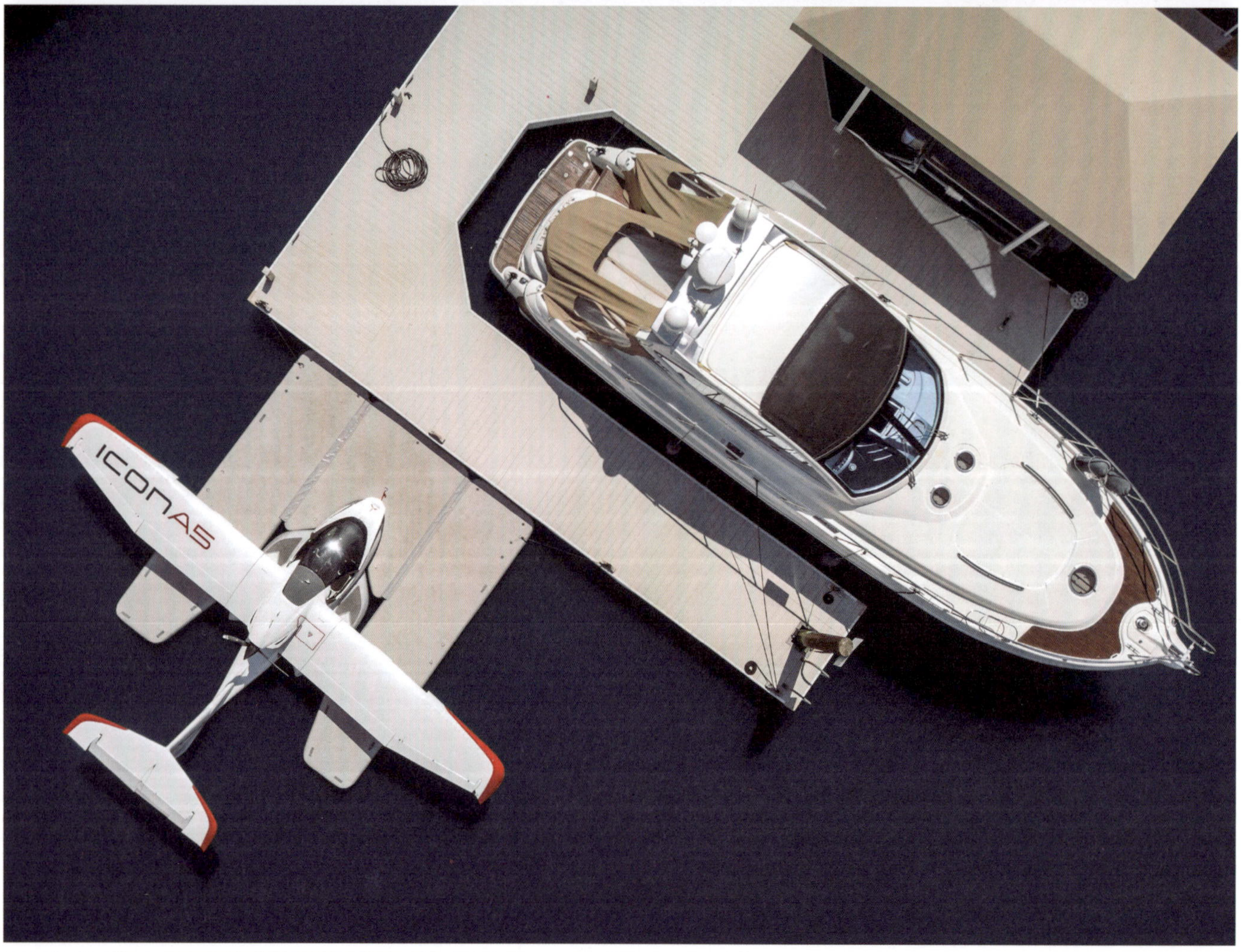

ICON Aircraft

The ICON A5 is an amphibious light sport aircraft that is designed for recreational pilots. Sinuous and sleek, the aircraft is a sports car for the sky with a spin-resistant design and ergonomic interiors. The A5 is design-forward inside and out, and its smooth handling matches its good looks. The UV-coated canopy and the removable side windows allow the pilot and passenger unobstructed 180-degree views.

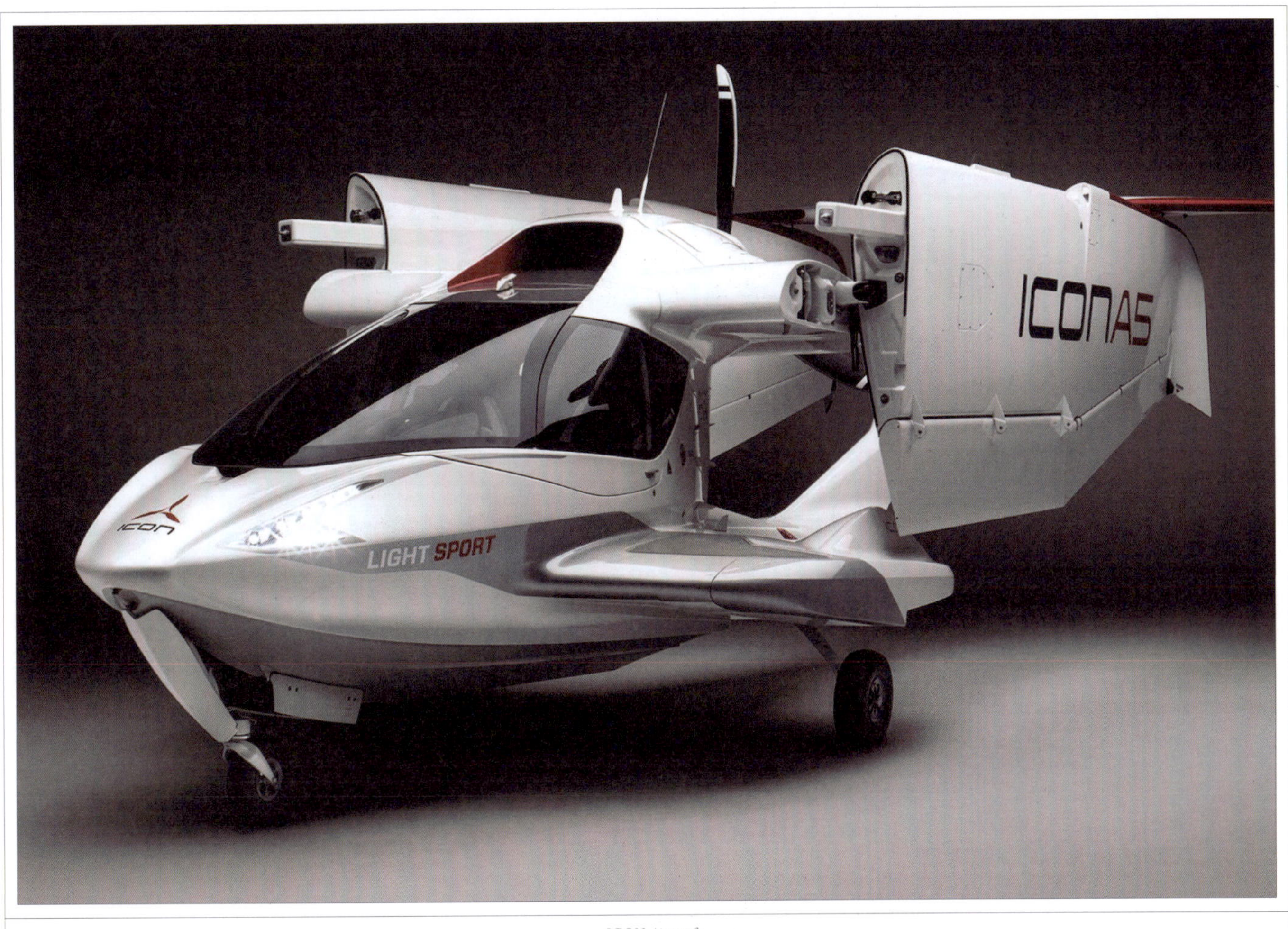

ICON Aircraft

Seats: Two	**Fuel:** 91 Octane Auto or 100LL Aviation	**Landing Distance:** Runway 590 ft / Water 700 ft	**Wingspan:** 34.8 ft (10.61 m)
Max Takeoff Weight: 1510 lbs (686.4 kg)	**Max Speed (Vh):** 95 KCAS (109 mph) (176 kph)	**Engine:** Rotax 912 (100 hp)	**Aircraft Length:** 23 ft (7.01 m)
Useful Load: 430 lbs (195 kg) (estimated)	**Range:** 427nm (45 min reserve)	*At standard conditions at sea level	**Aircraft Height:** 8.1 ft (2.47 m)
Baggage (Max): 60 lbs (27.2 kg)	**Takeoff Distance:** Runway 640 ft / Water 840 ft	**Interior Cockpit Width:** 46 in (116.8 cm)	**Price:** Starts at $359,000

Aimed at people who may have never flown before, the A5 is designed to be as simple as getting into a car and driving off, except this time, you're flying. Pilots who've taken the A5 for a flight describe the controls as intuitive and neither too difficult nor too sensitive to steer.

You'll only need a sport pilot license to fly the A5, which requires a minimum of twenty hours of flight time experience (compared to forty hours for a private pilot license) and which restricts pilots to flying two-seaters. In addition, sport pilot license holders can only fly during the day, in nice weather with at least three miles of visibility, and are limited to flights up to 10,000 feet above mean sea level or 2,000 feet above ground level.

The plane is designed to be easy to store; there's no need for an airport hangar. The wings fold so you can fit the plane in the garage. The company claims it takes one person just two minutes to unfold the wings and get ready for takeoff. Buy a trailer from the company and you can easily tow the plane to the nearest runway or waterway. In fact, the plane can even run on regular unleaded automobile fuel with a range of 450 miles on twenty gallons.

The A5 starts at $359,000 and all planes are built at the company's Vacaville, California headquarters.

EXPERIENCING THE WORLD FLYING AT 1,000 FEET WITH THE WINDOWS OUT IN AN A5 WILL CHANGE YOUR LIFE. **Jerry Meyer,** *Marketing Director, ICON Aircraft*

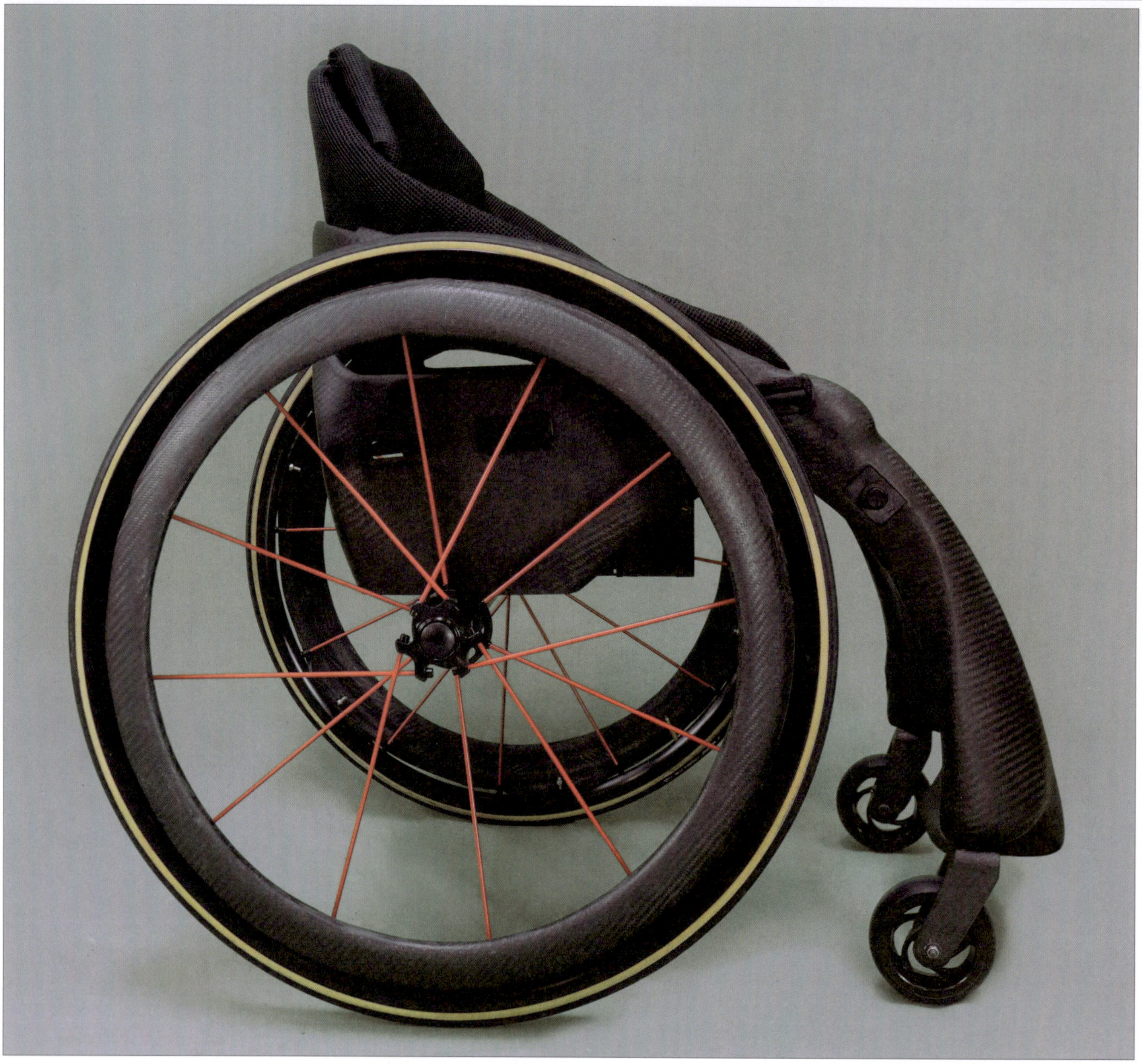

Phoenix i

re you ready to roll in style? Scottish designer Andrew Slorance, founder and CEO of Phoenix Instinct, who developed the first wheelchair compatible luggage system, is now developing the Phoenix i, the world's first ultra-light smart wheelchair. The winner of the Mobility Unlimited Challenge, a design competition for paralysis mobility devices hosted by the Toyota Mobility Foundation and the Nesta Challenge Prize Center, the Phoenix i received a $1,000,000 prize that helped fund the wheelchair's creation.

The frame is made of carbon fiber, making it lightweight and easily portable. Its smart technology is mainly incorporated in the adjustable axle. Built-in sensors can detect if the user is leaning forwards or backwards, and they constantly adjust so the wheelchair and user have the same center of gravity. This reduces the risk of falling backwards, thus creating a never-before-seen interactive user experience and a wheelchair that's able yet stable, which would be impossible without smart systems.

Once the Phoenix i is ready to sell, Phoenix Instinct will sell it at a price similar to regular wheelchairs since the company wants smart wheelchairs to become widely used.

"Wheelchairs are largely funded through reimbursement programs, so raising the ceiling on what insurers will pay means providing life-enhancing benefits and bringing greater savings to insurers in the long term — fewer injuries, greater independence, etc.," says Slorance. "We intend to price the new wheelchair in line with conventional wheelchairs so as to speed up smart wheelchairs becoming the norm."

THE JUDGES WERE IMPRESSED BY HOW THE DEVICE INCORPORATED INTELLIGENT SYSTEMS THAT REPRESENTS A TRUE ADVANCE FOR THE WHEELCHAIR. **Ryan Klem,** *Director of Programs for Toyota Mobility Foundation*

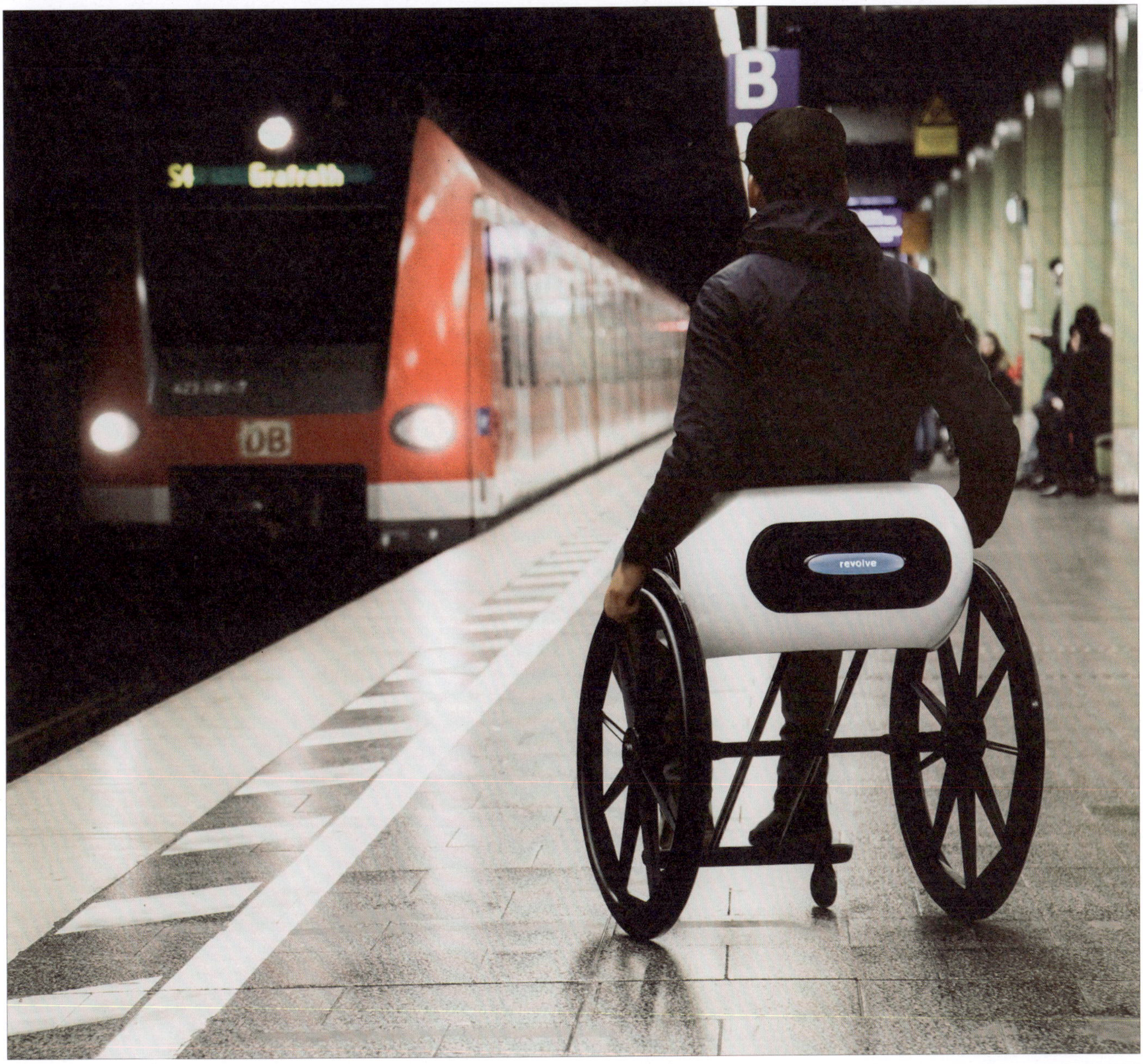

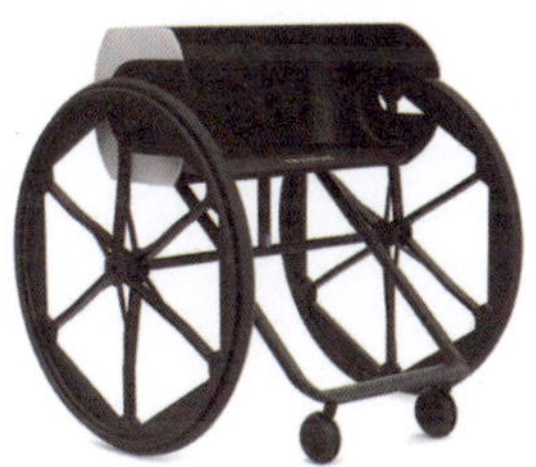

Photography by Matteo Mocellin

There's no wheelchair more travel-worthy than the Revolve Air. Created by Italian inventor Andrea Mocellin, this wheelchair folds in the same amount of time as a regular collapsible wheelchair, but saves 60% more space. The secret is Mocellin's foldable Revolve wheels; built with a unique hexagon structure and with a 24-inch circumference, these airless tires have won awards such as the Asia Design Prize and the Green Product Award. The seat and backrest also require little action and no equipment to open or fold. When folded, the Revolve Air easily fits into the trunk of a car as well as standard cabin baggage dimensions, allowing wheelchair users to keep the chair with them instead of checking it, reducing the risk of in-flight damage and saving valuable travel time before and after flying. While the price is currently unknown, the Revolve Air will be available in 2022 and can be reserved at www.revolve-wheel.com.

REVOLVE AIR AIMS TO GIVE A TOTAL NEW INDEPENDENCE TO ALL ACTIVE WHEELCHAIR USERS WHO COMMUTE AND TRAVEL EVERY DAY.

Andrea Mocellin, *Founder & Inventor of Revolve Air*

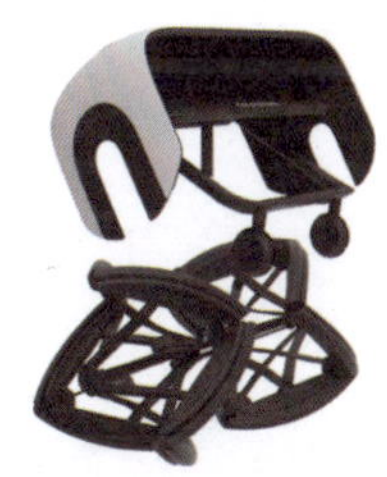
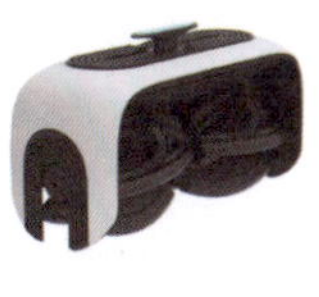

A

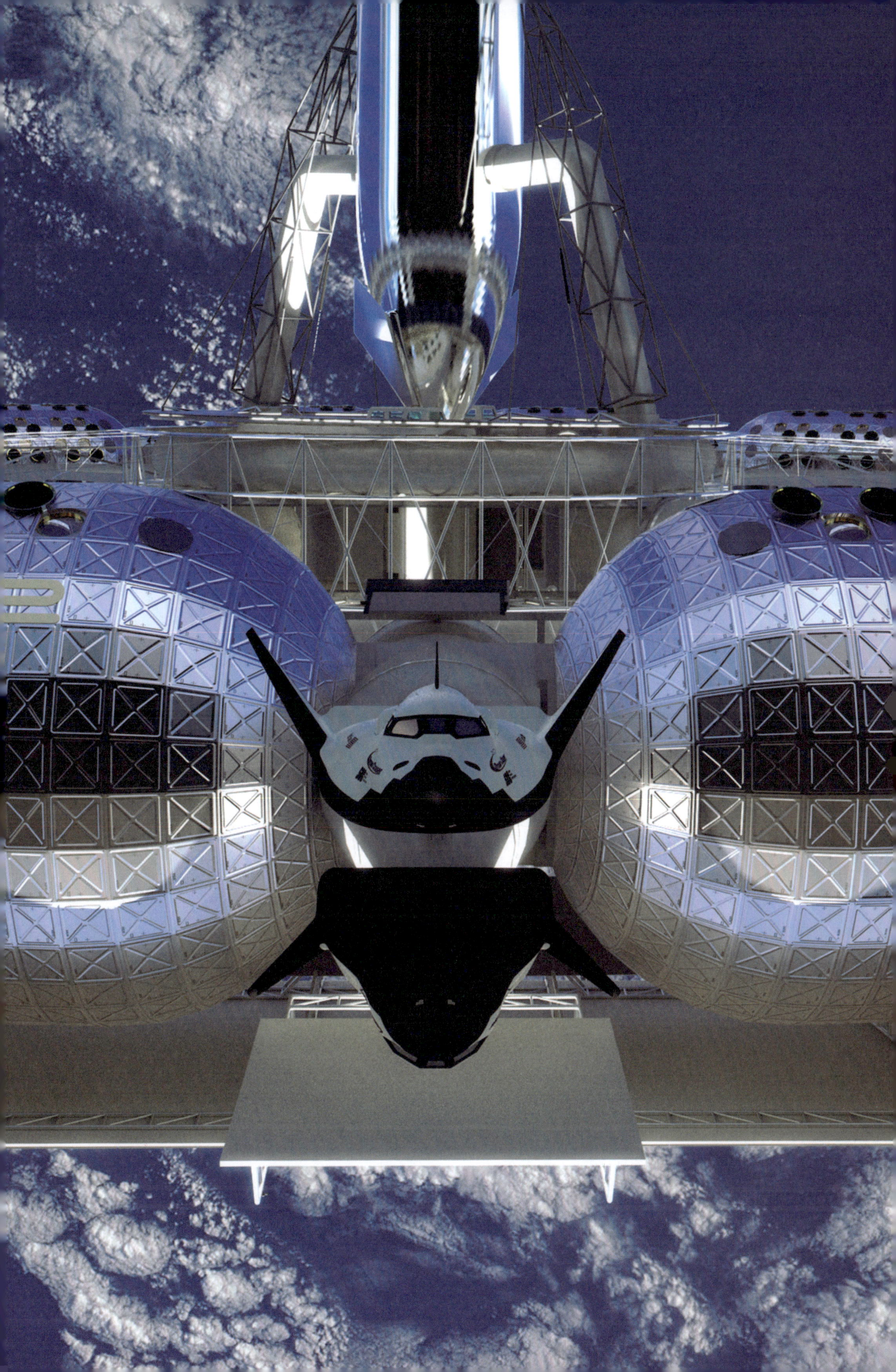

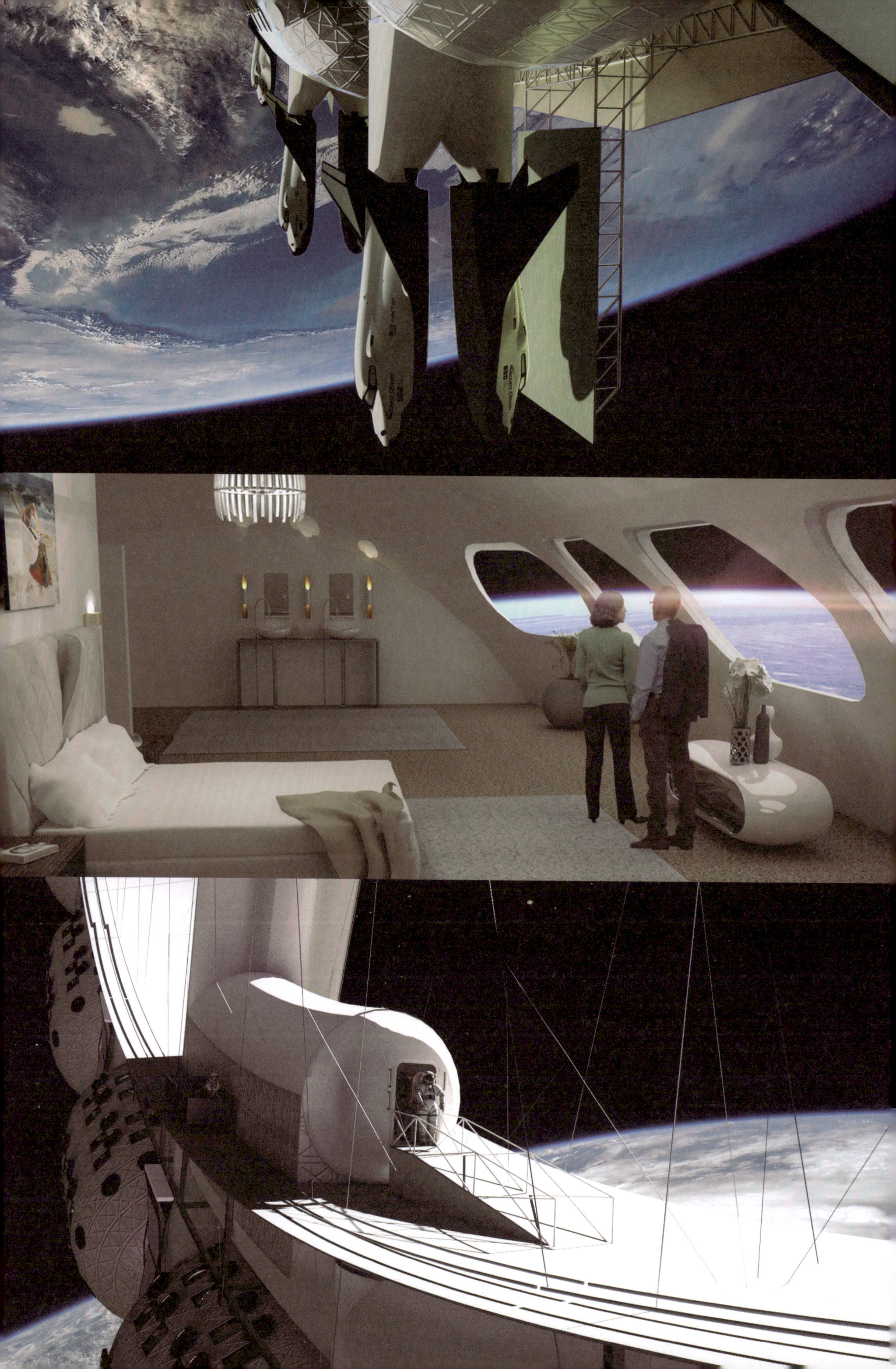

The Voyager Station, developed by the Gateway Foundation and its construction arm, the Orbital Assembly Corporation (OAC), hopes to be the world's first spaceport. The space station's design and technology is inspired by Wernher von Braun, a pioneering German-American rocket scientist who worked for Nazi Germany and NASA. Von Braun was an early proponent of creating a gently orbiting space station that would use centrifugal force to generate gravity for those inside.

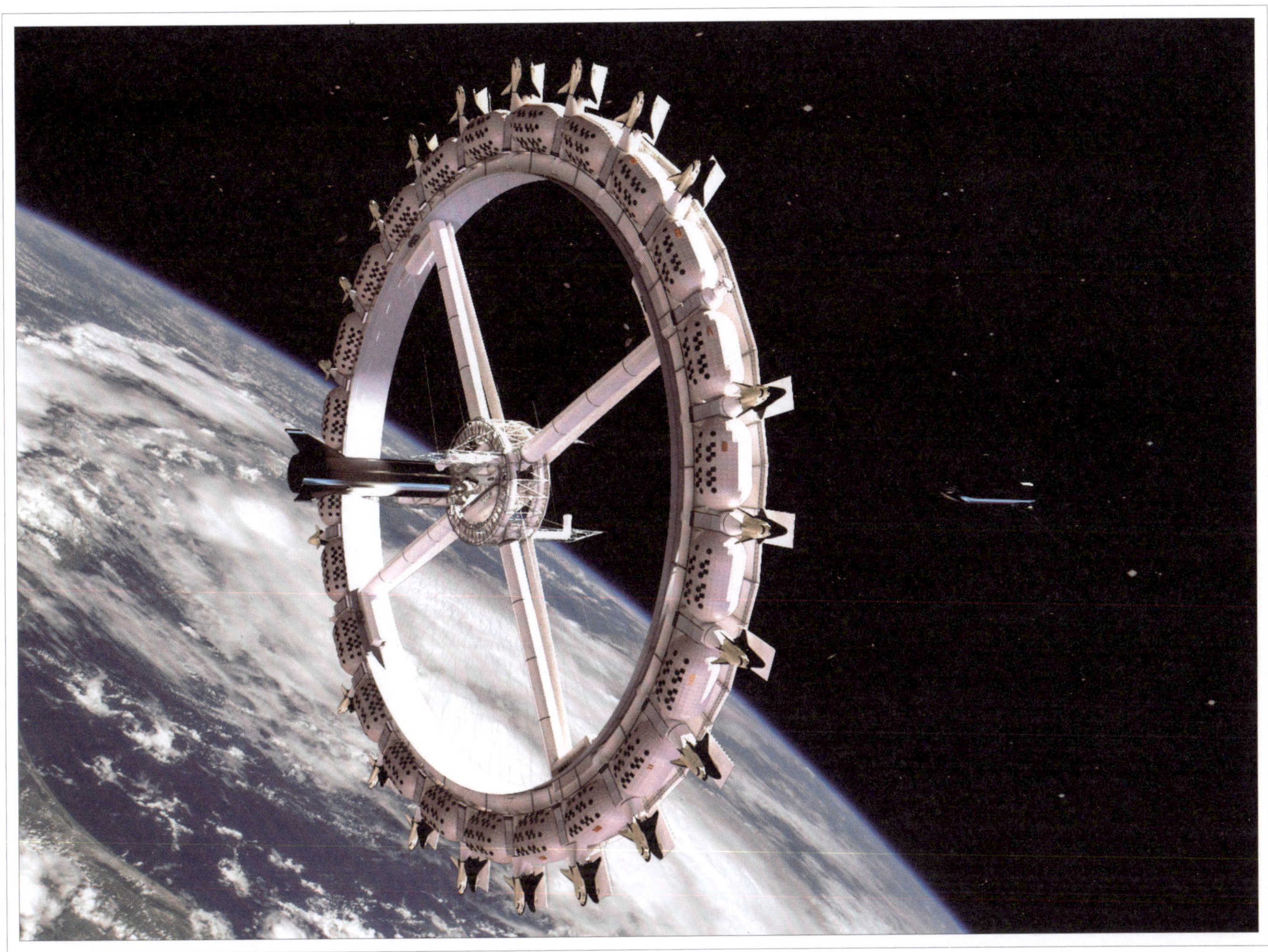

(Page 105) Voyager Station will offer unprecedented views of Earth for tourists and researchers. / (Opposite page, top to bottom) Voyager Station will be equipped with emergency escape vehicles; Luxury villas will offer style, comfort, and an unprecedented experience; An astronaut emerges from the air lock. / (Above) Voyager station with approaching SpaceX Starship.

The OAC envisions the Voyager Station as a place where scientists and tourists can experience life in space, but with all the amenities of Earth — including restaurants, bars, gyms, and concerts. But visitors will also participate in activities with reduced gravity, allowing people to jump and move in completely different ways than they do on Earth.

The Voyager Station will consist of two concentric structural rings fixed together with a set of spokes, which in turn will support a Habitation Ring. The inner ring, or docking hub, would allow visiting spacecraft to unload passengers and cargo. The outer ring truss would serve as structural support, with solar panels, radiators, and a rail transport system, as well as a pedestrian access tube. Finally, the Habitation Ring would be made up of individual pods that could be used as eating and entertainment areas or as privately owned modules, which could be rented out for space vacations.

OAC is planning for the majority of the station to be built in space, using robots. The company is projecting that the basic structure of the Voyager will be finished in 2025 and have full operations beginning in 2027.

WE'RE TRYING TO MAKE THE PUBLIC REALIZE THAT THIS GOLDEN AGE OF SPACE TRAVEL IS JUST AROUND THE CORNER.

John Blincow, *Gateway Foundation*

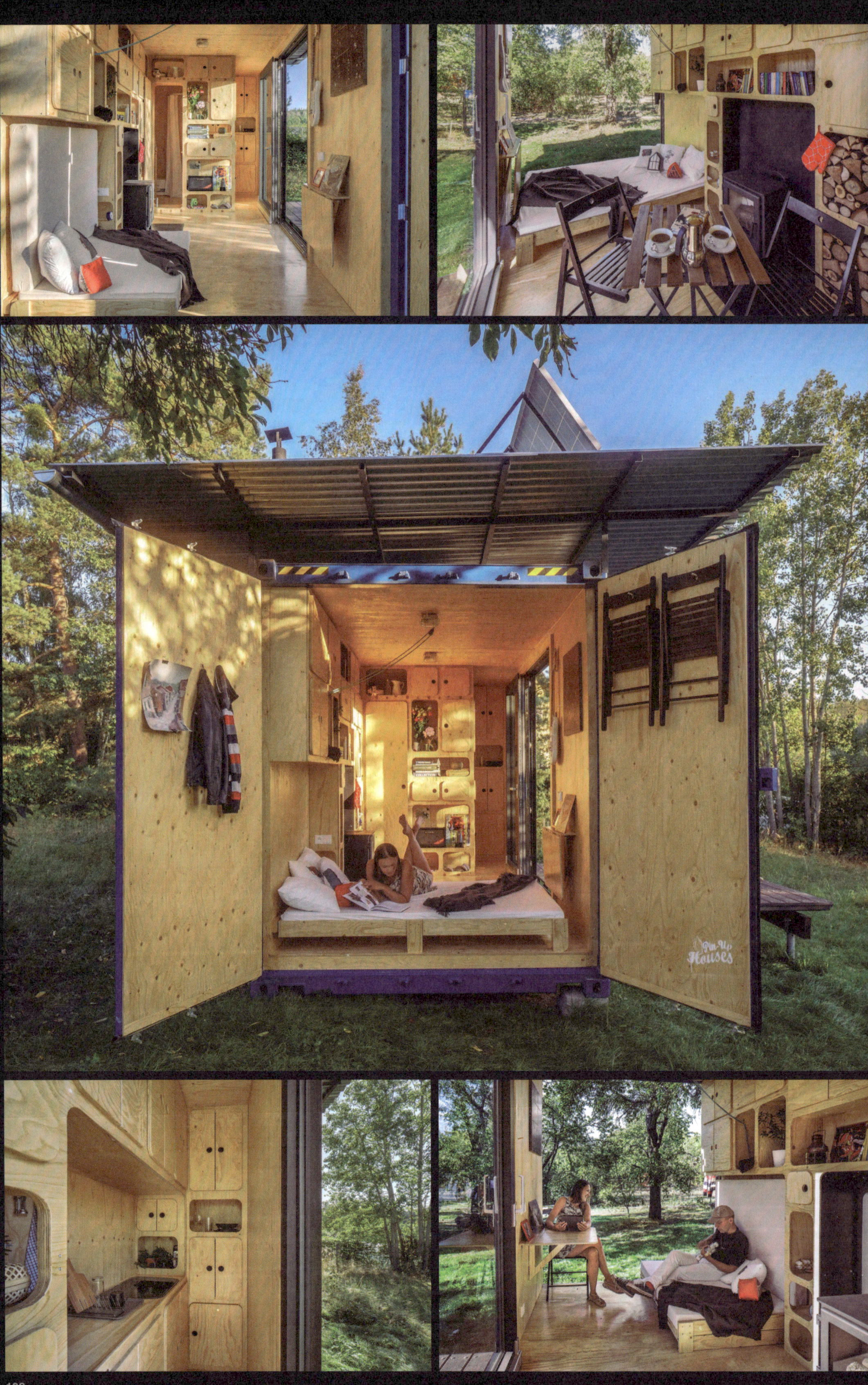

Pin-Up
Houses

Architect Joshua Woodsman of Pin-Up Houses designed this ingenious and self-sufficient house, using a shipping container as a base. Everything has a place, including a convertible sofa bed and an outdoor terrace that can be folded up to cover the sliding glass doors during inclement weather. The terrace and the open doors at one end of the house help to let in light and air for the small living space. There are cleverly designed built-in storage nooks throughout, as well as room for a small table and two chairs.

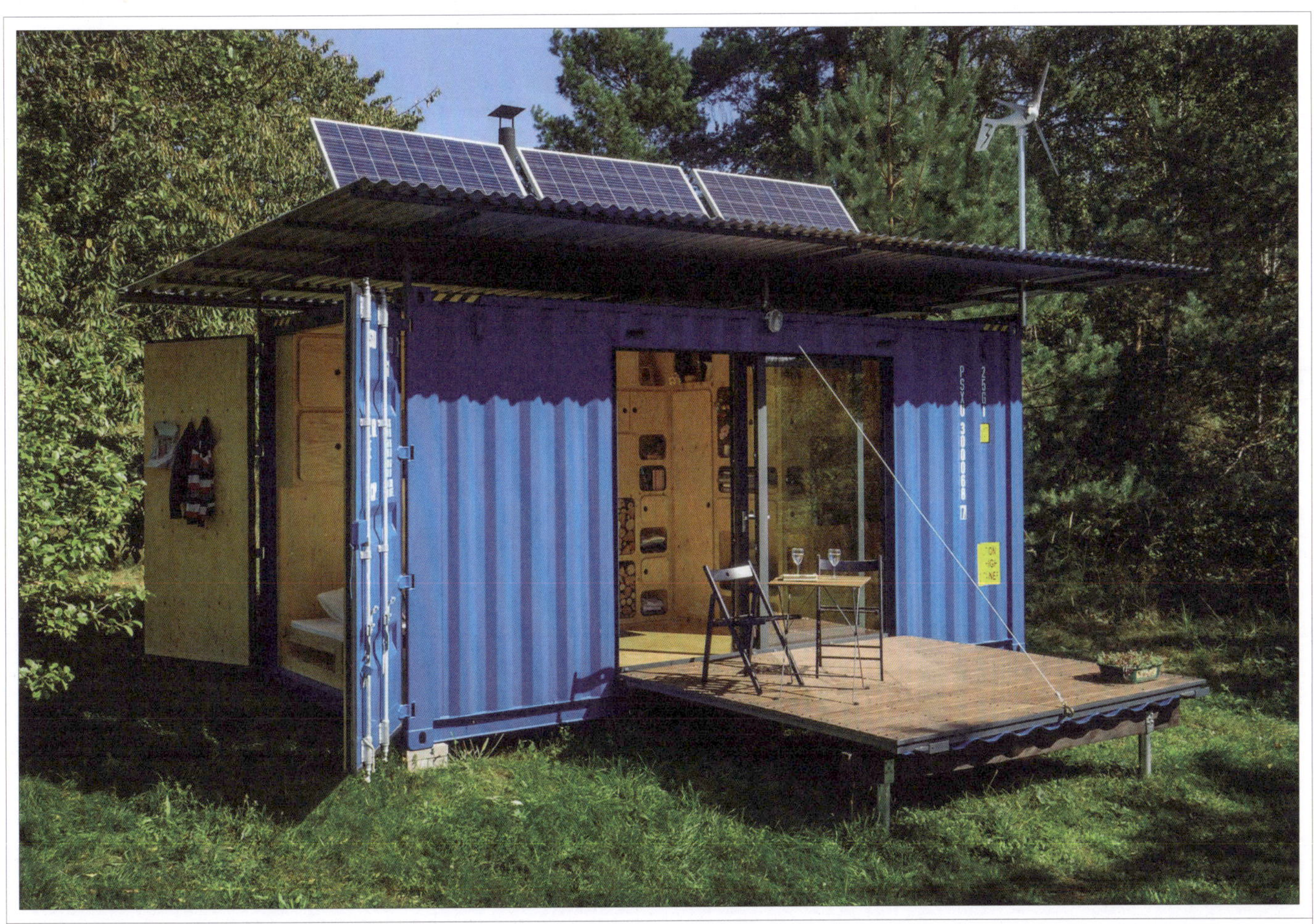

Photography by Jakub Zdechovan

The house does not need any external sources of energy or water, (though the owner will have to figure out a way to tap into Wi-Fi), as it has solar panels and a wind turbine, which power the refrigerator, water heater, and other appliances. The power level can even be monitored through a mobile app. The roof is covered with a galvanized corrugated metal sheet for additional protection, and it extends beyond the container's structure to increase rainwater capture. The rainwater is then filtered and stored in a 1,000-liter water tank and distributed for use in the kitchen and the bathroom.

Gaia is created using a 20' or 6-meter shipping container, with 132-square feet of interior living space. The inside uses spruce plywood and wooden studs, and is sprayed with thermal insulation to ensure a comfortable temperature throughout the year. There's even room for a small wood-burning stove. "I've slept in Gaia when it's -15ºC and it's comfortable," said Woodsman.

Woodsman estimates it takes about $21,000 and three months to build Gaia.

I WAS PRIMARILY INSPIRED BY CARAVAN AND SAILBOAT EQUIPMENT WHEN I WAS DESIGNING GAIA. IT IS A MACHINE FOR LIVING, AND THE TILTING TERRACE GIVES THE HOUSE TWO COMPLETELY DIFFERENT FACES. **Joshua Woodsman,** *Architect, Pin-Up Houses*

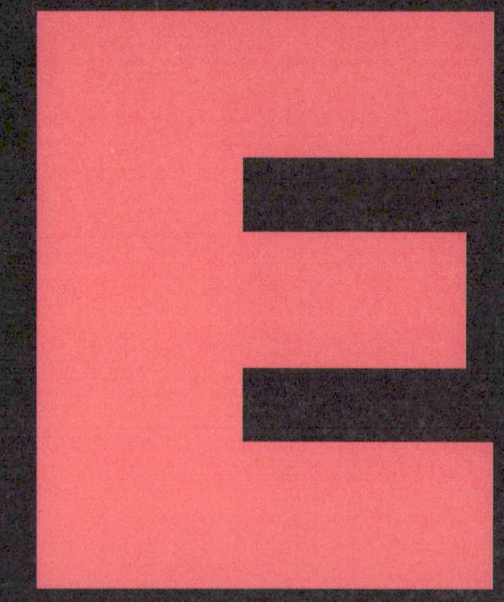

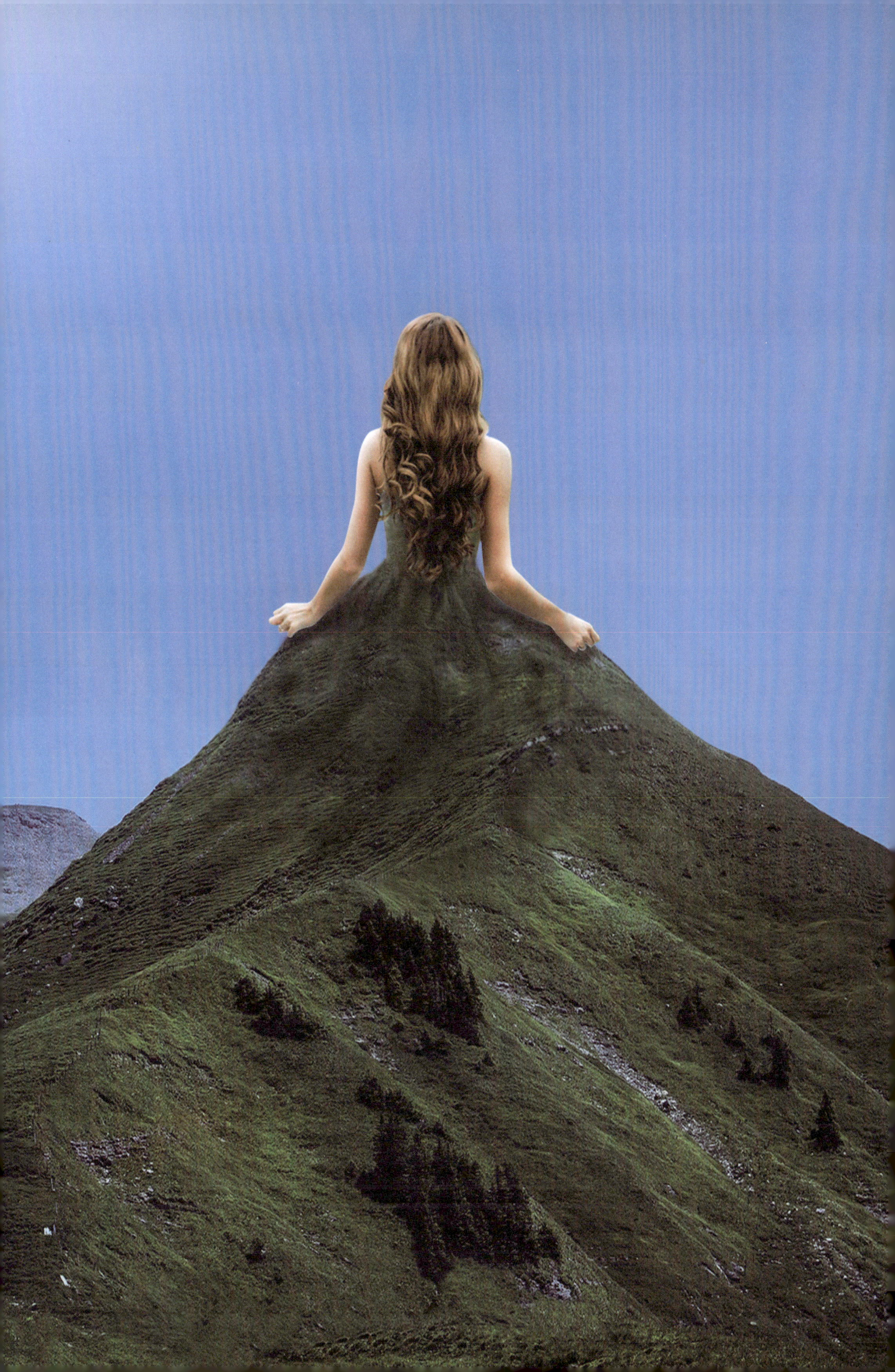

THEY'VE CONSISTENTLY WON EXCELLENT EDUCATIONAL AWARDS FOR OVER TEN YEARS AND HAVE GREATLY INFLUENCED DESIGN SOCIETY. THEIR UNIQUE TEACHING METHOD HAS SET A STRONG EXAMPLE IN THE EDUCATIONAL WORLD.
Young-Joo Jung, *Creative Director, Pulmuone Design Center*

THEY GIVE VALUABLE FEEDBACK ON THE DESIGN DIRECTION THAT STUDENTS WANT TO DO. ALSO, THEY GIVE PASSIONATE LECTURES AND TRY TO SHARE AS MUCH DESIGN INFORMATION AS POSSIBLE WITH THEIR STUDENTS
Sang Hee Han, *Design Student*

THEY HELPED ME FIND THE KEY IDEAS IN MY PROJECT AND LED ME TO CONDUCT CREATIVE GRAPHIC REPRESENTATION EXPERIMENTS. I WOULD LIKE TO THANK THEM FOR ENCOURAGING ME TO ENTER INTERNATIONAL CONTESTS EVERY YEAR.
Ji Young Moon, *Design Student*

GRAPHIS WAS MY FIRST NATIONAL COMPETITION, AND AT FIRST, I FELT NERVOUS, BUT MY PROFESSORS ENCOURAGED ME AND GAVE ME HELPFUL ADVICE. THANKS TO THEM, I COULD ENTER MY WORK SAFELY AND WITH PEACE OF MIND.
Eugene Kim, *Design Student*

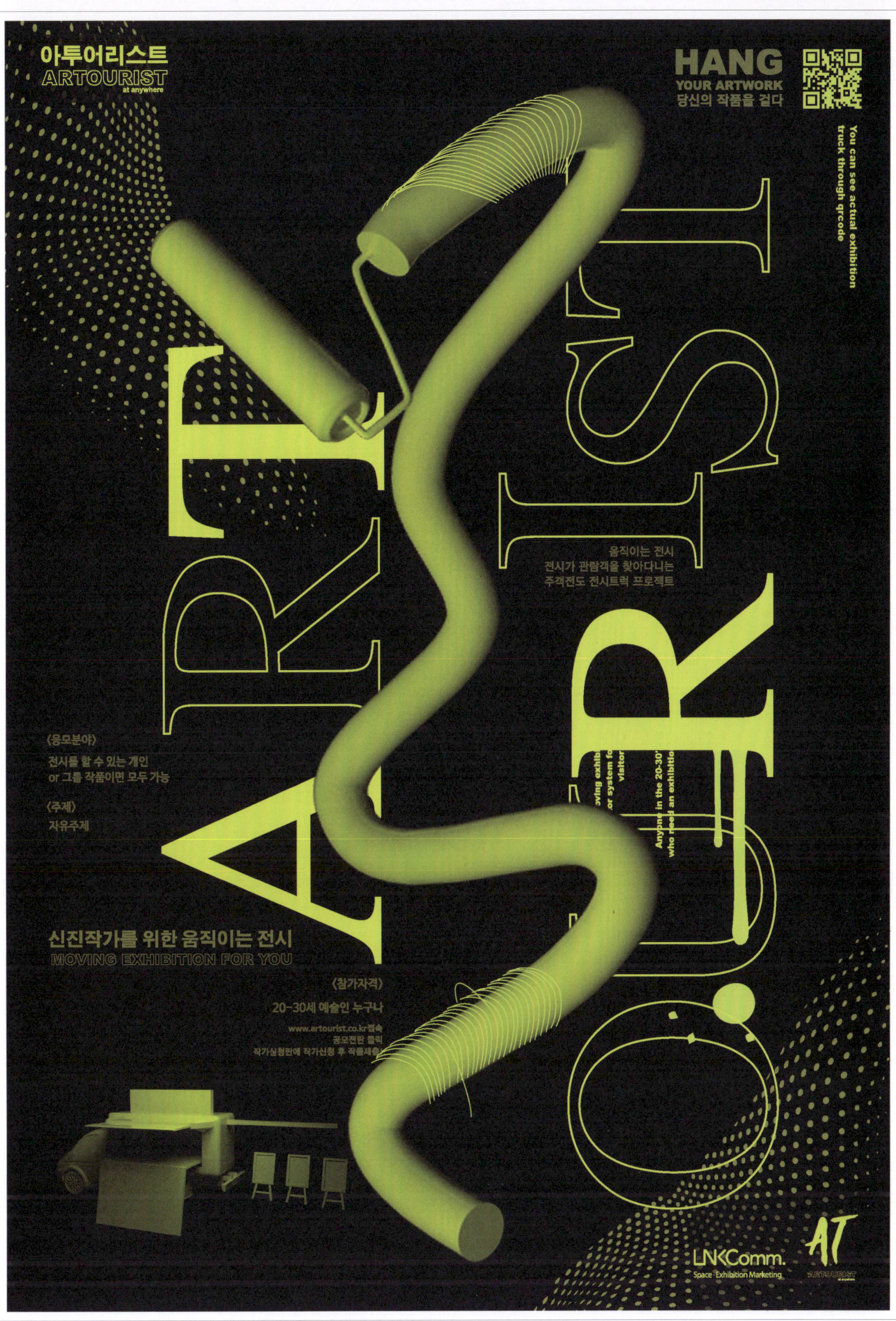

(Page 111) OUR DRESS CODE IS NATURE, New Talent Annual 2019. Platinum-winning students: Kim Su Bin & Hong Ye Rim
(Above) Exhibition Trucks, Artourist, New Talent Annual 2018. Platinum-winning student: Dan Bi Kim

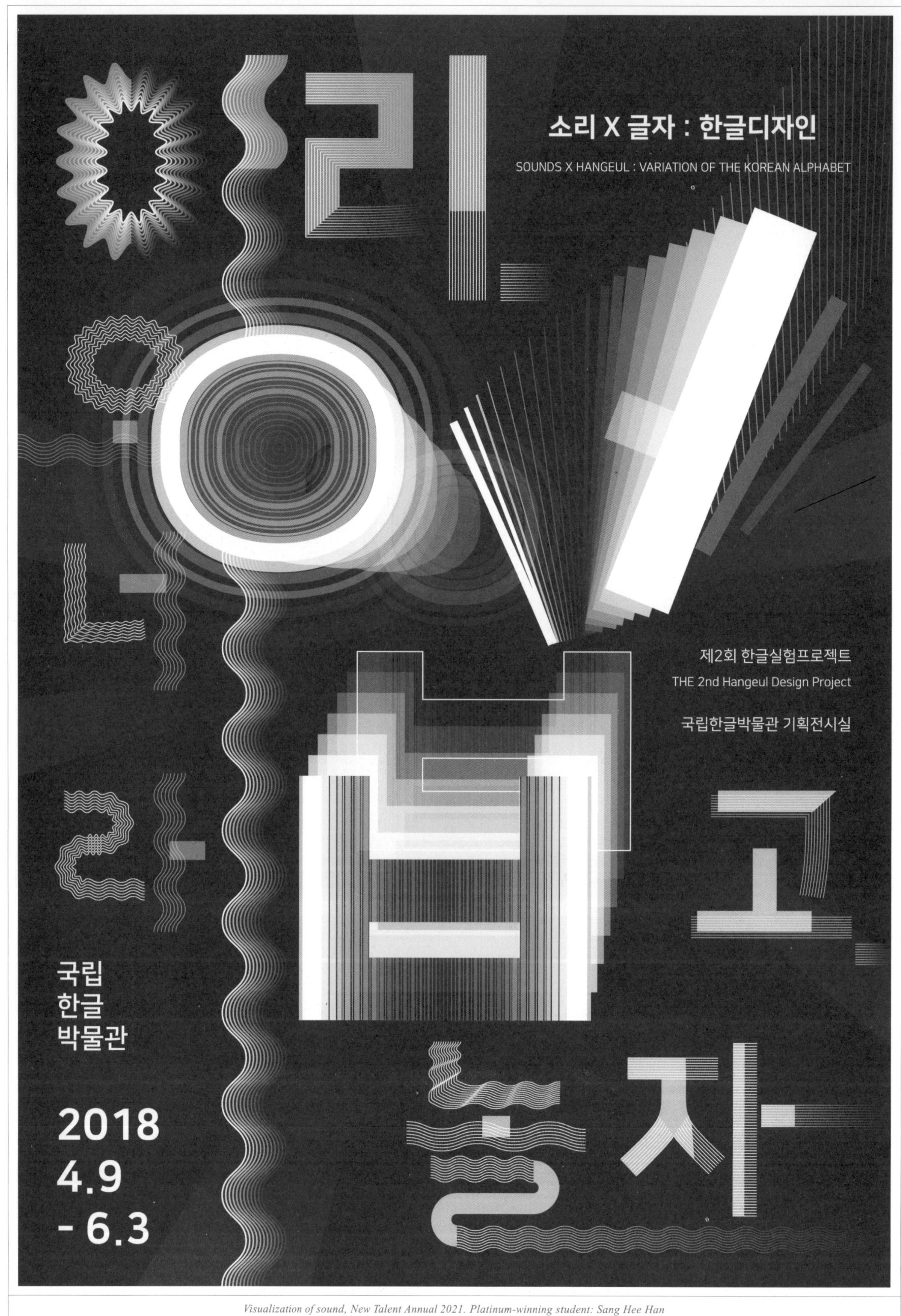

Visualization of sound, New Talent Annual 2021. Platinum-winning student: Sang Hee Han

Introduction by Yumi Jung *Brand Consultant, Daehong Communications, Design Marketing Center*

The professors Dong-Joo Park and Seung-Min Han have consistently produced outstanding results through their many kinds of design guidance for four years. Their work is a combination of creative talent and experience gained from not only commercial projects, but also diverse, self-initiated projects. They always produce creative results because they fearlessly enjoy challenges. Their works inspire a variety of people. As I worked with them, I admired their great leadership. I always give them my unwavering support, and admire their enthusiasm and creativity. I hope to work with them for a long time, and I always look forward to their next work.

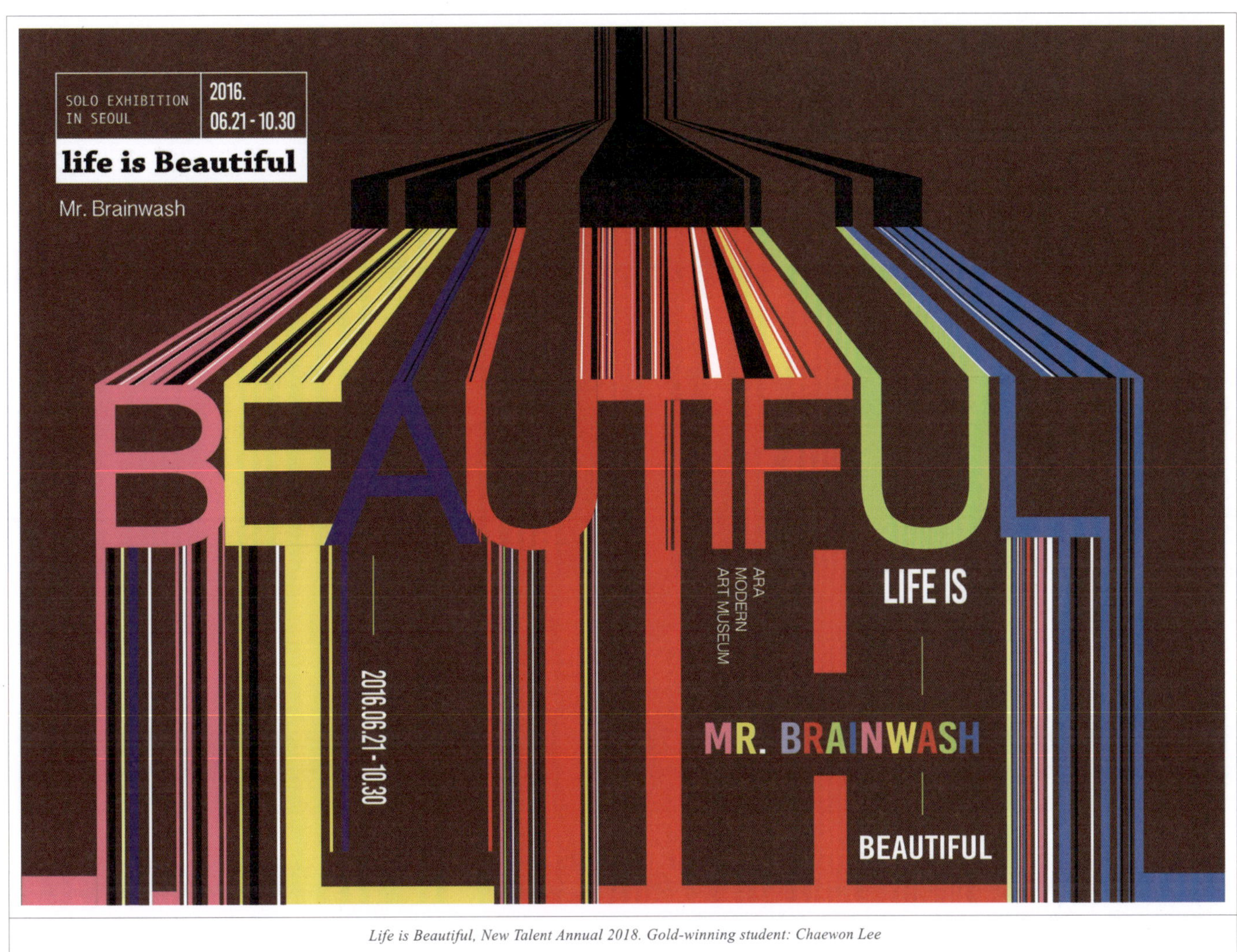

Life is Beautiful, New Talent Annual 2018. Gold-winning student: Chaewon Lee

I BELIEVE EVERYTHING HAS THE POTENTIAL TO HAVE NEW VALUES AND MEANINGS. THEREFORE, IT IS ADVISED TO CONSTANTLY ATTEMPT THE PROCESS OF EXPLORING, ANALYZING, AND EXPERIMENTING.

Seung-Min Han, *Visual Communication Design Dept. Professor, Hansung Univerisity Design & Arts Institute*

What is your process for selecting students from your class to apply for the Graphis competitions?
Dong-Joo Park (D.P.) & Seung-Min Han (S.H.): We always encourage our third and fourth year students to submit their final projects to the Graphis New Talent Annual. The juniors have mostly focused on communication design, while the seniors have been working on their senior projects that they need to complete for graduation.

Our third year class is about experimenting with graphic design and focusing primarily on developing clear and effective graphic communication. Any student who has passed their freshman and sophomore classes in graphic design can register for that class.

It's different for the seniors. They can only apply to be in the senior seminar if they've completed more than ninety credits. Students in senior seminars have to go through three stages of review: the first planning stage, the second design review, and a third and final portfolio review. Even if a student has completed all of the credits required for graduation, they cannot graduate if they fail their final portfolio review.

What do students need to do to succeed in your class?
D.P.: We expect students to understand the basic concepts of visual design and to develop and explore their own style. They should be able to create effective designs that demonstrate experimental thinking and a creative approach to any given concept. We want the students to think creatively and to consider multiple possibilities and methods in their approach. ·
S.H.: In the third and fourth year classes, the students work with us to answer these questions:
- What is the central idea of this project? What makes it unique?
- How can we find a solution or answer the question at the heart of this project?
- How can we incorporate different perspectives in our design?
- How do we create a visual language that can clearly communicate its purpose?
- Considering reality and objectivity, how can we create a visual language that we can relate to and understand?
- How can we create a visual language that has a clear point of view?

Students in our classes need to be constantly thinking creatively to solve problems. A student who wants to join our class should have a process-oriented desire to explore and to experiment. They should also be comfortable having a strong point of view.

What might be a typical first assignment?
D.P.: We start by having the students discover different ways to solve problems through visual design. We encourage them to develop clear visual communication using basic principles of graphic design, but also to experiment and to consider different perspectives as they work.
S.H.: Whether a student takes our class to improve their overall design skills, to improve their creativity, to improve their problem-solving skills, or to improve the aesthetics of their work, all these goals have something in common: always have a clear purpose and goal in your work. Whether a student is working on solving a problem from a conceptual angle or a visual angle, I think it's important for each student to carefully analyze and establish the purpose and the goal of their project.

Typically, the first assignment in all my classes is to do keyword research on the concepts that we focus on in class. It's essential that the students have this conceptual and analytical base for their work so that they feel comfortable building on this to present their own point of view.

Are real clients suggested?
D.P. & S.H.: In the first year course, we start with basic skills in visual communication design, and in the second year, we introduce real-life examples of design challenges. In the third year, the projects are more focused on actual clients, and by the time they're seniors, students have had internships and lots of industry-related project experience. This allows a lot of students to work on an actual corporate client project as a graduation project.

By the time students reach their junior and senior years, they've had a chance to plan and produce a number of real client projects in partnership with actual companies, which gives them valuable experience for the real world.

Do you work with students individually?
D.P.: Yes, throughout the course of the class we spend one-on-one time with the students to help guide them through the design process.
S.H.: I work with different companies and public institutions to present real-life client cases to our students. In the class, I am like an orchestra conductor, directing the entire project and the students' work with my guidance and coaching. We, the professor and the students, work and breathe together as a team, rather than working individually.

Do you present the student's work to the whole class so that everyone can critique it?
D.P.: Students freely share their ideas and work with each other during class. The students are inspired by each other during this process.
S.H.: I believe that when the work is freely shared, the scope of thinking can be greatly broadened. Students get the chance to hear many different opinions and are pushed to think about questions from different points of view. When everyone's work is included in the critiques, that's when we can develop the most creative and effective solutions. So, yes, we encourage all of our students to participate in the critiques.

How do you develop and raise your students' visual and verbal skills?
D.P.: We encourage our students to experiment without restrictions. Through the process of trying to solve design problems, they improve visually and verbally.
S.H.: To improve their visual and verbal skills, I suggest the following:
- Try to understand the problem from the student's perspective.
- Once you understand their point of view, encourage them to explore different concepts and designs.
- Next, students can propose different graphic methodologies after doing structural analysis.
- Have each student make their own checklist to include different perspectives and concepts that should not be forgotten.
- Organize the methodologies that were discovered through structural analysis, and based on those methodologies, experi-

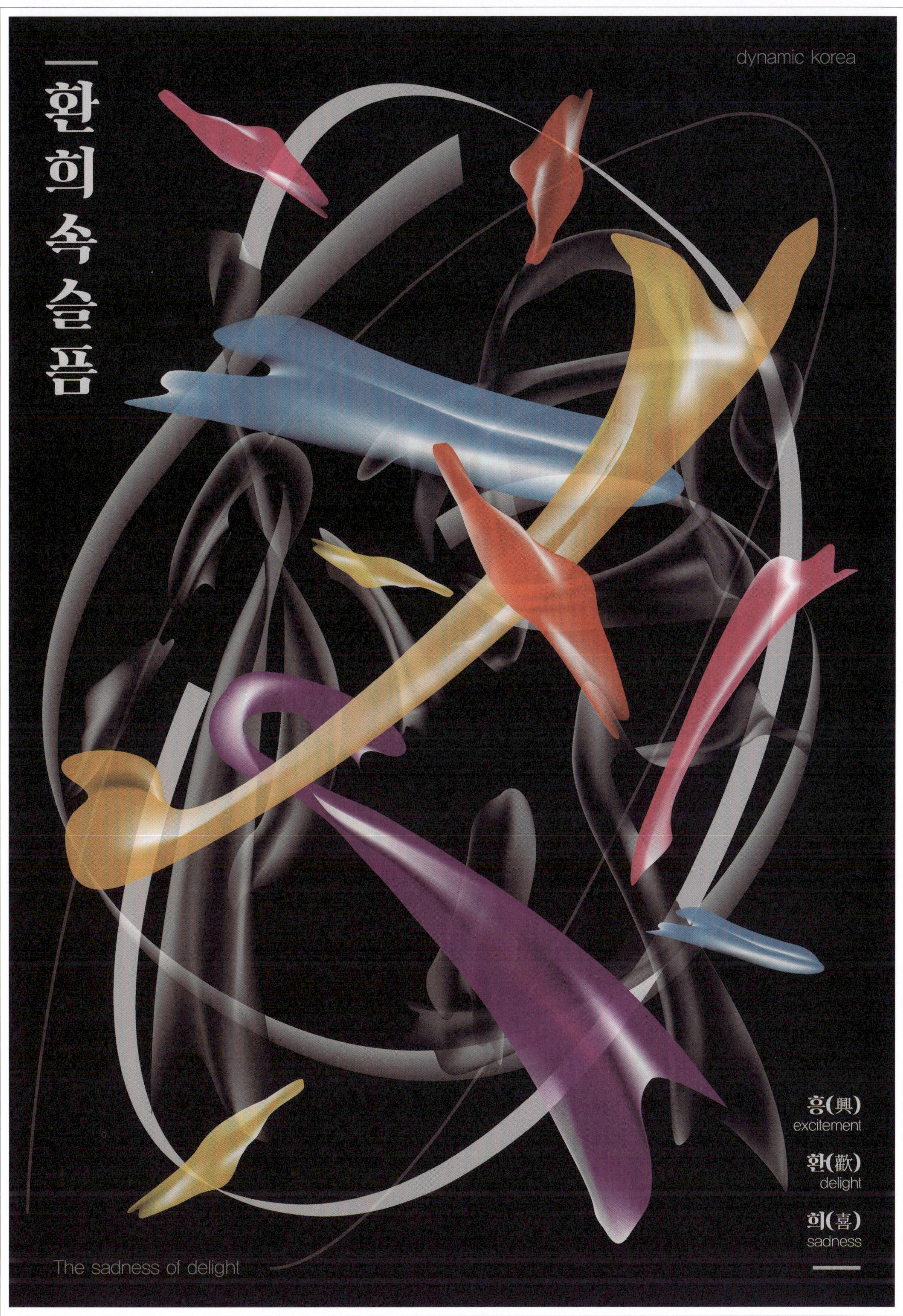

Dynamic Korea, New Talent Annual 2019. Platinum-winning student: Yeji Kim

ment so that new solutions can be found.
- Improve the students' problem-solving abilities by encouraging different elements of potential designs to be combined in different ways.
- Have the students practice summarizing, writing, and explaining the different steps that they took to come up with the final design.
- Finally, have the students present their projects with well-designed and persuasive presentation materials that clearly explain their thinking process.

What percentage of your students have received an award?
D.P. & S.H.: In our classes, we encourage all of our juniors and seniors to submit their final projects to the Graphis New Talent Annual Competition. I think the process of participating in an international design competition helps to improve the students' skills, whether they win or not. So, I always encourage everyone to submit their work, regardless of the quality. However, students who feel the quality of their work is not good enough can choose to withdraw their entries.

For the past four years, from 2018 to 2021, most of the students who submitted work have won. Here is a list of winners:
• 2018 Award-winning work: 18. Total students: 18.
  Platinum: 2, Gold: 4, Silver: 4, Honorable Mention: 8.
• 2019 Award-winning work: 22. Total students: 31.
  Platinum: 3, Gold: 7, Silver: 8, Honorable Mention: 4.
• 2020 Award-winning work: 11. Total students: 16.
  Platinum: 1, Gold: 2, Silver: 2, Honorable Mention: 6.
• 2021 Award-winning work: 16. Total students: 23.
  Platinum: 1, Gold: 2, Silver: 8, Honorable Mention: 5.

Can you name a few of your past students
who have gained success?
D.P. & S.H.: For the past four years, the names of the students who have won Platinum in the Graphis New Talent Annual are:
• 2018: Dan Bi Kim & Hyuk-June Jang
• 2019: Kim Su Bin & Hong Ye Rim (team), Yeji Kim, Jumi Park
• 2020: JeeHee Shin
• 2021: Sang Hee Han

Most of the students who have already graduated are working as designers at large international corporations.

At the semester's end, what kind of advice do you
give to the class?
D.P.: A successful idea expressed through graphic design begins with free thinking and imagination. Experimenting with many different mediums and methods will lead to better design outcomes.
S.H.: I believe everything has the potential to have new values and meanings. Therefore, I advise students to constantly explore, analyze, and experiment.

How do you define success in your classes? Is there any additional information you would like to share with readers?
D.P.: Our classes teach design thinking and design principles to communicate concepts and messages clearly through effective research and storytelling.
S.H.: When students are stuck, I encourage them to try doing some step-by-step, yet over-the-top style of thinking. I encourage them to look at the research and the data that they've collected and to talk with each other about different possibilities. I also encourage them to think from a variety of perspectives and to write down these possible ideas in structured notes. Once they've hit upon the core essentials of the design, I continue to guide them so they can draw a conceptual map of their thoughts. I also encourage them to replace keywords with common images. This way, the students can continue to talk to each other to find unexpected images that have similar semantic structures.

During this process of visualizing the core concepts, and by referring back to their conceptual map and keyword notes, the students try to develop visual logic and new perspectives. I try to speak with them mid-project so that the developing concepts and emotional characteristics of the project remain related and not too far off from their central axis of thought.

These class discussions, one-on-one dialogues, and brainstorming sessions encourage students to form a structural framework for their ideas. We find that this participatory method of learning allows our students to develop their own ways of creating a unique, graphic language.

Hansung Univ. Design & Arts Institute edubank.hansung.ac.kr
See their Graphis Master Portfolio on graphis.com.

IN THE CLASS, I AM LIKE AN ORCHESTRA CONDUCTOR, DIRECTING THE ENTIRE PROJECT AND THE STUDENTS' WORK WITH MY GUIDANCE AND COACHING. WE, THE PROFESSOR AND THE STUDENTS, WORK AND BREATHE TOGETHER AS A TEAM.

Seung-Min Han, *Visual Communication Design Dept. Professor, Hansung University Design & Arts Institute*

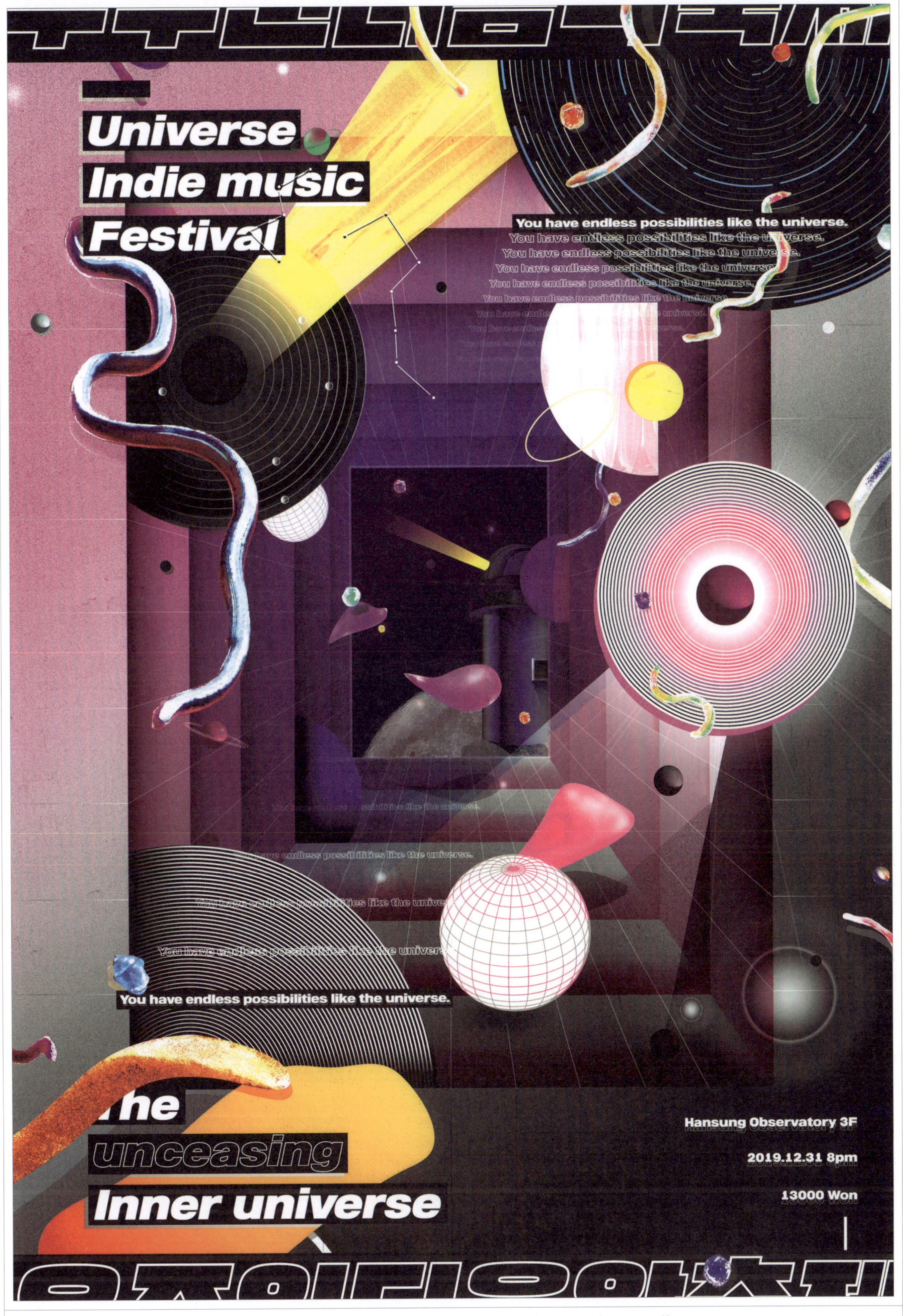

Universe Indie Music Festival, New Talent Annual 2020. Platinum-winning student: JeeHee Shin

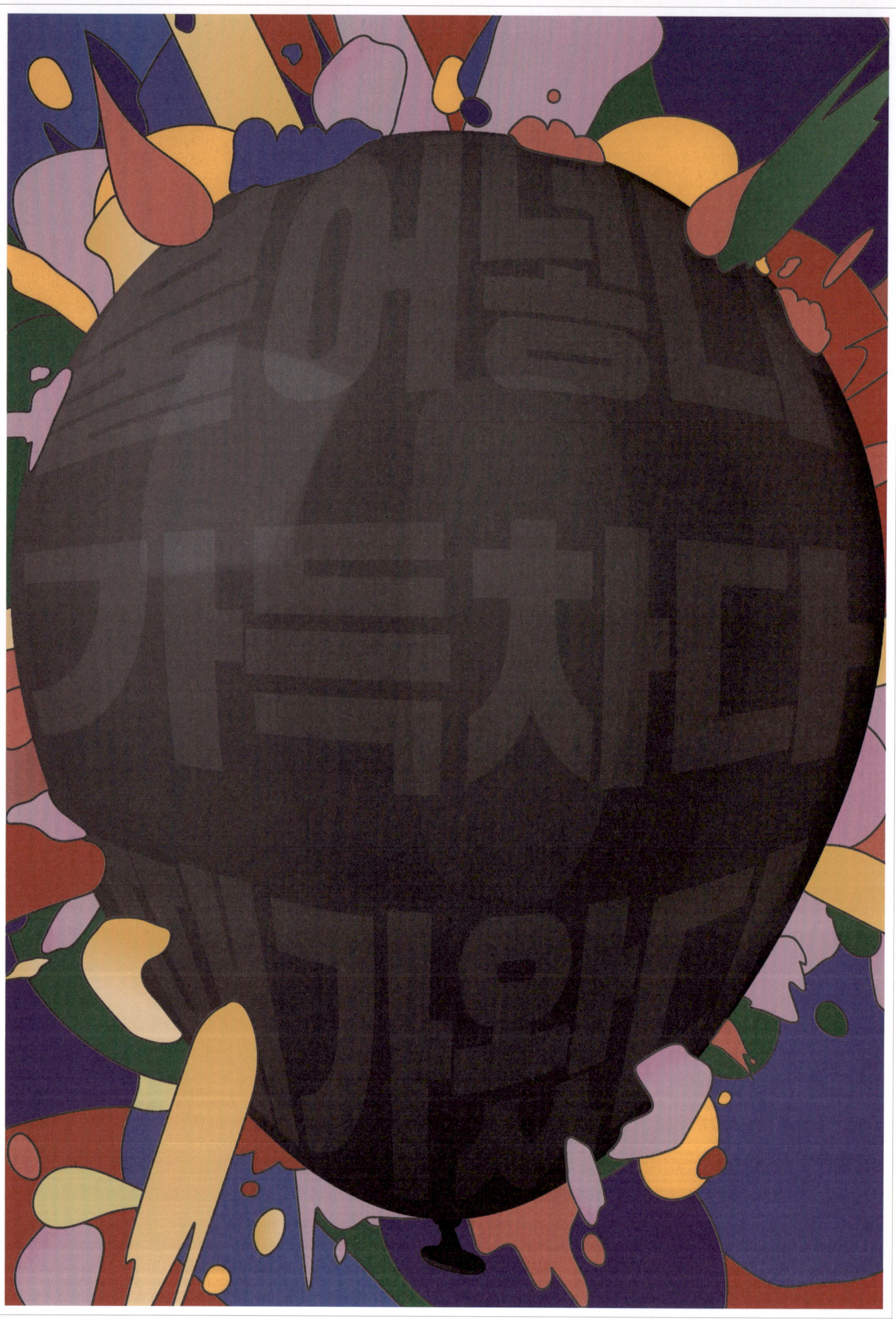

Hansung Uni. Design & Art Institute Graduation Poster, New Talent Annual 2018. Gold-winning students: Chan Kyu Lee, Min Gi An, Bong Hee Park, & Min Soo Kim

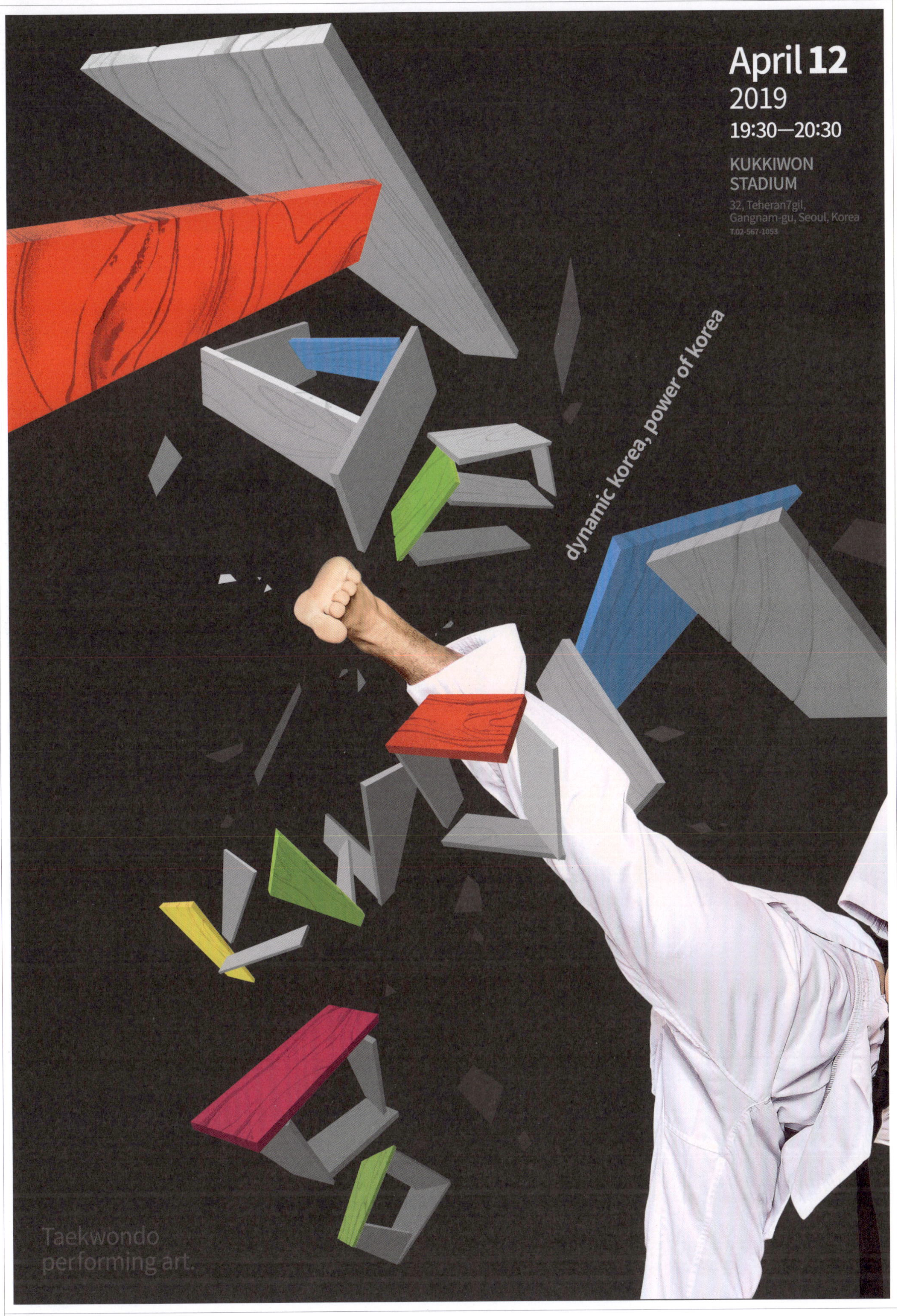

Dynamic Power of Korea, New Talent Annual 2021. Gold-winning student: Ji Young Moon

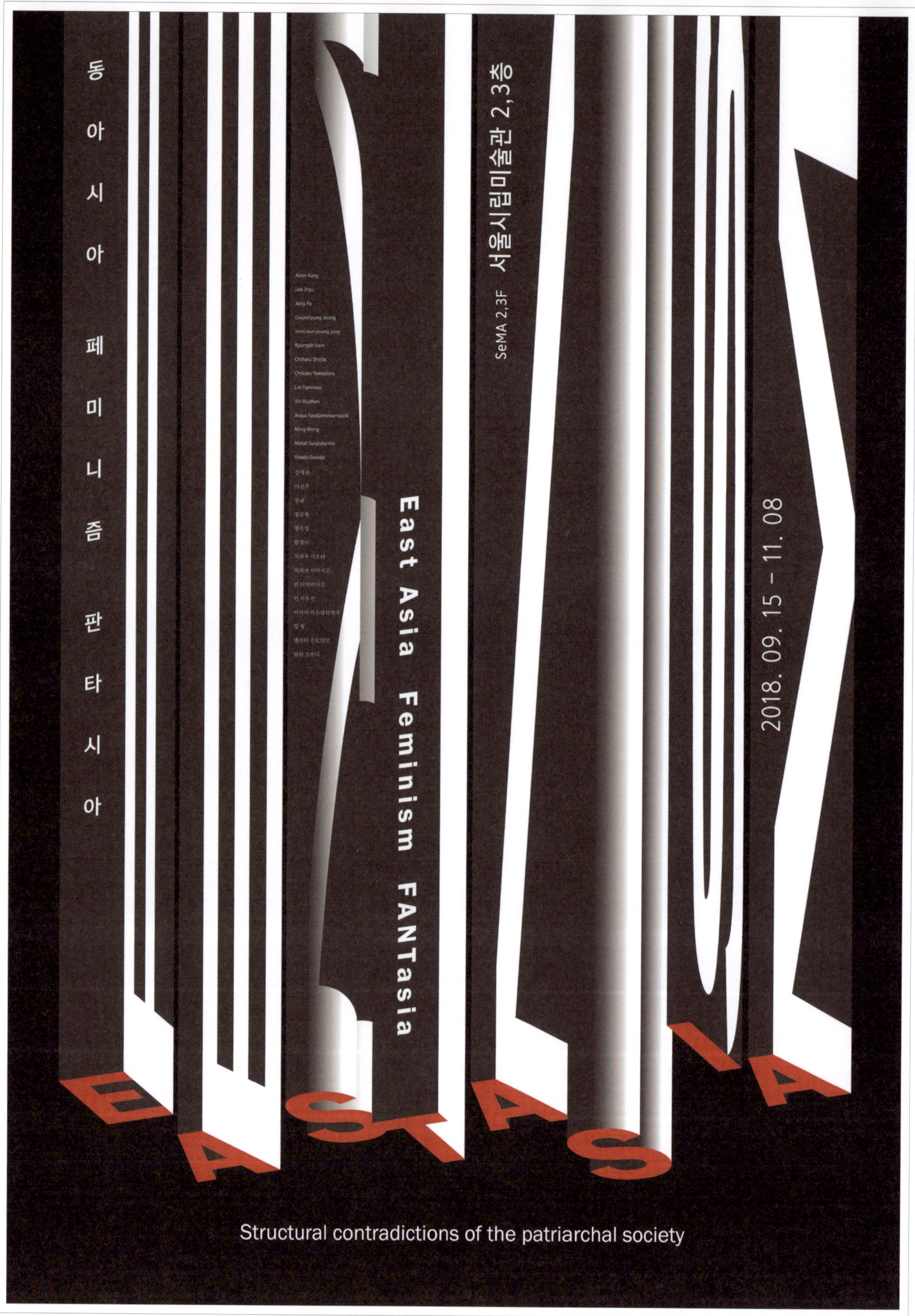

East Asia Feminism, New Talent Annual 2019. Platinum-winning student: Jumi Park

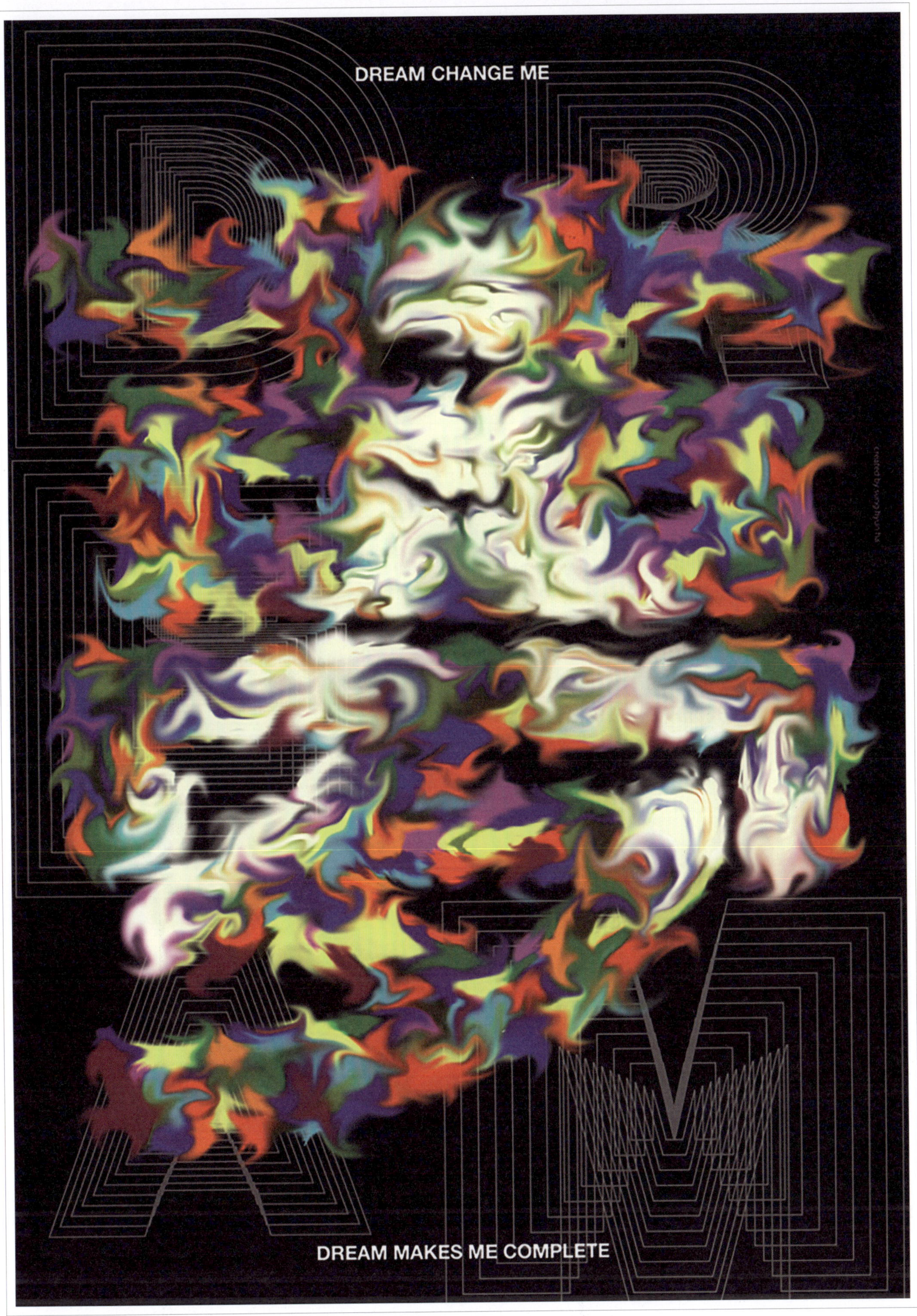

Dream Makes Me Complete, New Talent Annual 2018. Gold-winning student: Sung Hyun Ha

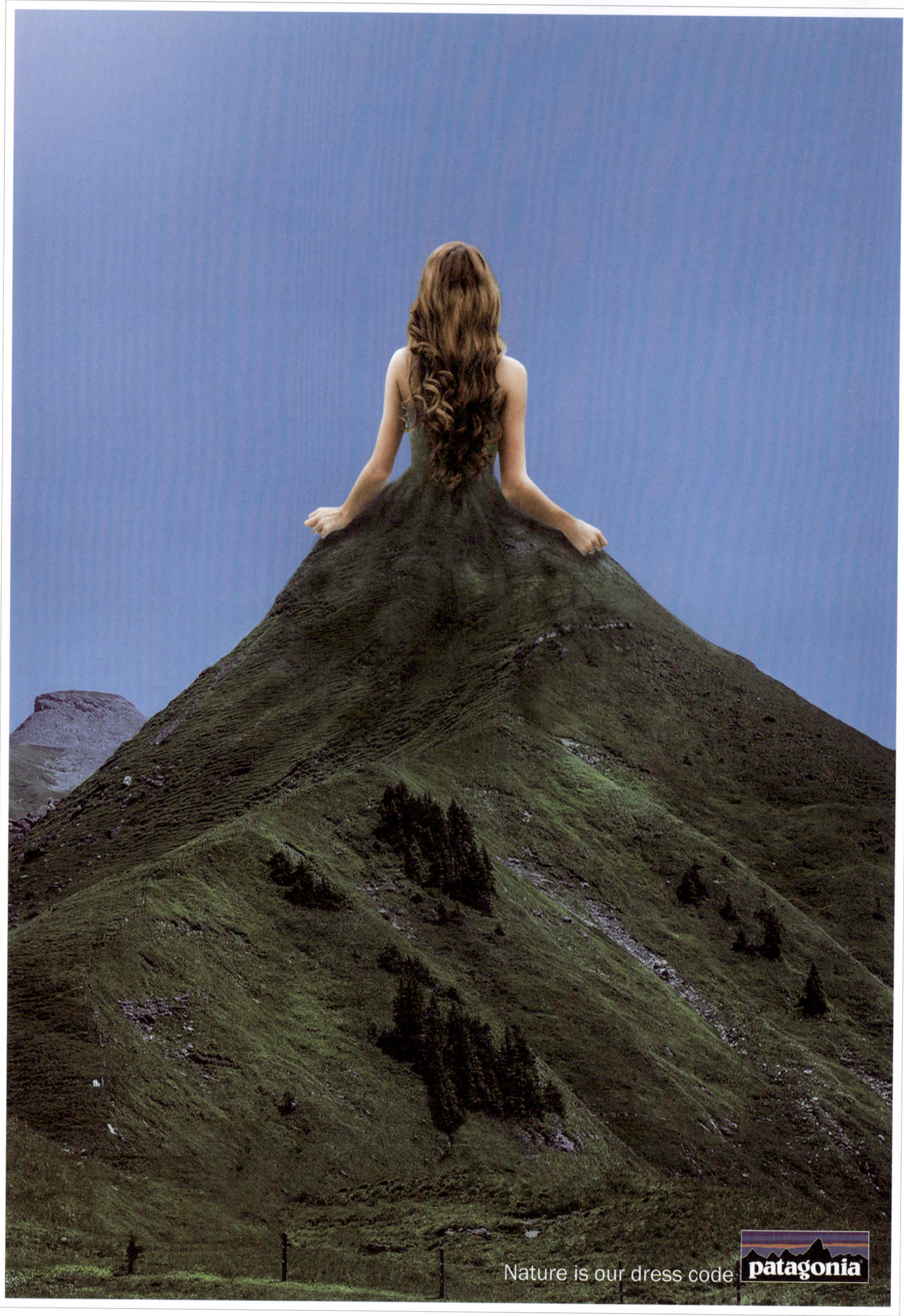

OUR DRESS CODE IS NATURE, New Talent Annual 2019. Platinum-winning students: Kim Su Bin & Hong Ye Rim

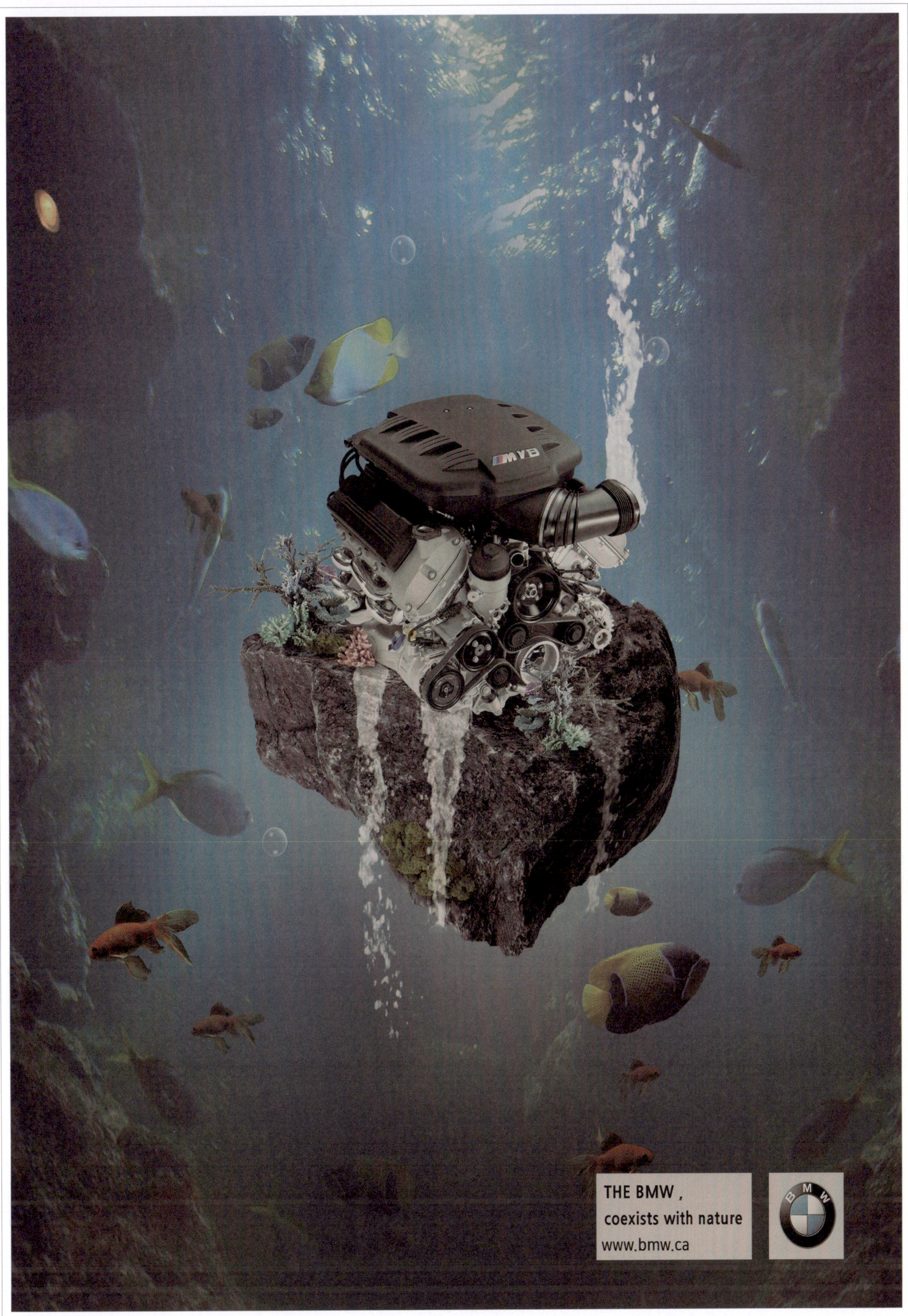

The BMW Coexists with Nature, New Talent Annual 2018. Platinum-winning student: Hyuk-June Jang

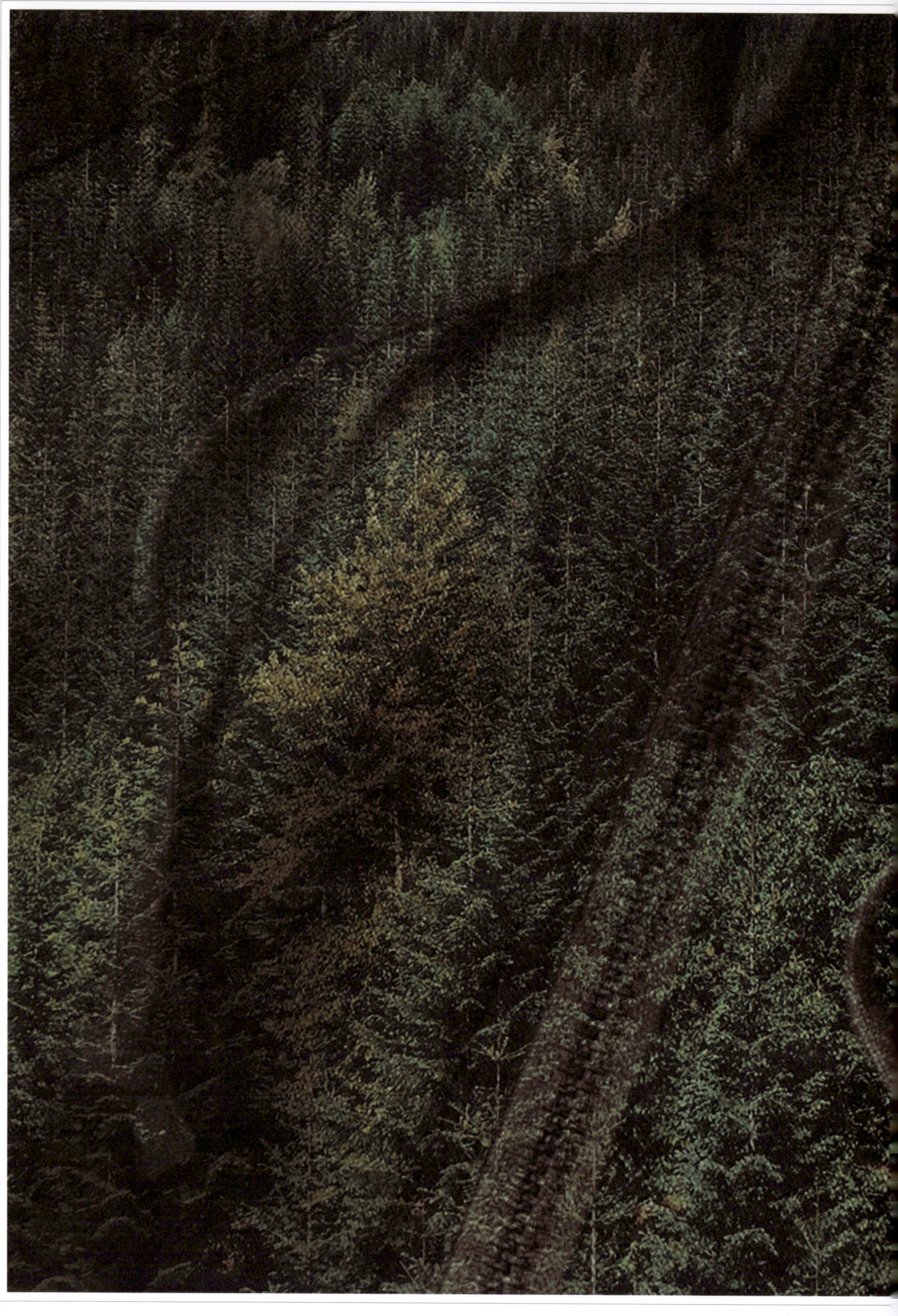

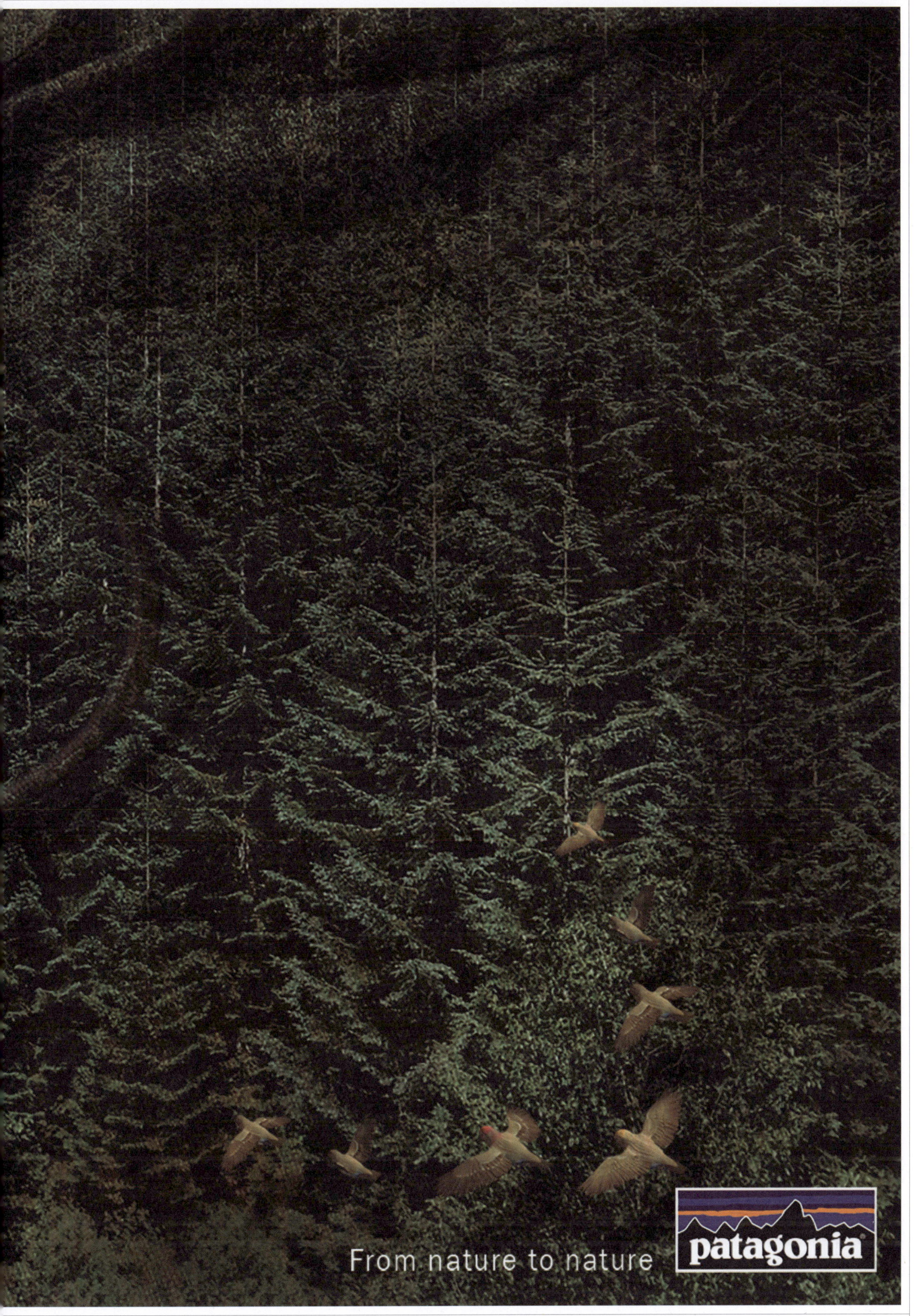

From Nature to Nature, New Talent Annual 2019. Gold-winning students: Kim Su Bin & Hong Ye Rim

At $90 each, these books present award-winning talent. Become a Professional Member and get a copy for only $45.

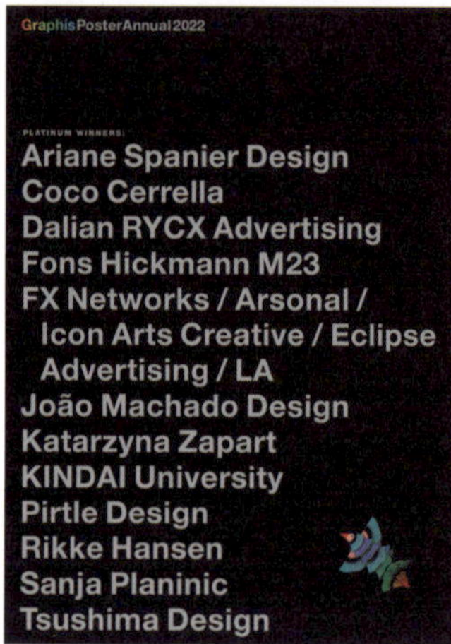
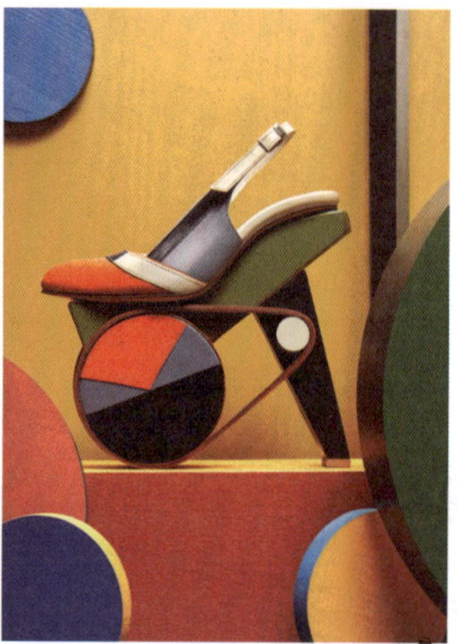
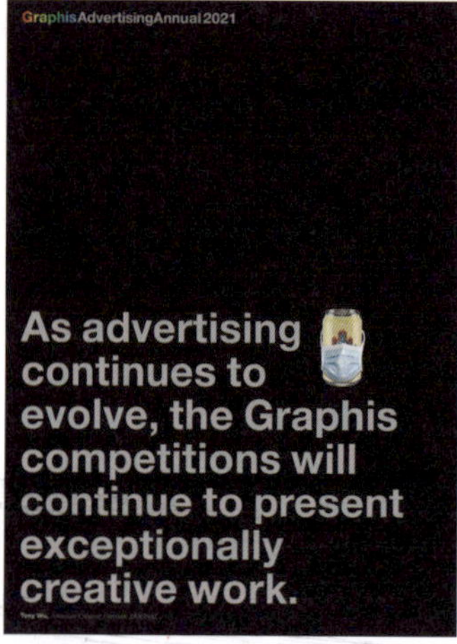

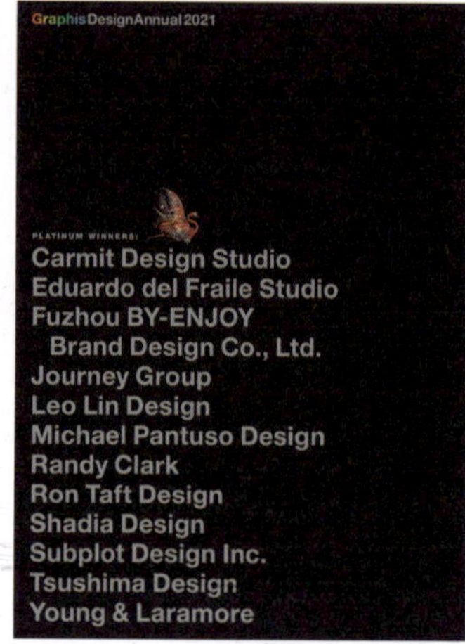

POSTER ANNUAL 2022 PLATINUM WINNERS:

Ariane Spanier Design
Coco Cerrella
Dalian RYCX Advertising
Fons Hickmann M23
FX Networks / Arsonal /
  Icon Arts Creative /
  Eclipse Advertising / LA
João Machado
Katarzyna Zapart
KINDAI University
Pirtle Design
Rikke Hansen
Sanja Planinic
Tsushima Design

PHOTOGRAPHY ANNUAL 2021 PLATINUM WINNERS:

Ashley Camper
Dylan Coulter
Craig Cutler
Bruce DeBoer
Ricardo de Vicq
  de Cumptich
Colin Douglas Gray
Lennette Newell
Joseph Saraceno
Howard Schatz
Tyler Stableford.

ADVERTISING ANNUAL 2021 PLATINUM WINNERS:

72andSunny Los Angeles
ARSONAL
The Beacon (Kohler Co)
Colin Corcoran
The Designory Inc
FOX Entertainment
INNOCEAN USA
Judd Brand Media
Young & Laramore

DESIGN ANNUAL 2021 PLATINUM WINNERS:

Carmit Design Studio
Eduardo del Fraile Studio
Fuzhou BY-ENJOY
  Brand Design Co., Ltd.
Journey Group
Leo Lin Design
Michael Pantuso Design
Randy Clark
Ron Taft Design
Shadia Design
Subplot Design Inc.
Tsushima Design
Young & Laramore

Books are available at www.graphis.com/store

I AM ALWAYS INSPIRED TO BE ABLE TO SEE THE BROAD ARRAY OF WORK COMING INTO THE GRAPHIS AWARDS FROM AROUND THE WORLD; TO SIT IN JUDGMENT OF SUCH AN AUGUST COLLECTION IS AN INCREDIBLE PRIVILEGE.

Jonathan Knowles, *Photographer, Jonathan Knowles Photography, Photography Annual 2021 Judge*

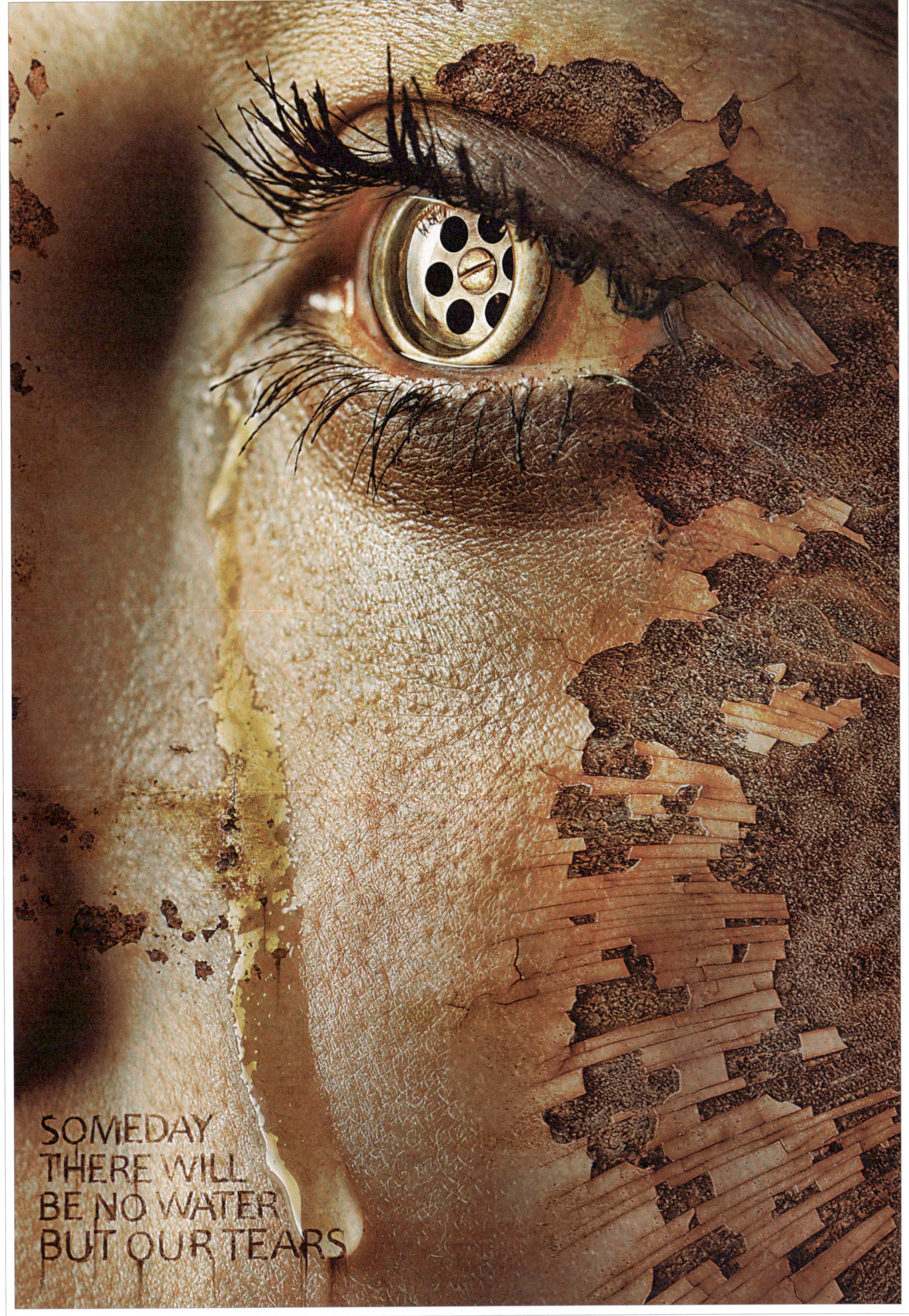

Designer: **Wesam Mazhar Haddad** | Client: **The Museum of Cultural Heritage**

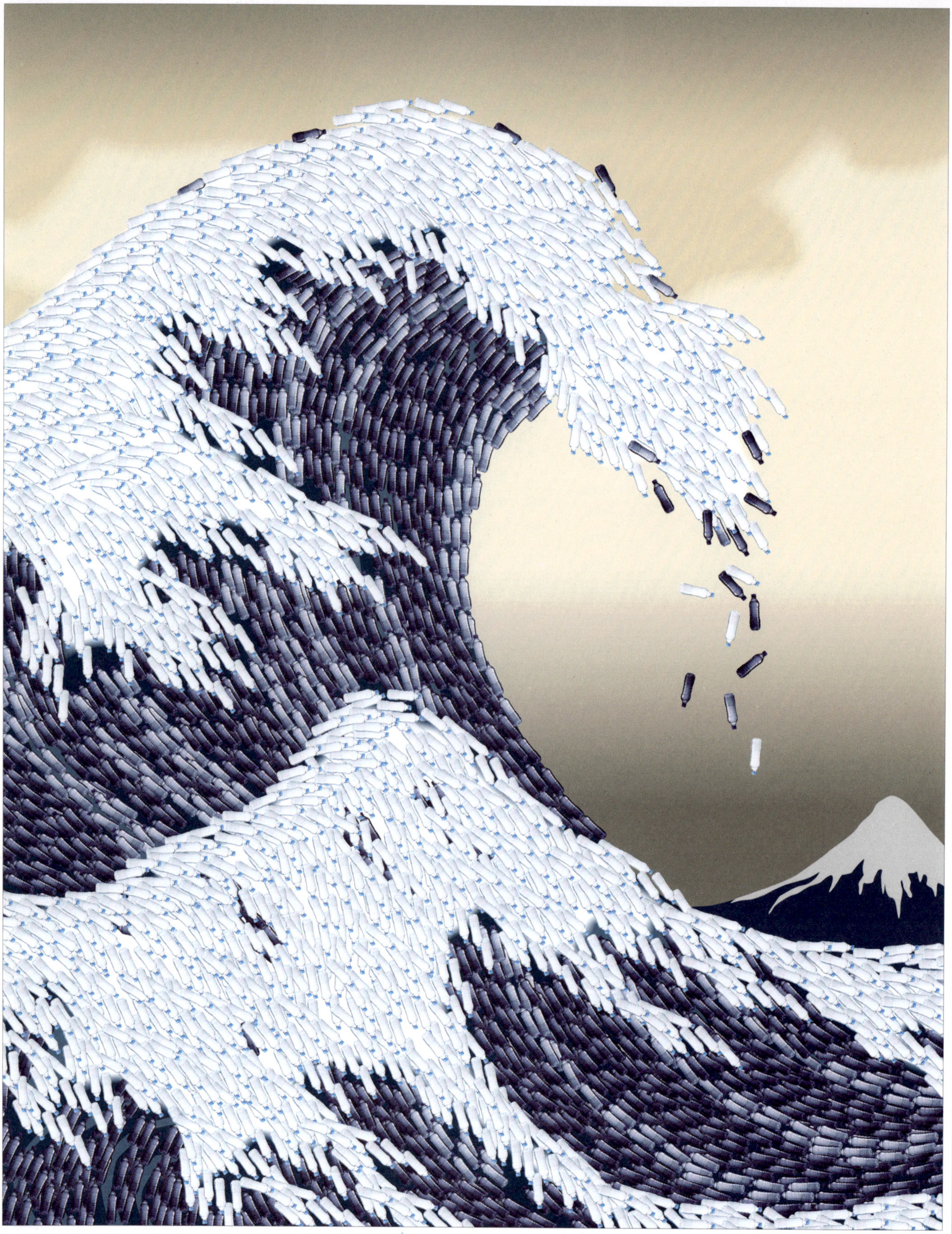

Designer: **Andrew Sloan** | Client: **Self-initiated**

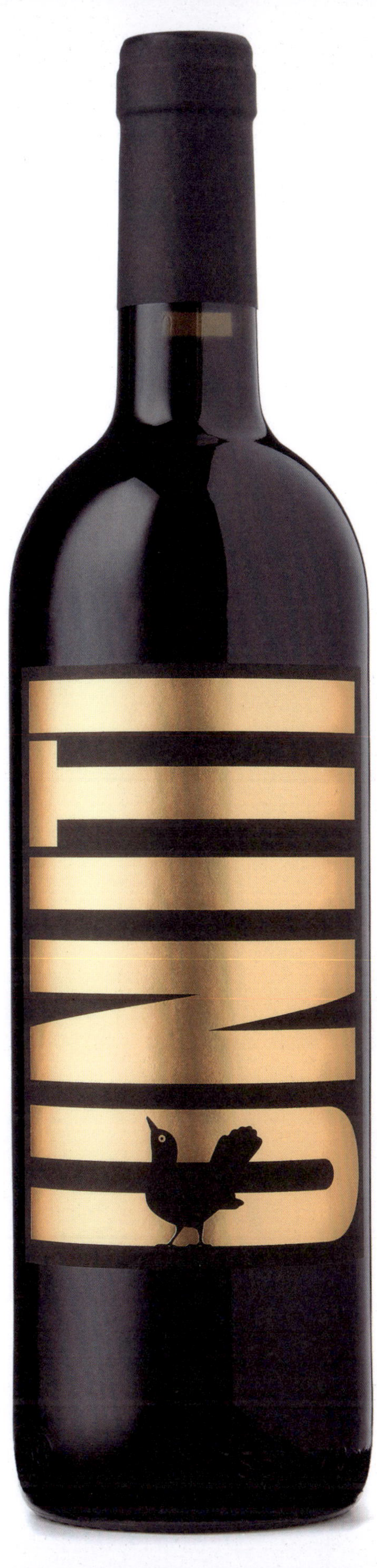

Designer: **Mattia Conconi** | Design Firm: **Gottschalk+Ash Int'l** | Client: **Ticinowine**

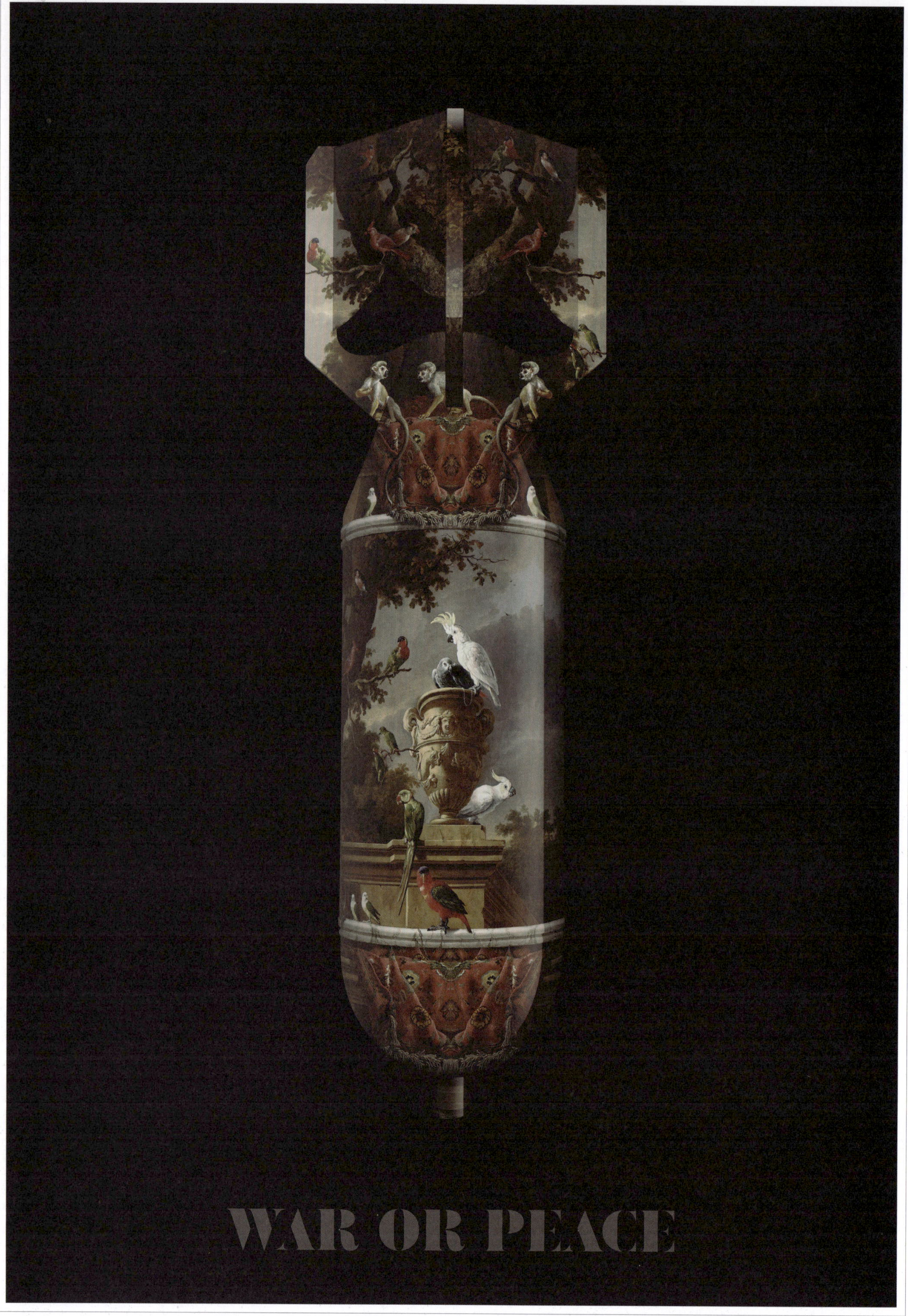

Designers: Toshiaki Ide, Hisa Ide, Magnus Gjoen | Design Firm: IF Studio | Client: Self-initiated

IT IS SIMPLY STUNNING! THE PUBLICATION COMES BURSTING BACK WITH SUCH NEW VIGOR.

Richard Danne, *Founder, Danne Design*

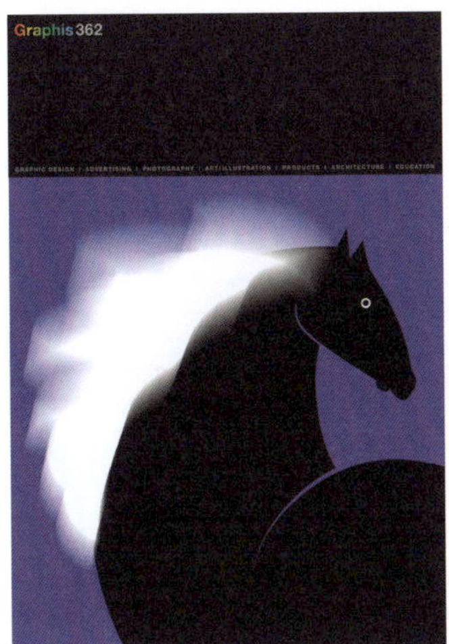

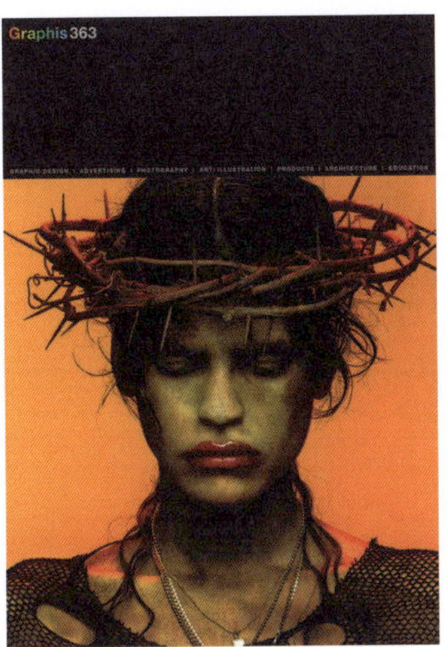

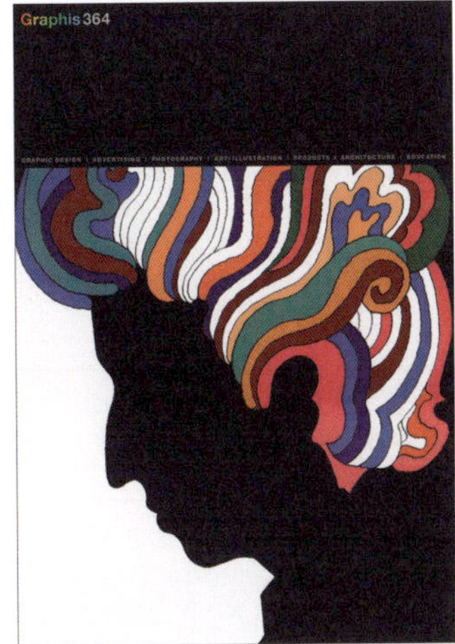

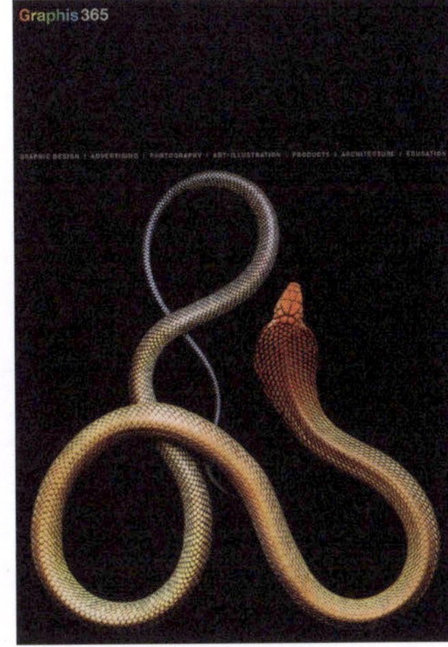

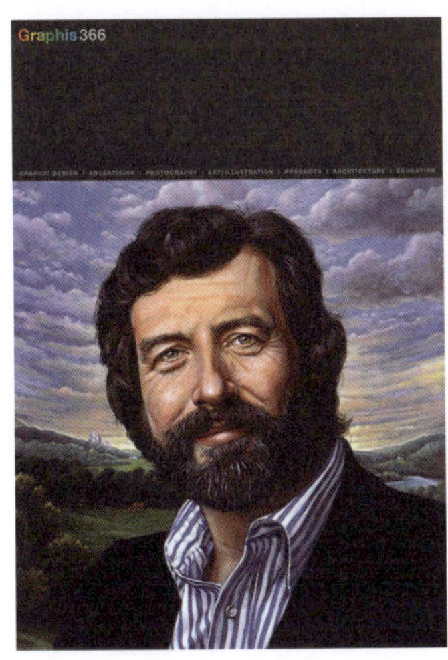

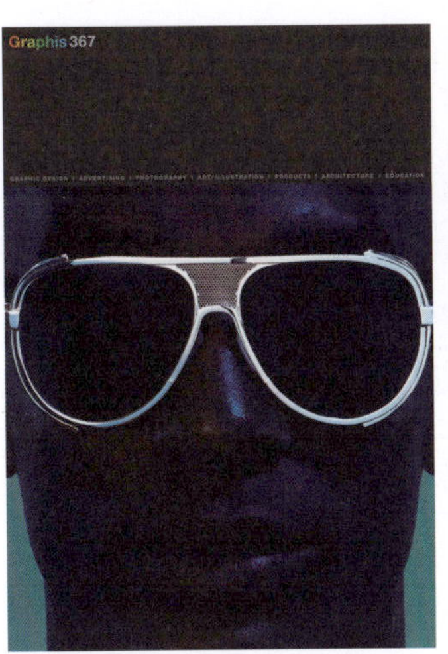

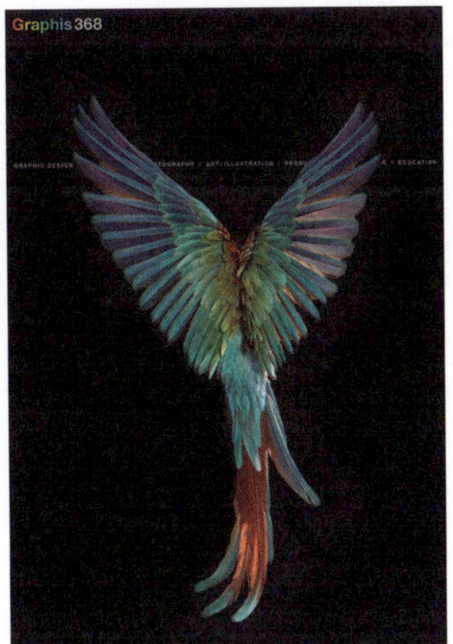

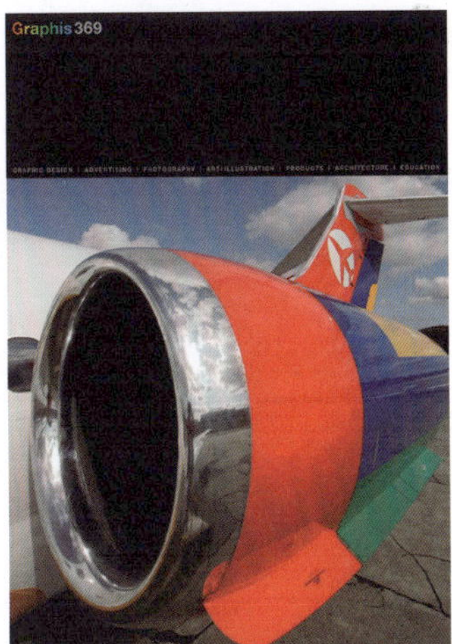

HE IS ONE OF THOSE PEOPLE THAT EVERYONE REALIZES IS ON ANOTHER LEVEL. IT'S BEEN A PLEASURE WATCHING HIM SUCCEED AND EXCEL AT MOST ANYTHING HE APPLIES HIMSELF TO, ALL WHILE SHARING HIS GIFT WITH OTHERS AROUND HIM.

Marcus White, *Creative Director, Grow*

HE'S A DESIGNER AND CREATIVE MASTERMIND WHO'S A COLLEAGUE AND A FRIEND. HIS LEADERSHIP AND HELP FORGING A BRANDED IDENTITY LED TO GREAT SUCCESS. WE ADMIRE HOW HE BRINGS PEOPLE TOGETHER; PEOPLE ARE THEIR BEST SELVES WHEN HE'S AROUND.

Brian Watson & Miles Dotson, *Co-founders, HellaCreative*

HE EXCELS AT CREATIVE INNOVATION. TIME AND TIME AGAIN HE BRINGS BRAND IDENTITY TO LIFE, TRANSLATING A BRAND'S PURPOSE INTO A VISUAL DESIGN AN AUDIENCE CAN FEEL AND RELATE TO.

Love Beach, *VP of Creative Strategy, Blavity Inc.*

QUINNTON'S AN EXCEPTIONAL LEADER AND CO-FOUNDER. HE'S ALWAYS READY TO THINK BIG, BUT EQUALLY READY TO GET HIS HANDS DIRTY. HE ALSO MAKES PEOPLE FEEL AT HOME AND HEARD, WHICH HELPS HIM ATTRACT AND ELEVATE COMMUNITY WHEREVER HE GOES.

Joy Ekuta, Ajene Green, & Chijioke Amah, *Co-founders, Retrospect*

Opposite page: Portrait of Neko Harris. Chicago, IL, USA. August 2018. Kodak Portra 800, 35mm.

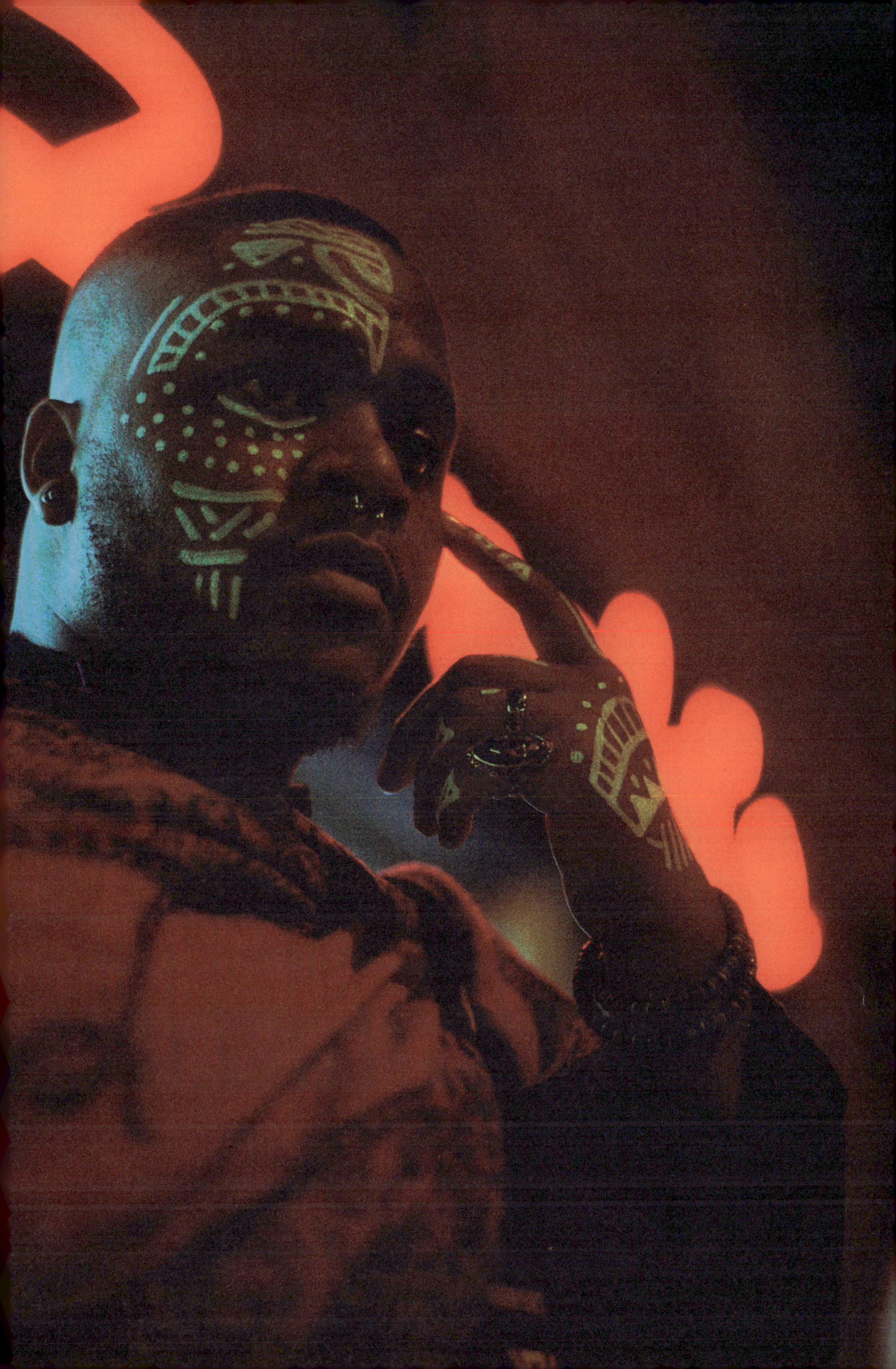

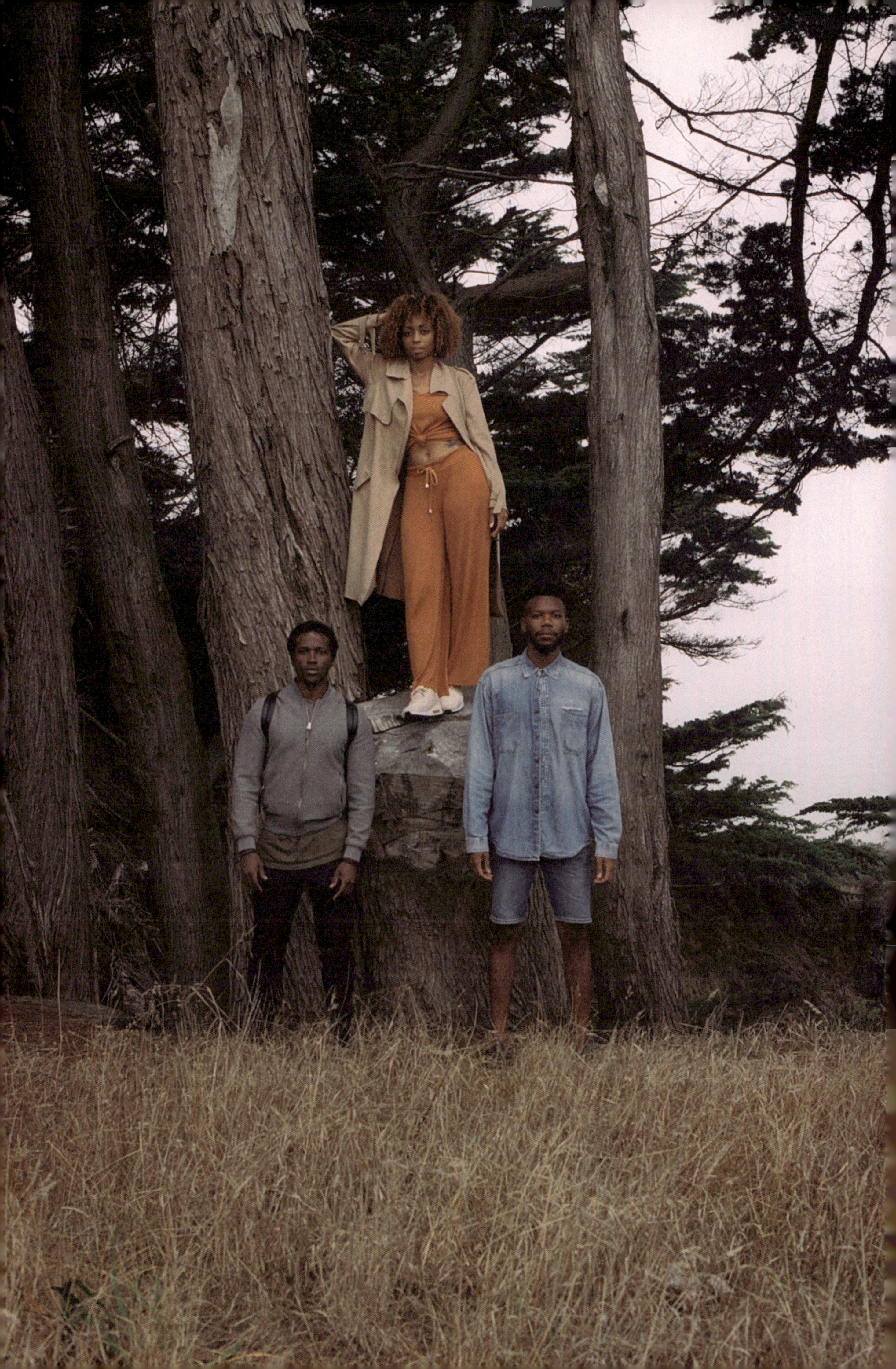

Quinnton Harris is both a card-carrying MIT mechanical engineer and a classically-trained architect. He represents the vanguard of a new generation of designers who are deeply rooted in their understanding of technology but not overly enamored by it. Rather than spend all of his time waxing poetically about the future of machine learning, Harris' approach is decidedly analog, human, and unapologetic. That's because his lived experience has shown him how technology can serve the elite with intimacy while simultaneously widening the gulf to their ability to stay connected to reality. People. Hope. Accountability. That's how I read Quinnton Harris.

Q&A: Quinnton Harris

You are an MIT alum with a SB in mechanical engineering and dual minors in architecture and visual arts. What led you to create that conversation and what advice would you give to yourself back then or to current students today?

I love the way you phrase it as "the conversation" because I can interpret it in a couple of different ways: what conversation was I having with myself, and then also what conversations was I trying to have in my life path in those moments that I might not have thought I was having or desiring.

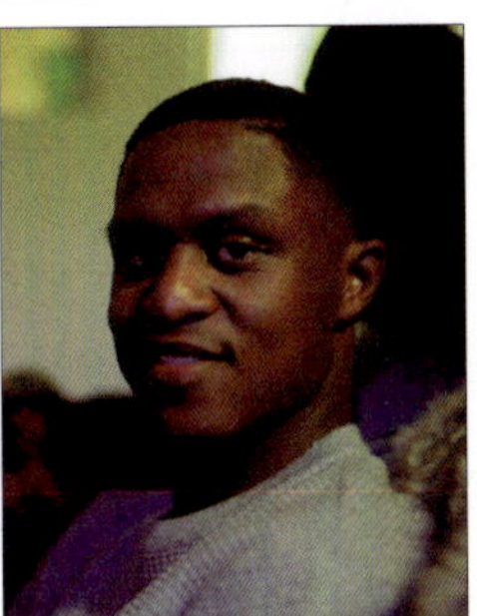

As a kid I think I was insecure in my creative abilities and didn't really understand myself, partly because everybody in my family was very expressive in their creativity. I didn't realize that the way I put together things — particularly my approach to math and science in school — was my expression of creativity. So I was deeply insecure about those things, but I loved being in proximity to my people, whether it was my older brother who's a musician, my mom who's a singer, or my twin who's an illustrator. I loved to be in proximity to their artistic expression and the really interesting conversations they were having as artists.

I got to MIT and I longed for that type of conversation I had with my family. I wasn't having that human connection or conversation with my engineering curriculum. I didn't know this conversation would come from "design" or architecture or studying form and function. I didn't know any of that, so I just started to go on this quest to try to have these mini conversations with myself. I love the phrase "conversation" because it's a dialogue. I became friends with an older student who was into graphic design and roller-coasters, so I had conversations with him and he taught me how to use Photoshop which I used for a job on campus. My older brother was living in New York as an artist at the time, so I would go spend time with him in search of the dialogue I knew as a kid.

The advice I'd give to myself back then and to students facing challenges now is that it's okay to have those conversations. Even if you are scared of the outcome, it's good to embrace the notion that "it might not work out." I don't like to say "failure" because in my current understanding, failure is a word that wasn't designed for the human experience — it was designed to describe financial transactions or things within the banking system that did not work. Failure is very empirical, but the human experience is full of trial and error. Life is about learning from discovery. It's experimentation. And I am working to remove "failure" from my lexicon.

So, looking at my younger self, I would just say, chill out, dude. It's okay to make the mistakes you deem as failure, and you have the privilege of being at a place like MIT to experiment more in ways that other people can't.

How did you become the creative director of the Publicis Sapient Group and the Experience and co-leader of Global Computational Design? Of all the pathways you took to get here, how did that happen?

Back in 2019 I was burned out, dealing with mental health issues, and was just tired. I decided to take a step back from working and running so hard. By that point I was eight years into my career as a designer, had worked at several start-ups, and hadn't been taking the proper rest. I wanted to take this time away to recenter and think about what was next. I had visions for what those things would be, but I also believed that those visions wouldn't necessarily manifest immediately. I was simply ready to surrender to the process for discovery and healing, and whatever winding roads I'd end up on.

All of the experiences I've had to date have been at the intersection of preparedness and opportunities that seem like luck. I only could take advantage of those opportunities because of my level of preparedness, which I was often coached into realizing my potential.

My sabbatical from work started in April 2019, and it became an intentional moment for me to prepare for the next thing even though I had no clue what it was. I just knew I wanted to be better and heal. It was a painful sabbatical — I was unlearning habits and dealing with new normals for how mental illness shows up in my life. I was feeling so many emotions that I didn't allow myself to feel. One of my best friends from college, Wayne Hollman, died in 2015 at the age of twenty-four. I remember how much it hurt me, but 2019 was the first time I actually grieved his death because I finally allowed myself to feel it.

I initially gave myself three months before heading back into the workforce. I spent the first two months freaking out that I didn't have anything else to do. It wasn't until month three that I was able to finally settle in and rest. And three days before the end of my planned sabbatical, I got a DM on Twitter from John Maeda. John was someone who I had only known as one of the most decorated designers of our time, a thought leader and philosopher, the former president of RISD, and an MIT alum. He essentially said hi and asked if I would like to come work with him at Publicis Sapient.

Our first phone call was over two hours long, and we shared all kinds of stories with each other. He opened himself up to me in a way that, up until that point, I hadn't experienced a leader doing. We shared our childhood experiences and our respective paths to MIT. Through it all, I recognized that it was a heart-connection and he was someone that I needed to learn from and be around. He was curating an *Ocean's 11*-level team and had identified me as a great storyteller and someone who understood the power of brand. I accepted his invitation to join him and was one of the five people he eventually hired on his global leadership team, being the youngest of the group and the only black person.

Two days before my start date, he asked me to be his chief of staff. While I had been completely taken aback by the request, he showed me his appetite for experimentation and provided the space for me to learn and fail, too. Eventually John prepared to move on from his role at Publicis in September 2020, and before he left he helped me connect the dots on my next opportunity. This led me to starting a company that Publicis Group became a seed investor for. Starting my own thing was the vision I had during my sabbatical, and now I have the opportunity to build it in a way I didn't know it could be built.

What do you hope to achieve as an advisory board
member with Graphis?
Graphis is one of the most beloved institutions for design in the world, and I have come to love its history, its owner Marty, and its global community. Graphis has an enormous potential for its future, and I am excited for how even more colorful it can become — increasing its representation of designers from diverse and historically marginalized backgrounds will make Graphis the most comprehensive archival of modern design history in the world. And I'm so honored to commit time and energy to making the world's best designs and creativity accessible to people from all walks of life. Furthermore, as we become more of a digital world, Graphis has the opportunity to preserve and codify a sustainable relationship and elevated experience with the physical world, specifically print. I hope to work with Graphis to strengthen its connection to its global community, inject new ways of thinking about the overall brand experience, and build new pipelines for creative enthusiasts and professionals to participate in the vision.

What is your work philosophy?
If my work philosophy had to be summarized into one word, it would be vulnerability, specifically the process of becoming vulnerable. There's a deep level of introspection that I like to take when it comes to my work, and when I'm working with clients and other colleagues, I really need to get intimate with the problem we're trying to solve. I work to peel back my own biases to be as open as possible with what we are trying to accomplish — I believe I have to remove myself then add myself back into the equation, which is a process of surrender.

In practical terms, I start with questions big, small, tactical, and conceptual, and then I identify people who can answer them, whether they be present with me or distant ancestors. It's important to me that I consider people who have asked these questions before me. After I curate these people

and their thoughts, I start the process of synthesizing their perspectives and making decisions. Decision-making in the design process is so important because the quicker you make a decision, the quicker you can get feedback from the audience you're designing for, and that feedback lets you know if you are getting the desired result or if you have to go back and do the process over again.

Who do you find yourself going to for answers?
Right now my inner circle mostly; my immediate family are one of the earliest layers I turn to when I need support across the board. Then there's a layer of people who I consider to be experts in my world that I look to bounce ideas off of. I'm part of a group called Trillicon Valley which is made up of men of color at various stages of their careers — some have been CEOs, some are tech folks, some are artists, etc.; I turn to social media at times, particularly content I've curated from designers and thought leaders; and I listen to a lot of conversations, for example Brene Brown's *Dare to Lead* podcast and Jemele Hill's *Unbothered* podcast. I specifically love listening to documentary-style podcasts and storytelling.

Sports commentators are also a big inspiration to me. When these folks talk about sports, there's a stat line that is undebatable — it's a fact — but then there is the interpretation of that fact … and I find the different personalities extremely entertaining. I'm usually listening to brilliant black thinkers like Stephen A. Smith or Jalen Rose build complete stories around these data points as they mix in more context and borderline gossip. I see their takes as super creative, and most of them are doing this in real-time. I ask myself, do they even believe the story they're telling? Or are they just saying what they're saying to antagonize another broadcaster? I'm reading and contextualizing all of these different data points, as I do with everything that I work on creatively, and I thoroughly enjoy the richness of the conversation.

I think I love storytelling so much because as a kid there were always people in our house talking back and forth, telling stories to each other. I'd just be a fly on the wall listening to these conversations, developing a demeanor that held space for storytelling and dynamic debate.

What are the most important ingredients you require
from a client to do successful work?
Vulnerability is top of mind for me when it comes to doing client work. I've never been a very transactional person … I sometimes think when we're overly transactional we might not see the humanity of the others. I put a lot of passion, a lot of love, and a lot of care into the things I do. And I like to care for my clients.

When I had a vision for an agency a long time ago, I called it "Birth" and I thought of myself as a doula or midwife because I was essentially helping people give birth to their ideas. And there's a level of intensity, intentionality, and nurturing that you need to have. The people you serve need to be able to trust you, be vulnerable with you, and be as invested as you are in what they're asking you for help with.

And so my greatest ask of my clients is to be vulnerable and to be willing and open to doing something they've never done before. By virtue of my service, they are not able to do what they want to do without me, and I am not able to create the things that I want to create without my clients. So vulnerability and understanding needs to be at the foundation of our relationship.

I think the other piece is trust, which is built over time and built very intentionally. However, I believe you can't have that trust without vulnerability. A famous theologian named Michael Todd has a quote that I think about all the time — "Trust is lost in buckets and it is earned back in drops" — how do

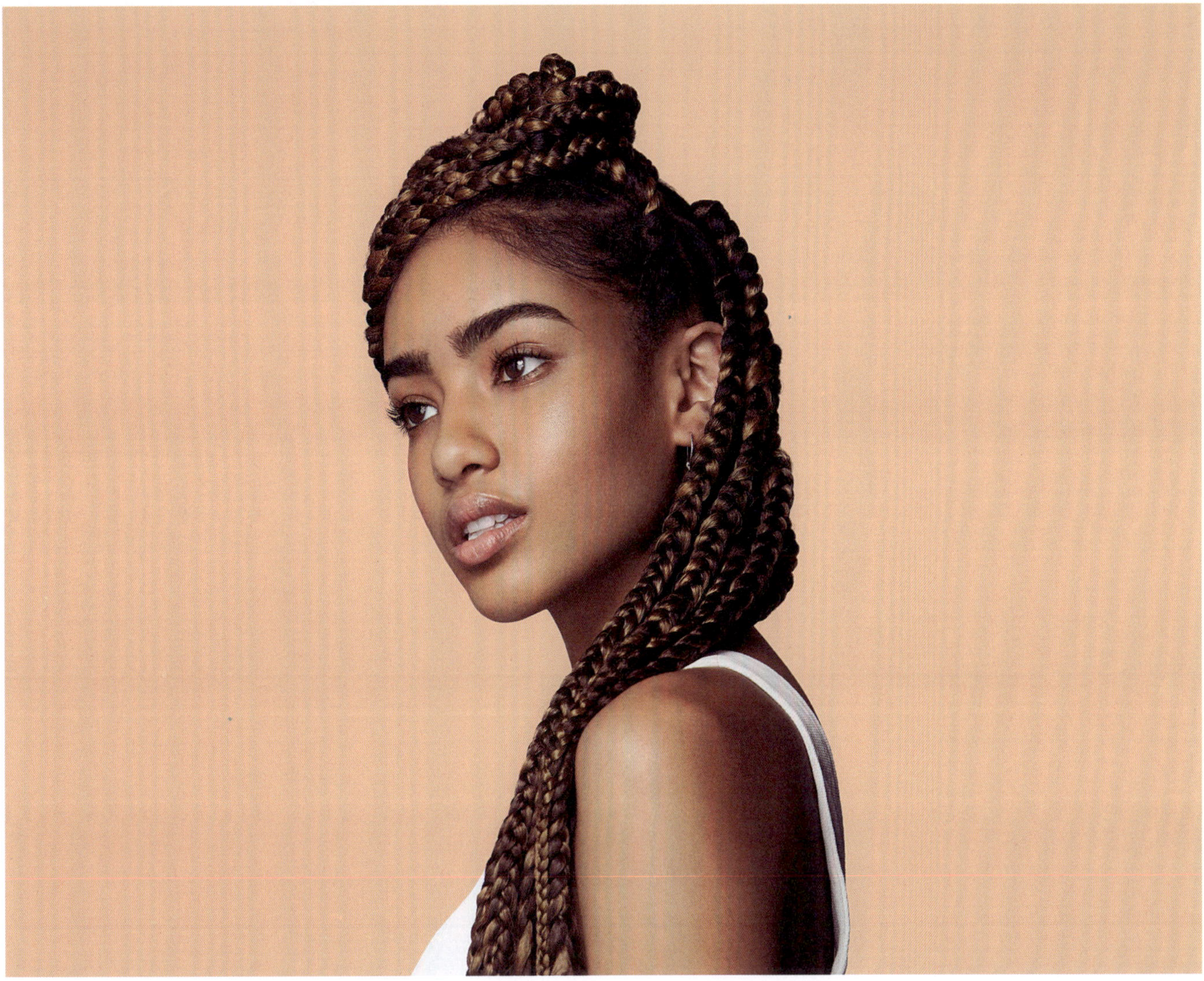

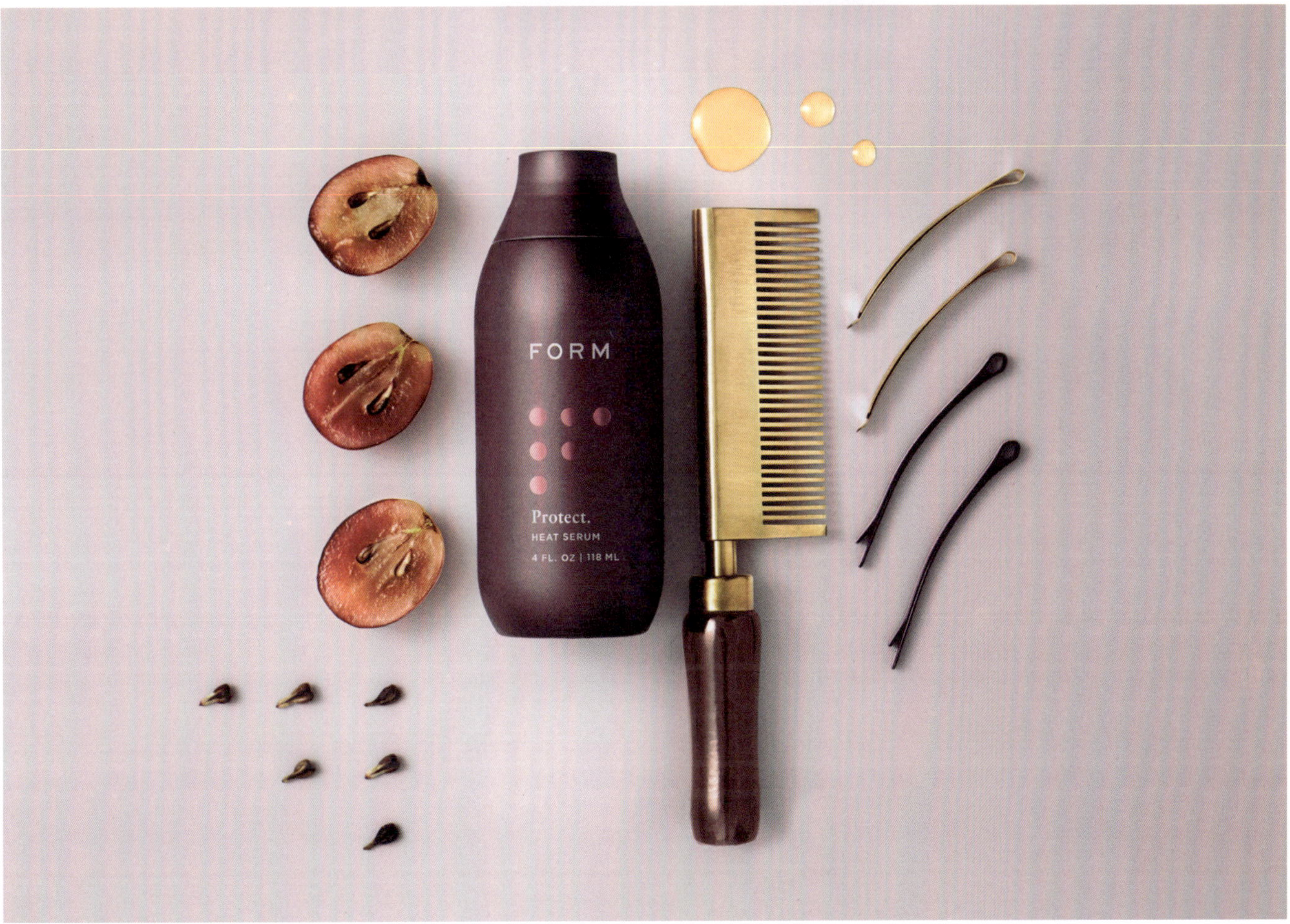

Form Beauty Brand Photography, August 2017. Courtesy of Walker and Company Brands.

we make sure we honor this principle so that we don't create distrust during this process?

What part of your work do you find most demanding and what part provides the greatest satisfaction?
For me, communication is the most demanding. What I mean by this is making sure that I am communicating my process and my intention at every step of the way because there is no space for distrust. I believe distrust comes when there is a lack of consistent and thoughtful communication.

To be honest, I treat my work like any intimate relationship. I see a lot of parallels in my work to how I show up as a partner in my marriage, or even in my family, where nurturing good relationships is just as important as the work itself. The work, in many ways, is an output of the relationship and how it's nurtured. Thus, the communication piece is the hardest thing for me, and oftentimes the most rewarding, too, because making sure that the communication is what it needs to be not only ensures the product is delivered effectively, but it also creates some level of fulfillment that can be shared within the partnership.

The greatest satisfaction that I get from my work is to see an idea come to life and then have an impact on people.

I'm now getting more honest with myself because before, I just would say that "creating just to create" was enough for me, but I think I'm actually more driven by the response — did it have some meaningful impact in someone's life?

What would be your dream assignment? If someone said, "Alright, blank check. Let your mind run free and wild," what would you love to be able to work on?
My dream would be to create a studio — or studios — where creative professionals have the ability to tell stories and craft experiences they care deeply about in the world, where their greatest motivation for creation is their lived experience, nothing more, nothing less.

I believe people care about the things they've experienced in their lives, good or bad.

For me, I care about black people. I'm a black man who has a very specific lived-experience, and I tend to create things or take part in creating things that are aligned with this lived experience, particularly as it relates to overcoming oppression in America or equal rights and equal access to justice.

And you know, I am kind of in the first phase of realizing this dream right now. I call what I want to create a "studio" because it helps define the output, but I think it's more than a studio. It's bigger. I think of it as a revolutionary idea, similar to "Black Lives Matter." It's a powerful idea that warrants so much action and challenges people to create authentically and boldly from their vantage point — whether they're doing political work, commercial work, or community work. So what I'm striving to think about is, what is that big idea that I can get people behind where it becomes bigger than me?

How has your definition of success changed over time and what prompted that change?
There was a time where I considered success to be a result or a material manifestation of hard work (e.g., a degree from MIT, a high-paying job, etc.). It was very surface-level, and my main goal was to be held in high regard for the work I'd done.

Now I define success as the pursuit of purpose. It's on-going, it's a process, it's showing up to do the thing that you believe in your heart is the thing you should do. Success to me now is a decision that you have to make every single moment of your life, and when you forget it's a decision you have to

make, you slip back into that performative, material definition.

I liken it to love. Before, I thought love was the #couple-goals photos or the lovey-dovey notes or sex everyday … it was always about an output instead of an input or process. Now I see that love is a conscious decision to show up and demonstrate care, regardless of how you feel and whether or not someone deserves it. So it's the same for success where, instead of thinking about output, I think about process and how to stay aware of it because that awareness takes work.

The tipping point for me has been happening all throughout my life in various phases. Whenever I find myself being disconnected from purpose, I'd wrestle and struggle to find that "thing," and the pursuit of such purpose usually leads me to the next phase of my life. In this pursuit process, I ask myself intense, highly reflective questions, and generally I am able to find what I was looking for.

As it relates to my mental wellness, I've recently discovered that my battle with anxiety is partly a result of me not being fully connected to myself and my purpose. The gap created from this disconnection, or what I perceived as the distance between who I truly am and a shadow of who I think I should be, leaves me grappling with intense emotions and identity issues. Furthermore, anytime I feel like I'm trying to perform or do something that doesn't feel authentic to myself, I get anxious and fearful. My body physically reacts to this disconnection from myself and my understanding of myself.

Let's talk a little bit about the #hellaJuneteenth movement — how would you summarize what it was? Was it an idea? Was that a concept? What was that?
Fittingly, it was an idea that became bigger than I could ever imagine. The holiday of Juneteenth became a vehicle to celebrate liberation and joy during a time where black Americans experienced widespread trauma by the police state.

April into May and June 2020 was a tipping point in a way, where, over the last ten years or so, we've just been completely inundated with public lynching after public lynching after public lynching after public lynching. Amidst all of this, we've had mixed responses from our government in the pursuit of justice, fairness, and equality. It was a tipping point last summer because not only were we experiencing the same trauma for the umpteenth time, but we were all locked in the house because of COVID-19. America was actually forced to have even more conversations about this, and the aperture was a lot wider for people of all backgrounds, especially white folks, to reconcile with what they were seeing. So there was this moment where damn, we're hurting so bad, AND everybody else wants to talk about it. It was a nightmare for me personally. It was a nightmare to be black in a corporation, it was a nightmare to be black in the street, it was a nightmare to just be black. And it was just taxing and heavy.

Prior to all those things happening, a few friends and I got together to create a collective called HellaCreative as a response to shelter in place with COVID — we could no longer gather physically, so we used a Slack channel and started doing Thursday happy hours on Zoom to stay connected. Sometimes we'd be online together for six, seven hours just talking.

And there was one particular happy hour after the back-to-back murders where we were all just downtrodden. We used the space to just talk about it. As we talked about how we planned to take care of ourselves, someone brought up the idea of getting together for a socially-distanced picnic, followed by someone else sharing that Juneteenth was coming up and it was his birthday. We started discussing Juneteenth and came to find out that half of the group didn't know about it, also citing that it's not nationally recognized. Eventually, we decided to make the day ours. We collaboratively created a social media post that basically said, look y'all, we're taking this day off, we need this, it's our "calling in black" day. We designed a few graphics on the spot and pulled together some resources such as writing templates to help other people who wanted to take the day off, too. Things moved very quickly — the conversation in our group happened during happy hour on Thursday, a simple landing page went up on Saturday, and on Sunday it went viral.

I spoke with my boss at the time, John Madea, about the project, and he shared how cool it was that we were empowering other people to make the day theirs. He then suggested, wouldn't it be cool if we empowered companies to join in the

Company mentor and confidant Ajene Green, and creative collective peer Chijioke Amah signed on to co-found a new incarnation for what the industry calls a "studio."

We formed our company as a response to a simple question: what happens when you have black, queer, indigenous, women, neurodivergent, or any other historically marginalized people in a room and are authentically driving business impact from their lived experience? Retrospect seeks to reframe "inclusivity" so that we can honor cultural brilliance and drive business impact for social and economic empowerment. Conversations across industries for inclusivity often can be surface-level, performative, and derivative. True inclusivity is making the excluded be seen, heard, and empowered, and time and time again, the process to realize these markers reveals a brilliance only authentic to the culture of those people.

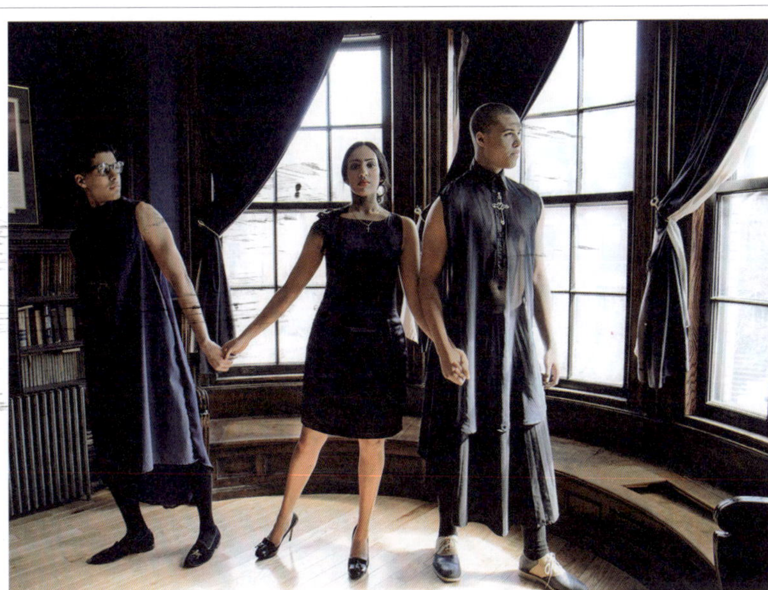

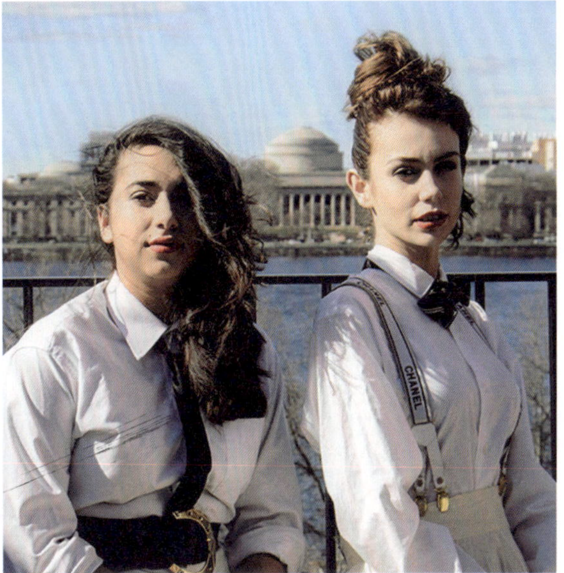

Portraits from the "The L'Académie Project." Boston, MA, USA. March 2013. Digital.

conversation, too? Immediately this sparked an idea to showcase companies officially observing the holiday by including their logo on our website.

Friends started sharing the resource with their companies. Jack Dorsey tweeted it out and gave his commitment for Twitter and Square. We created clear criteria for their inclusion and when it was all said and done, over 600 companies joined in, forty publications organically published the initiative in the media, and four states passed legislation to make it a paid state-wide holiday. As for our core group, we had our picnic.

Moving forward, I would love for this to be an annual conversation, whether it be led by our group or not. The timing of COVID-19 and the events of that summer made this conversation extremely relevant and timely. We struck gold; the moment allowed for us to be heard in a very specific way. That being said, the most important thing for me is that it showed us our collective power. All of us [the members of the collective] sometimes exist in our own separate worlds, work at different companies, come from these different life paths — but we found our collective voice in this moment, and it was powerful. It showed that if there's a clear call-to-action and we feel motivated to do something, we could do it uniquely our way.

What's on the forefront for you?
Working at and developing my new company Retrospect, a black-owned venture that builds platforms for economic empowerment and technological innovation, alongside my long-time friends. My MIT schoolmate Joy Ekuta, Walker &

We're cultivating a global platform to inspire creators and technologists of all colors, shapes, and sizes to make things their way while looking to use radical reflection and historical context to boldly charter a legacy for the world we collectively need and want.

When you think about your work, when you think about your life, when you think about your impact, what five words describe it? And what comes up as you think of them?
Six words :). Beloved. Beautiful. Culture. Connected. Passionate. Honest.

I don't know how to describe the emotion I feel right now as I say those words … there's a deep sense of responsibility and graciousness that I feel.

This moment reminds me of my grandmother. She had such a tender soul. I remember her stoic, well-poised facade, but I also remember that at a drop of a dime she would cry. She'd have a single tear run down the side of her cheek. I'd always wonder what would suddenly move her to tears. Toward the end of her life I remember her talking more about God's goodness and the blessings He's shown our family. And I think now, putting two and two together, I believe she was experiencing God's presence in those moments. I think I just felt God and even her spirit when I thought about those words. I'm just trying to learn how to surrender to them.

If I'm doing this [the new venture] right, I'm gonna feel God, the people around me are going to feel God, and they're going to feel these words. That's the ultimate goal.

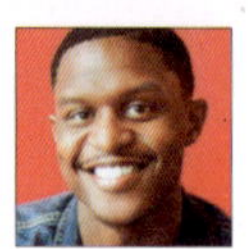

Quinnton Harris

Retrospect co-founder and chief executive officer, Quinnton J. Harris is a creative leader and entrepreneur living in Brooklyn, New York. His new venture focuses on building products and digital experiences that are radical, culturally nuanced, and more accessible for untapped or overlooked market opportunities. Previously, he served as Publicis Sapient Group creative director within experience design as well as co-leader of global computational design, which focused on evolving the organization's design systems practice. He played a critical role in accelerating CXO John Maeda's vision for fostering a more inclusive, multidimensional, and cohesive experience design capability. He also served as head of Experience for San Francisco. In early 2020, he completed a short tenure as John Maeda's chief of staff, finding much success in pushing critical CXO initiatives, implementing systems for global collaboration, and enhancing internal communication strategies. Quinnton recently led the #hellajuneteenth movement and got over 600 companies committed to observing Juneteenth as a paid holiday for its employees. Prior to joining Publicis Sapient, he served as inaugural creative director at Blavity, Inc., and before that led design at Walker & Company Brands, a start-up consumer products and tech company notably acquired by Procter & Gamble. He is an MIT alum, graduating with a SB in mechanical engineering and dual minors in architecture and visual arts.

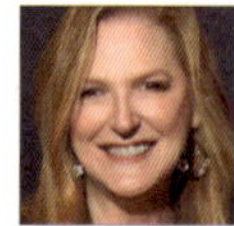

Patti Judd

Award-winning creative director, accomplished marketing and film executive, and co-founder of the San Diego International Film Festival, Patti recently joined Graphis as chief visionary officer. A key initiative was forming the Graphis Industry Advisory Board to promote greater industry insights and connections globally. Patti blends business savvy gained from twenty plus years at her agency with the entertainment biz acumen garnered from working in music and film. Her studio, Judd Brand Media, champions her passion for creating innovative work, receiving over 100 awards in design, advertising, and marketing. Her work includes notable global brands such as WME, Disney, Mattel, Montreux Jazz Festival, Century 21, Aramark, Service America, and Hilton, alongside numerous emerging brands, recording artists, and filmmakers. Her influence goes from helping launch a major live music venue, where she was a key player in its growth to one of the top live jazz venues in the world, to co-founding the San Diego International Film Festival. She holds two executive producer credits for a children's TV series on Nickelodeon and a feature film in association with the BBC, which premiered at Sundance (acquired by Universal Pictures). Currently, she is in development as executive producer on an exciting new animated children's series. Patti's nonprofit work includes being a foster youth board member and a past president of an arts and culture board benefiting Balboa Park, the largest urban cultural park in the U.S. Recently, she was awarded as an Altruist Honoree by *Modern Luxury* magazine.

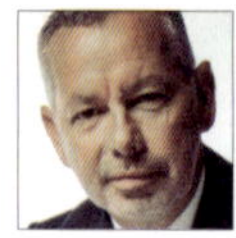

Duncan Milner

Born in Kingston, Jamaica, Duncan was drawn to the world of advertising, intrigued by the clash of art and commerce. This led to art school in Toronto and the launch of his career at small, but creatively respected shops in San Diego, where his good work caught the eye of Chiat/Day. Various roles in the Chiat/Day network included stints in the Toronto, St. Louis, and New York offices on blue-chip brands like Nissan, Pepsi, Mars, and Levi's. This led to Duncan being handpicked to co-found TBWA/Media Arts Lab, where, as chief creative officer, Duncan worked closely with Steve Jobs to help re-build the Apple brand, launching the iPod, iPhone, iPad, Apple Watch, and Apple TV. Duncan's work has been recognized at numerous awards shows, including the iconic "Mac vs. PC" campaign, which was named Campaign of the Decade by Adweek, won the 2013 Cannes Press Grand Prix, and earned the 2014 Emmy Award for Best Commercial, and Apple's "Shot on iPhone 6" campaign, which won the 2015 Cannes Grand Prix and Grand Clio for Outdoor. In 2015, he was named to Fast Company's Creative 50. In 2017, TBWA\Media Arts Lab and Apple were awarded the One Show's Penta pencil, recognizing the successful partnership and outstanding body of work between agency and client over five years. Currently, Duncan consults with numerous brands and has also taken on a new role sharing his experience and the occasional funny story speaking at corporate events.

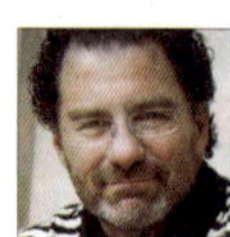

Michael Pantuso

As a multi-disciplined graphic designer and artist, Michael Pantuso thrives at the intersection of creative thinking, artistic expression, and strategically inspired ideas. Throughout his career, Michael has managed his own design practice, partnered with the branding agency IDEAS360°, and held positions inside TBWA Worldhealth (formerly CAHG) and Discover Financial. Located in the Chicago area, Michael is focused on creating design and art for clients, collectors, and organizations that make a social impact — these include charities, not-for-profits, NGOs, educational and arts bodies, social enterprises, and for-profit businesses who want to do more good. Michael's practice creates all the usual outputs of a branding agency — design identities, advertising, social media, print literature, websites, email, e-newsletters, photography, etc. But he does so in the context of a bigger picture — a vision for what the brand is, and, more importantly, what it can become. It's a passion that comes from a desire to make things better. Michael's art is an extension of this passion, but it's revealed and expressed in a more visceral way. One example of this can be seen through his "Mechanical Integration" work, where he explores nature and humanity through a series of fine art illustrations that integrate natural life forms with the inner workings of mechanical components. Part of this collection was recently celebrated as a solo exhibition which began in Paris, France, followed by a tour of Europe that concluded in early 2020. Much of that work now remains in galleries and private collections.